The Political Economy of Terrorism

Vani Kant Borooah

The Political Economy of Terrorism

A Quantitative Analysis for India

palgrave
macmillan

Vani Kant Borooah
Faculty of Social Sciences
University of Ulster
Belfast, UK

ISBN 978-3-032-08552-8 ISBN 978-3-032-08553-5 (eBook)
https://doi.org/10.1007/978-3-032-08553-5

This Palgrave Macmillan imprint is published by the registered company Springer Nature Switzerland AG
The registered company address is: Gewerbestrasse 11, 6330 Cham, Switzerland

In Memory of Shanti Priya Chakravarty, 1945–2023

Preface

The theme of this book is terrorism in India in its three main theatres of conflict: *Jammu and Kashmir* in the North; *The Red Corridor* which is a swathe of districts cutting across seven states of Eastern, Central and Southern India; and the seven states which comprise India's *Northeast*.

The quantitative analysis in this book is based on data from the Global Terrorism Database which contains an event-by-event record of all known terrorist incidents in the world from 1972 till June 2021 (which, at the moment of writing, was the latest period for which data was available) with ancillary information about the nature of these incidents: *inter alia* the country, and the country sub-region, in which the incident occurred; the terrorist group involved; the intended target; the weapons used in the incident; and the casualties (if any) that resulted from the incident in terms of deaths of the perpetrators, security personnel, and civilians.

Circumstances in India provide a natural experiment for studying inter party-in-government differences in the effectiveness of dealing with terrorists and terrorism. Between the period 2004 and (June) 2021 (which is the last year for which GTD data were available) India had two governments of different ideological make-ups. The United Progressive Alliance, headed by the Congress Party, and led by Prime Minister, Manmohan Singh, governed India between 2004 and 2013 and, in the subsequent general elections of 2014, 2019 and 2024, was followed by a Bhartiya Janata Party government with Narendra Modi as Prime

Minister. The heart of this book lies in a quantitative examination of the effectiveness of the two governments in combatting terrorism in India.

In writing this book, I am grateful to an anonymous referee for their comments and to my editor, Wyndham Hackett-Pain, for encouraging me to write this book and supporting me in doing so. Sincere thanks to Vidya Borooah and to Ashok Srinivasan for reading and commenting on the manuscript. I am also grateful to Arun Pratap Singh of *Burning Compass* and to Akhilesh Muraleedharan of *Mapping Digiworld* for supplying me with their maps, and permitting me to use these, for this book.

Notwithstanding these debts, I am solely responsible for the book's contents, for the analysis and views expressed in it and, indeed, for all its shortcomings. I have no competing financial or non-financial interests in the contents of this book.

Belfast, UK
August 2025

Vani Kant Borooah

Competing Interests The author has no competing interests to declare that are relevant to the content of this manuscript.

Contents

About the Author

Vani Kant Borooah, who was born in India, held the Chair in Applied Economics at the University of Ulster, 1987–2013. After taking his Ph.D. in 1977 from the University of Southampton, he worked for the next 10 years as a Senior Research Officer at the University of Cambridge's Department of Applied Economics and, concurrently, was a Fellow of Queens' College. He is a past President of the European Public Choice Society and of the Irish Economic Association and was also Honorary Professor of Economics at the University of Queensland. He was elected a Member of the Royal Irish Academy in 2006 and served as its Secretary from 2013 to 2015. His work has been mainly in the areas of economic development (with particular reference to inequality and poverty), political economy, and unemployment. Since retiring from his Chair in 2013, he was appointed Emeritus Professor at the University of Ulster. He is the author of several books, the most recent of which is *Economics, Religion, and Happiness*, Oxford: Routledge, August 2023.

Abbreviations

ADC	Autonomous District Council
AFDP	Association of Parents of Disappeared Persons
AFSP Act	Armed Forces Special Powers Act
AGP	Assam Gana Parishad
APHC	*All Parties Hurriyat Conference*
ATC	Autonomous Territorial Councils
BJP	Bhartiya Janata Party
COP	Chamber of Princes
CPI	Communist Party of India
CPI (M)	Communist Party of India (Marxist)
CPI (Maoist)	Communist Party of India (Maoist)
CPI (M-L)	Communist Party of India (Marxist-Leninist)
CRPF	Central Reserve Police Force
EDE	Equally Distributed Equivalent
FPTP	First Past the Post
GoI	Government of India
GTD	Global Terrorism Database
HUM	Hizbul Mujahideen
ISI	Inter-Services Intelligence (Pakistan)
JeM	Jaish-e-Mohammad
JI	Jama'at-i-Islami
JKLF	Jammu and Kashmir Liberation Front
LeT	Lashkar-e-Taiba
LWE	Lef-Wing Extremists
MCC	Maoist Communist Centre
MNF	Mizo National Front

MUF	Muslim United Front (Jammu and Kashmir)
NC	Jammu and Kashmir National Fron
NEFA	North-East Frontier Agency
NRC	National Register of Citizens
NSCN	National Socialist Council of Nagaland
NSCN (I-M)	National Socialist Council of Nagaland (Isak-Muivah faction)
NSCN (K)	National Socialist Council of Nagaland (Khaplang faction)
PDF	Jammu and Kashmir Peoples Democratic Party
PF	Plebiscite Front
PLGA	People's Liberation Guerrilla Army
PoK	Pakistan Occupied Kashmir
PWG	Peoples War Group
RCC	Revolutionary Communist Committee
SP	Synthetic Probabilities
SRE	Security Related Expenditure
ST	Scheduled Tribe
STIR	Strategy and Tactics of the Indian Revolution
SULFA	Surrendered United Liberation Front of Assam
ULFA	United Liberation Front of Assam
UPA	United Progressive Alliance

List of Figures

List of Maps

List of Tables

CHAPTER 1

Setting the Scene: An Overview of Terrorism in India

1.1 Introduction

On 14 February 2019, a suicide bomber, affiliated to the *Jaish-e-Mohammad* (JeM) group, mounted a vehicle-based attack on a convoy of vehicles carrying Indian security personnel on the Jammu Srinagar National Highway at Lethpora in the Pulwama district of Jammu and Kashmir (hereafter, J&K) in India: 40 members of India's Central Reserve Police Force , along with the bomber, were killed. What was significant about this attack was not that it happened—it was after all, the latest in deadly litany of such bombings in J&K. This attack stood out for the carnage that it inflicted—the 16 suicide attacks between 2005 and 2018 in J&K had resulted in 67 deaths whereas, in Pulwama, a single attack had killed 41 people.[1] But it was even more remarkable for the response it elicited from Prime Minister Modi's Bhartiya Janata Party (BJP) government.

On 26 February, twelve days after the Pulwama attack, fighter jets of the Indian Air Force flew 50 miles across the de facto international border between India and Pakistan, known as the Line of Control (LoC), and

[1] The death toll refers to the total of security personnel and terrorists killed. Of the 16 suicide attacks in J&K between 2015 and 2018, six were in 2015, four in 2016, four in 2017, and two in 2018. https://www.satp.org/satporgtp/countries/india/states/jandk/data_sheets/Suicide_attacks_Jammu_Kashmir_2015.htm (accessed 28 March 2018).

V. K. Borooah, *The Political Economy of Terrorism*,
https://doi.org/10.1007/978-3-032-08553-5_1

bombed what was alleged to be a JeM training camp near Balakot in Pakistan's Khyber-Pakhtunkhwa province. Since this was the first time since the Indo-Pakistan war of 1971 that the Indian Air Force had conducted airstrikes in Pakistan this muscular response by the BJP government was a radical departure from the more muted responses of earlier governments and it signalled a willingness on the part of the Modi government to risk war, if necessary, in order to punish both terrorist groups and their sponsor.

It is generally accepted that the robustness of India's reaction to the Pulwama attack won the 2019 elections for the BJP by successfully portraying its leader as the guardian of national security. In the words of an opposition Member of Parliament, Shashi Tharoor of the Congress Party, "Had performance been a factor, the BJP would have never won…There was nothing in the economy that was going right… but we were wrong because indeed Pulwama and Balakot were very good examples of how the national security issue was used to support the BJP's [election] effort".[2]

This observation then leads to the central purpose of this book which is to ask whether India's strong post-Pulwama riposte to Pakistan was simply an electoral tactic by the BJP, designed to win votes against the backdrop of a faltering economy, and that the BJP's attitude towards terrorism and terrorists, in the six years that it had been in power, was no different from that of the preceding Congress government? Or was it the case that the post-Pulwama airstrike was simply further evidence of the BJP government's willingness to take a harder line against terrorism than their more timorous Congress predecessor?

This book offers *quantitative* answers to this brace of questions. These answers are based on a general methodology, articulated in this book, for evaluating the effectiveness of a government's anti-terrorist policies: are governments more effective in dealing with certain types of terrorists? In certain regions of the country? Against certain types of weapons? The answers to these questions then result in a more nuanced comparison of inter-government differences—specifically here between the BJP (in government since 2014) and the Congress (in government, as the largest member of a coalition, between 2004 and 2014) in India.

[2] https://www.indiatoday.in/india/story/pulwama-balakot-bjp-national-security-profit-shashi-tharoor-1601489-eventas2019-09-20 (accessed 29 March 2020).

An irony of terrorism analysis is while anti-terrorist policies depend upon a rigorous analysis of data, statistical analysis was rarely employed in articles published in terrorism journals.2F[3] Indeed, it has been found that this figure was as low as 3% for articles in terrorism journals and this compared poorly with the fact the 86% of articles in psychology and 60% of articles in criminology were underpinned by statistical analysis.3F[4] Similarly, in a review of over 14,000 article abstracts from peer-reviewed sources, only 3–4% of these were based on studies that employed empirical analysis on terrorism data or information: consequently, there was an almost complete absence of evaluation research on counter-terrorism interventions.4F[5] These observations make the quantitative analysis in this book particularly important and apposite for the study of terrorism.

1.2 The Global Terrorism Database

The analysis is based on analysis of data from the Global Terrorism Database (GTD). These data are described in some detail in Lafree and Dugan (2007)5F,[6] Lafree et al. (2015)6F,[7] and Global Terrorism Database (2019)7F[8] and so, for the purposes of this paper, a summary will suffice. The GTD contains an event-by-event record of all known terrorist incidents in the world from 1972 till June 2021 (which, at the moment of writing, was the latest period for which data was available) with ancillary information about the nature of these incidents: *inter alia* the country, and the country sub-region, in which the incident occurred; the terrorist group involved; the intended target; the weapons used in

[3] Lafree et al. (2015).

[4] Silke (2003).

[5] Cynthia Lum, Leslie W. Kennedy, and Alison Sherley (2006), "Are Counter Terrorism Strategies Effective? The Results of the Campbell Systematic Review on Counter-Terrorism Evaluation Research", *Journal of Experimental Criminology*, 2 (2006): 489–516, https://doi.org/10.1007/s11292-006-9020-y.

[6] Gary Lafree and Laura Dugan (2007), "Introducing the Global Terrorism Database", *Terrorism and Political Violence*, 19 (2007): 181–204, https://doi.org/10.1080/09546550701246817.

[7] Gary Lafree, Laura Dugan, and Erin Miller (2015), *Putting Terrorism in Context: Lessons From the Global Terrorism Database* (Abingdon: Routledge, 2015).

[8] Global Terrorism Database (2019), *Codebook: Inclusion Criteria and Variables* (Maryland: University of Maryland, 2019).

the incident; and the casualties (if any) that resulted from the incident in terms of deaths of the perpetrators, security personnel, and civilians.

The GTD regards an event as a "terrorist incident" if the event was committed by nonstate actors, was violent, and was intentional. In addition, the act should have met two of the following three criteria: (i) it should have been aimed at attaining a political, economic, religious, or social goal with the caveat that, in terms of economic goals, the exclusive pursuit of profit did not satisfy this criterion; (ii) there must have been evidence of an intention to coerce, intimidate, or convey some other message to a larger audience (or audiences) than the immediate victims; and (iii) the action must have been outside the context of legitimate warfare activities, that is, the act must have been outside the parameters permitted by international humanitarian law (particularly the admonition against deliberately targeting civilians or noncombatants).

The GTD also contains information on whether a particular incident, *from the perspective of terrorists*, was a "success". This is a binary variable in the GTD, associated with *every* terrorist incident, termed *success*. It indicated whether, *from the perspective of the terrorists*, the incident had been successful *(success = 1)* or unsuccessful *(success = 0)*. As the GTD makes clear, "the success of a terrorist attack is defined according to the tangible effects of the attack and not in terms of the larger goal of the perpetrators. An incident involving multiple attack types (firearms, explosives, etc.) would be regarded as a success if any of the attack types were successful".[9]

1.3 Definitions of Terrorism

The GTD definition is not the only possible definition of terrorism. The Eighth Report of the Second Administrative Reforms Commission of the Government of India (Second Administrative Reforms Commission, 2008) contains a comprehensive overview of the various definitions in circulation. The gist of these definitions is that terrorism is the use, or

[9] Global Terrorism Database, *Codebook: Inclusion Criteria and Variables* 26–27. For example, a bomb that explodes would be counted as a success even if it did not hit the intended target. An armed assault is successful if the attack occurs and a target is hit (people and/or property). A hijacking is successful if the hijackers obtain control of the vehicle. Hostage taking is successful if, at any point, the terrorists take control of individuals. An attack on infrastructure is successful if the facility is damaged. An unarmed assault is successful if there is a victim who has been injured.

threatened use, of violence against persons (private or officials) or property with the aim of intimidating governments and their polity to achieve political, religious, or ideological ends. It very important to distinguish between terrorist acts and those that are purely criminal—though often they are carried out by persons who moved seamlessly between the two worlds of terrorism and criminality.

To help clarify this distinction Hoffman (1998) set out the following conditions for an act to be regarded as a "terrorist" act: (i) it should be ineluctably political in its aims and motives; (ii) it should be violent—or threaten—violence; (iii) designed to have far-reaching psychological repercussions beyond the immediate victim or target; (iv) conducted by an organisation with an identifiable chain of command or conspiratorial cell structure (whose members wear no uniform or identifying insignia); and (v) perpetrated by a sub-national group or non-state entity.

1.4 A "Natural Experiment" in Indian Politics

An important tool of research in economics is provided by the existence of what are termed "natural experiments". These are situations in which rules governing behaviour of agents, starting from a position of identity, change to affect some persons but not others. The consequence of this change may be interpreted as a "treatment effect", operating on one part of the population but not the other, and, under the right circumstances, may be regarded as a random effect. Rosenzweig and Wolpin (2000) provide several instances of such natural experiments and one, which has bearing on this study, is that of Card and Kreuger's (2000) study of minimum wages and employment for the USA: on 1 April 1992, the minimum wage in New Jersey rose from $4.25 to $5.05 per hour but that in neighbouring east Pennsylvania remained unchanged. This then constituted a natural experiment which allowed them to study the effect of minimum wages on employment.

Circumstances in India provide a natural experiment for studying inter-party-in-government differences in the effectiveness of dealing with terrorists and terrorism. Firstly, between the period 2004 and (June) 2021 (which is the last year for which GTD data were available) India had two governments of different ideological make-ups. The United Progressive Alliance (UPA), headed by the Congress Party, and led by Prime Minister, Manmohan Singh from the Congress, governed India in the decade between 2004 and 2013. Hereafter, this government is referred to as the "Congress government". The subsequent general elections of 2014 and 2019 saw the BJP swept into power and, since 2014, the BJP, led by Prime Minister Narendra Modi, has been India's party of government.[10]

The Congress and the BJP could not have been more different in their social and economic views. First, the Congress was committed to the idea of a secular India which gave equal importance to all religions whereas the BJP's vision was (is) that of a Hindu India in which non-Hindu minorities—of which Muslims, comprising about 14% of India's population, were the most numerous—had to accept a subordinate status. Second, the Congress derived its economic policies from the socialist tradition emanating from India's first Prime Minister, Jawaharlal Nehru, while the BJP's economics, reflecting the interests of its business-oriented supporters, were rooted in a free market ideology. Third, the Congress' attitude towards state violence was tempered by the non-violent tradition of India's freedom movement, whose architect Mohandas ("Mahatma") Gandhi was a member of the Congress party; the BJP, on the other hand, admired the militant tradition of Subhas Bose's Indian National Army which collaborated with the Japanese during the Second World War to overthrow British rule in India.

1.5 The Position of India in World Terrorism

The title of this book raises the question as to why, in the context of terrorist incidents, India should be of interest. The short answer is that, as Tables 1.1 and 1.2 show, 10,328 of the 138,487 terrorist incidents (7.5%) in the world, as recorded in the GTD for the period 2004–2021 occurred in India and that India came fourth in a ranking of countries by the number of terrorist incidents. Table 1.1 shows that, between 2014–2021, the 5935 incidents in India followed Pakistan (6262 incidents), Afghanistan (14,423 incidents), and Iraq (15,947 incidents); Table 1.2 shows that, between 2004–2013, the 4393 incidents in India followed Afghanistan (5660 incidents), Pakistan (7398 incidents) and Iraq (11,839 incidents). In turn, over 2014–2021, India was followed by Nigeria and the Philippines in fifth and sixth positions (Table 1.1: respectively, 4460 and 4111 incidents) and, over 2004–2013, it was followed by Thailand and the Philippines (Table 1.2: respectively, 2379 and 1939 incidents).

[10] Though the BJP lost its parliamentary majority in the 2024 General Election, it continued in government as part of a coalition.

Table 1.1 The ten countries of the world with the largest number of terrorist incidents: 2014–2021 (BJP Government)

	Number of incidents	*Number of deaths*	*Number of terrorist deaths*	*Deaths per incident*	*Terrorist deaths per incident*	*Success rate of terrorist incidents* (%)*
Iraq	15,947	44,938	11,015	2.82	0.69	83.9
Afghanistan	14,423	56,353	25,771	3.91	1.79	84.8
Pakistan	6262	7840	1411	1.25	0.23	81.7
India	5928	2879	444	0.49	0.07	76.1
Nigeria	4460	25,215	5168	5.65	1.16	91.6
Philippines	4111	3053	600	0.74	0.15	79.2
Somalia	3806	9895	3100	0.60	0.81	88.9
Syria	2476	15,949	3498	6.44	1.41	95.2
Libya	2147	2665	295	1.24	0.14	88.2
Egypt	1787	1787	830	1.72	0.46	79.3
Total for 10 countries	**61,354**	**170,574**	**52,132**	**2.78**	**0.85**	**84.0**
World total	**89,301**	**223,872**	**65,200**	**2.51**	**0.73**	**84.2**
Percentage of world total	***68.7***	***76.2***	***80.0***			

* The *success rate*, indicated whether, *from the perspective of the terrorists*, the incident had been successful *(success = 1)* or unsuccessful *(success = 0)*. As the Global Terrorism Database (2021) makes clear, "the success of a terrorist attack is defined according to the tangible effects of the attack and not in terms of the larger goal of the perpetrators. An incident involving multiple attack types (firearms, explosives, etc.) would be regarded as a success if any of the attack types were successful" (p. 26)
Source Global Terrorism Database: 1970–2021 (June)

If one expands the time frame to 1970–2021, India's position was equally dire. Over these 50 years, 14,164 of the 214,666 terrorist incidents (7%) in the world, as recorded in the GTD, occurred in India and, once again, India was fourth in the world when countries were ranked by the number of terrorist incidents: after Iraq (28,068 incidents), Afghanistan (20,373 incidents), and Pakistan (15,654 incidents) but now followed by the Philippines (8375 incidents), Peru (6116 incidents), Nigeria (5998 incidents), the United Kingdom (5553 incidents), and Somalia (5442 incidents).

The success rate of terrorist incidents during the period 2004 till 2013—during which India had a Congress-led coalition government—was 87.1% (Table 1.2) and this fell to 76.1% during 2014–2021 when

Table 1.2 The ten countries of the world with the largest number of terrorist incidents: 2004–2013 (Congress Government)

	Number of incidents	*Number of deaths*	*Number of terrorist deaths*	*Deaths per incident*	*Terrorist deaths per incident*	*Success rate of terrorist incidents* (%)*
Iraq	11,839	35,946	1801	3.03	0.15	94.6
Pakistan	7398	13,885	1730	1.88	0.23	90.4
Afghanistan	5660	14,655	3361	2.59	0.59	93.2
India	4392	5870	443	1.33	0.10	87.1
Thailand	2379	1826	50	0.77	0.02	95.6
Philippines	1939	1724	174	0.89	0.09	87.2
Somalia	1449	3351	580	2.31	0.40	93.7
Nigeria	1431	4869	784	3.40	0.55	91.7
Russia	1271	1788	172	1.41	0.14	82.9
Yemen	1042	2661	522	2.56	0.50	85.5
Total for 10 countries	**38,801**	**86,575**	**9617**	**2.23**	**0.25**	**91.6**
World total	**49,186**	**106,573**	**12,161**	**2.17**	**0.25**	**90.9**
Percentage of world total	*78.9*	*81.2*	*80.0*			

* The *success rate*, indicated whether, *from the perspective of the terrorists*, the incident had been successful. As the Global Terrorism Database (2021) makes clear, "the success of a terrorist attack is defined according to the tangible effects of the attack and not in terms of the larger goal of the perpetrators. An incident involving multiple attack types (firearms, explosives, etc.) would be regarded as a success if any of the attack types were successful" (p. 26)

Source Global Terrorism Database: 1970–2021 (June)

India had a BJP government. During the latter period, the success rate of terrorists, from the countries cited in Table 1.1, was lowest in India. The number of deaths per incident was higher under the Congress-led (Table 1.2: 1.33), than under the BJP (Table 1.1: 0.49), government; as with the success rate, the number of deaths-per-incident, of the countries cited in Table 1.1, was lowest in India (Fig. 1.1).

1.6 Terrorist Regions in India

There were three main theatres of terrorist activity in India (Map 1.1). The first was Jammu & Kashmir. The districts of Jammu and Kashmir are shown in the accompanying map (Map 1.2). The state is divided between

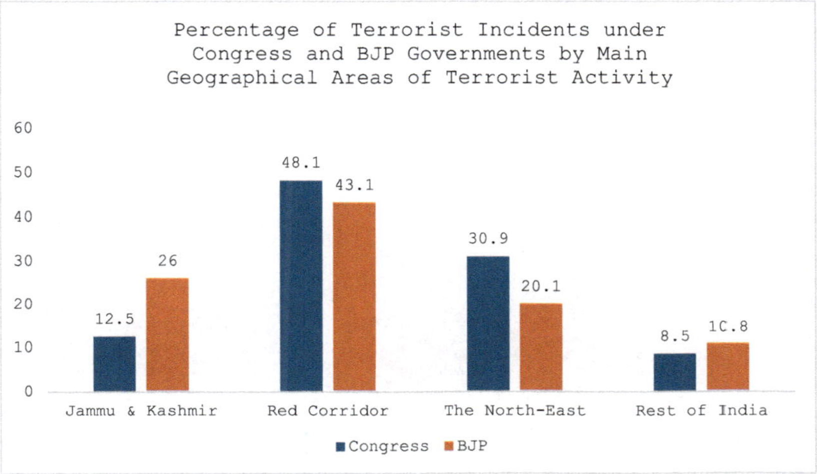

Fig. 1.1 Proportion of terrorist incidents occurring in India by government and main geographical area of terrorist activity

Pakistan Occupied Kashmir (PoK) and an Indian Administered Kashmir (IAK). Henceforth this latter part is simply referred to as Jammu & Kashmir (J&K). Map 1.2 delineates the Line of Control (LoC) separating PoK from J&K. J&K is prey to Islamic terrorist groups—many with bases in PoK and in Pakistan and receiving support from the Pakistan Army's Inter-Services Intelligence (ISI)—whose aim is to force India to withdraw from J&K and bring into being—depending on the ideological inclinations of the terrorist groups involved - either an independent Kashmir or Kashmir as a part of Pakistan.[11]

The second was a swathe of districts in Eastern, Central, and Southern India (hereafter referred to as the *Red Corridor*) in which left-wing groups sought to usher in a Marxist regime through a violent overthrow of the Indian State.11F Hereafter, this collective left-wing groups are collectively referred to as Left Wing Extremists (LWE) or, sometimes, *Naxalites* after the district of Naxalbari in West Bengal which

[11] With the possible exception of the militant groups associated with *Jamaat-Islami*, the so-called Kashmir *tanzeems* (organisations) have been raised, nurtured, assisted, and trained by the ISI. See Fair (2014) for an account of the support that terrorist groups in J&K receive from the ISI.

Map 1.1 Map of India (*Source* Burning Compass)

spawned this movement. The Red Corridor encompasses (or encompassed) districts in the states of Andhra Pradesh, Bihar, Chhattisgarh, Jharkhand, Madhya Pradesh, Maharashtra, Orissa, Telangana, Uttar Pradesh, and West Bengal. Although identifying the districts in India

Map 1.2 Jammu & Kashmir showing line of control and Pakistan Occupied Kashmir (PoK) (*Source* Burning Compass)

affected by LWE is not without controversy (Borooah, 2008), an official answer was provided by the Minister of State for Home Affairs in the Indian Government, Hansraj Ahir on 18 July 2017. Replying to a Parliamentary question he said that 106 districts were affected by LWE activity and were covered by the Security Related Expenditure (SRE) scheme whereby expenditure incurred by State governments on counter-LWE operations were reimbursed by the Central government. Of these 106 districts 35 districts were the worst affected. These are identified in Tables 1.3 and 1.4 and illustrated in Map 1.3.

The third geographical area, shown in Map 1.4, affected by terrorist activity was the Northeast of India—comprising the seven states of Arunachal Pradesh, Assam, Manipur, Meghalaya, Mizoram, Nagaland, and Tripura—where, broadly speaking, terrorist incidents were motivated by a xenophobic desire to drive out foreigners, to repossess land owned by them, and in some cases establish independence from India.

Table 1.3 Districts in India affected by left-wing terrorist activity

State	*Number of affected districts*	*Name of district*
Andhra Pradesh	8	Anantapur, East Godavari, Guntur, Kurnool, Prakasam, Srikakulam, Visakhapatnam and Vizianagaram
Bihar	22	Arwal, Aurangabad, Bhojpur, East Champaran, Gaya, Jamui, Jehanabad, Kaimur, Munger, Nalanda, Nawada, Patna, Rohtas, Sitamarhi, West Champaran, Muzaffarpur, Sheohar, Vaishali, Banka, Lakhisarai, Begusarai and Khagaria
Chhattisgarh	16	Bastar, Bijapur, Dantewada, Jasper, Kanker, Korea (Baikunthpur), Narayanpur, Rajnandgaon, Sarguja, Dhamtari, Mahasamund, Gariyaband Balod, Sukma, Kondagaon and Balrampur
Jharkhand	21	Bokaro, Chatra, Dhanbad, East Singhbhum, Garhwa, Giridih, Gumla, Hazaribagh, Koderma, Latehar, Lohardagga, Palamu, Ranchi, Simdega, Saraikela-Kharaswan, West Singhbhum, Khunti, Ramgarh, Dumka, Deoghar and Pakur
Madhya Pradesh	1	Balaghat
Maharashtra	4	Chandrapur, Gadchiroli, Gondia and Aheri
Orissa	19	Gajapati, Ganjam, Keonjhar, Koraput, Malkangiri, Mayurbhanj, Navrangpur, Rayagada, Sambhalpur, Sundargarh, Nayagarh, Kondhamal, Deogarh, Jajpur, Dhenkanal, Kalahandi, Nuapada, Bargarh and Bolangir
Telangana	8	Adilabad, Karimnagar, Khammam, Medak, Mehboobnagar, Nalgonda, Warangal and Nizamabad
Uttar Pradesh	3	Chandauli, Mirzapur and Sonebhadra
West Bengal	4	Bankura, West Medinipur, Purulia and Birbhum
Total	106	

Source Government of India, Ministry of Home Affairs, Lok Sabha Question No. 241

This is not to suggest these were the only areas in India which saw terrorist activity. India has been bedevilled by a Sikh separatist movement demanding an independent state called *Khalistan* to be carved out of the northern state of Punjab. This movement gained significant momentum in the 1970s and 1980s as Sikhs sought greater recognition of their distinct religious and cultural identity within India allied to their feeling that their unique heritage was not sufficiently respected or protected. This was exacerbated by economic issues specific to Sikhs and the Punjab. Punjab, being an essentially agricultural state, felt more

Table 1.4 Districts in India worst affected by left-wing terrorist activity

State	*Number of affected districts*	*Name of district*
Andhra Pradesh	1	Visakhapatnam
Bihar	6	Aurangabad, Gaya, Jamui, Muzzafarpur, Banka, Nawada
Chhatisgarh	8	Bijapur, Sukma, Bastar, Dantewada, Kanker, Narayanpur, Rajnandgaon, Kondagaon
Jharkhand	16	Giridih, Gumla, Khunti, Latehar, Palamu, West Singhbhum, Bokaro, Hazaribagh, Chatra, East Singhbhum, Ranchi, Garhwa, Dumka, Ramgarh, Lohardaga, Simdega
Maharashtra	1	Gadchiroli
Orissa	2	Koraput, Malkangiri
Telangana	1	Khammam
Total	35	

Source Government of India, Ministry of Home Affairs, Lok Sabha Question No. 241

keenly than most other Indian states issues relating to inadequate agricultural prices, shortage of water for irrigation, and lack of modernisation in agricultural practices.

It is, however, fair to claim that, within India, support for Khalistan has dwindled considerably since 1984, when the occupation of the Golden Temple in India under the orders of the then Indian Prime Minister, Indira Gandhi, followed by her assassination by her Sikh bodyguards, and the anti-Sikh riots in Delhi sparked by this assassination, combined to crystallise Sikh grievances. Today, such demand for Khalistan as does exist is to be found among the Sikh diaspora, particularly in Canada.

Table 1.5 shows the distribution of terrorist incidents in India across four geographical areas: J&K, the Red Corridor, India's Northeast, and the Rest of India (RoI), for each year of the period 2004–(June) 2021, the number of terrorist incidents in India by terrorist region.12F[12] The first point of interest is that of the total of 10,320 terrorist incidents in India over 2004–2021, 45.2% occurred in the Red Corridor, 24.7% occurred in the, 20.3% occurred in J&K, and only 9.8% occurred in RoI.

[12] Since district-level data was not readily available from the GTD, the Red Corridor in Table 1.5 is defined as comprising the states of major LWE activity: Andhra Pradesh, Bihar, Chhattisgarh, Jharkhand, Orissa, West Bengal, and Telangana.

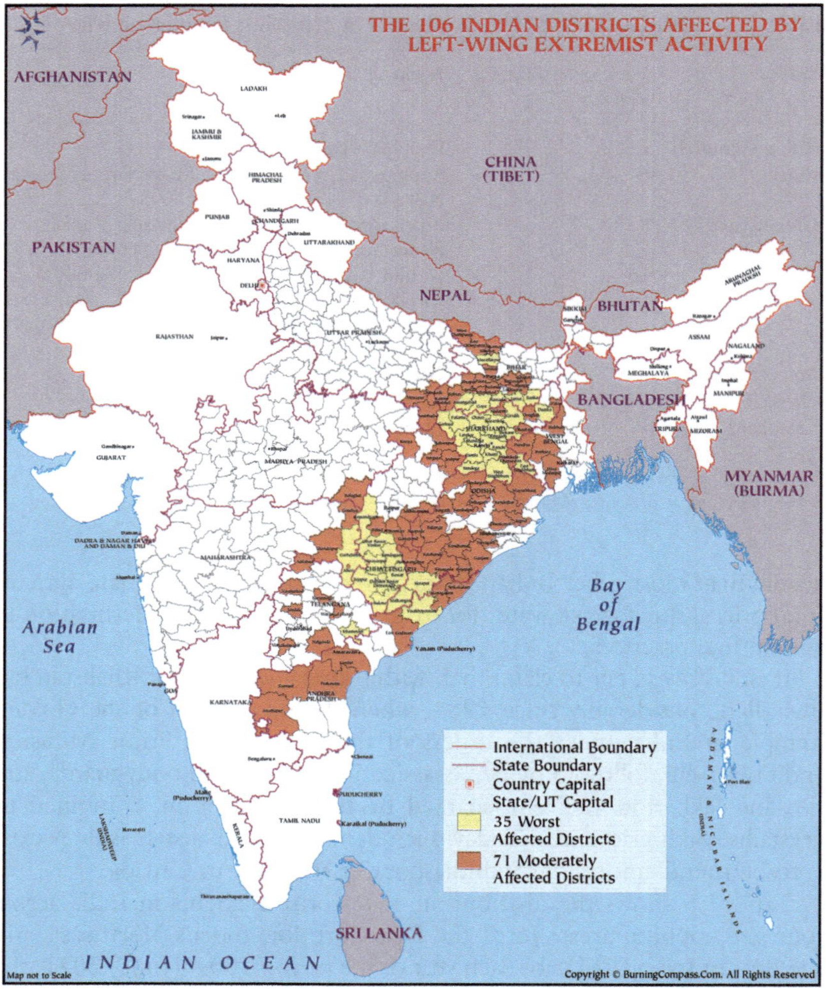

Map 1.3 Districts in India affected by left-wing extremist activity (*Source* Burning Compass. Map drawn according to a answer to Lok Sabha Unstarred Question 241 by the Minister of State for Home Affairs, Govt. of India)

Map 1.4 The Northeastern States of India (*Source* Maps of India)

The inter-regional distribution of terrorist incidents, however, was markedly different between the Congress and BJP regimes. As Fig. 1.1 (derived from Table 1.5) shows, during the period of Congress rule, 2004–2013, 12.5% of the total of 4392 incidents were in J&K, 48.1% were in the Red Corridor, 30.9% were in the Northeast, and 8.5% were

Table 1.5 Number of terrorist incidents in India by terrorist region and year

	Figures in italics are percentages of total				
	Jammu & Kashmir	*Red Corridor*	*Northeast*	*Rest of India*	*Total*
2004	73	11	22	2	108
	67.59	*10.19*	*20.37*	*1.85*	*100*
2005	89	13	31	13	146
	60.96	*8.9*	*21.23*	*8.9*	*100*
2006	78	35	44	9	166
	46.99	*21.08*	*26.51*	*5.42*	*100*
2007	37	33	68	12	150
	24.67	*22*	*45.33*	*8*	*100*
2008	52	177	217	89	535
	9.72	*33.08*	*40.56*	*16.64*	*100*
2009	24	418	196	34	672
	3.57	*62.2*	*29.17*	*5.06*	*100*
2010	13	514	98	38	663
	1.96	*77.53*	*14.78*	*5.73*	*100*
2011	38	403	160	44	645
	5.89	*62.48*	*24.81*	*6.82*	*100*
2012	68	234	240	71	613
	11.09	*38.17*	*39.15*	*11.58*	*100*
2013	78	275	279	62	694
	11.24	*39.63*	*40.2*	*8.93*	*100*
Total Congress: 2004–2013	**550**	**2113**	**1355**	**374**	**4392**
	12.52	***48.11***	***30.85***	***8.52***	***100***
2014	125	372	293	69	859
	14.55	*43.31*	*34.11*	*8.03*	*100*
2015	109	411	251	114	885
	12.32	*46.44*	*28.36*	*12.88*	*100*
2016	204	459	228	134	1025
	19.9	*44.78*	*22.24*	*13.07*	*100*
2017	257	444	175	89	965
	26.63	*46.01*	*18.13*	*9.22*	*100*
2018	408	310	98	72	888
	45.95	*34.91*	*11.04*	*8.11*	*100*
2019	200	253	72	97	622
	32.15	*40.68*	*11.58*	*15.59*	*100*
2020	167	177	53	53	450
	37.11	*39.33*	*11.78*	*11.78*	*100*

(continued)

Table 1.5 (continued)

	Figures in italics are percentages of total				
	Jammu & Kashmir	*Red Corridor*	*Northeast*	*Rest of India*	*Total*
2021	72	129	22	11	234
	30.77	*55.13*	*9.4*	*4.7*	*100*
Total BJP: 2004–(June) 2021	**1542**	**2555**	**1192**	**639**	**5928**
	26.01	***43.1***	***20.11***	***10.78***	***100***
Total: 2004–(June) 2021	2092	4668	2547	1013	10,320
	20.27	*45.23*	*24.68*	*9.82*	*100*

The Red Corridor comprises the states of: Andhra Pradesh, Bihar, Chhattisgarh, Jharkhand, Orissa, West Bengal, and Telangana
The Northeast comprises the states of: Assam, Arunachal Pradesh, Manipur, Meghalaya, Mizoram, Nagaland, and Tripura
Source Own calculations from the Global Terrorism Database: 1970–2021 (June)

in the RoI.13F[13] However, during the period of BJP rule, 2014–2018, 26% of the total of 5928 incidents were in J&K, 43.1% were in the Red Corridor, 20.1% were in the Northeast, and 10.8% were in the RoI. Thus, the major difference in the regional distribution of incidents between the periods of Congress and BJP governments was the increase in the proportion of total incidents that occurred in J&K (from 12.5% under Congress to 26% under the BJP) and the RoI (from 8.9% under Congress to 10.8% under the BJP) paralleled by a decrease in the proportion of total incidents that occurred in the Northeast (from 30.9% under Congress to 20.1% under the BJP) and the Red Corridor (from 48.1% under Congress to 43.1% under the BJP).

The second point of interest about the figures reported in Table 1.5 is the over five-fold increase in total terrorist incidents from150 in 2007 to 535 in 2008. This overall increase was mirrored in all the terrorist

[13] The fact that nearly half of terrorist incidents in India during the period of Congress rule was due to LWE led the then Indian Prime Minister, Manmohan Singh, to declare in 2006 that the LWE "were the single biggest internal security challenge ever faced by our country", *The Economist*, last modified 26 July 2006, accessed 6 April 2020, https://www.economist.com/news/2006/07/26/indias-deadly-maoists.

regions: from 37 to 52 in J&K; from 33 to 177 in the Rd Corridor; from 68 to 217 in the Northeast; and from 12 to 89 in the RoI. The next spurt in the number of terrorist incidents, from 694 in 2013 to 859 in 2014, was largely the product of an increase in the number of incidents in the Red Corridor, from 275 in 2013 to 372 in 2014 and, to a lesser extent, an increase in the number of incidents in J&K, from 78 in 2013 to 125 in 2014. This increase could well have been induced by the change of government that occurred between 2013 and 2014.

1.7 Terrorist Groups in India

In conjunction with the division of India into terrorist regions, terrorist organisations operating in the country were grouped as: Islamic Terrorists; Left Wing Extremists (LWE); Northeast Terrorists; and Other Terrorists (OT). An Appendix to this paper lists the terrorist organisations included in these broad groups. Table 1.6 shows, for each year of the period 2004–(June) 2021, the number of terrorist incidents in India by broad groups of terrorists. Of the total of 10,320 incidents: 4361 (42.3%) were due to LWE; 1385 (13.4%) to Northeast terrorists, 738 (7.1%) to Islamic terrorists and 3836 (37.2%) to other terrorists.

Comparing the Congress and BJP regimes, the point of interest about Table 1.6 is that the proportion of total terrorist incidents due to Islamic terrorists and to other terrorists rose (respectively, from 5.6% to 8.3% and from 31.2% to 41.6%) while the proportion due to LWE and to Northeast terrorists fell (respectively, from 47.4% to 38.5% and from 15.8% to 11.6%). These figures mirror those in Table 1.5 showing changes in incidents by terrorist region: the proportion of terrorist incidents in J&K and RoI rose while the proportion of terrorist incidents in the Red Corridor and the Northeast fell.

Table 1.7 compares the activity of the different terrorist groups by terrorist region. This Table shows that while terrorist groups, in the main, confined their activities to their areas of interest—83.3% of Islamic terrorist incidents were in J&K, 89.4% of LWE incidents were in the Red Corridor, and 91.3% of Northeast terrorist incidents were in that region—there were significant differences between the periods of Congress and BJP governments in the willingness of terrorists to step outside their territorial comfort zones.

During the period of Congress government, 2004–2013, 37.2% of incidents for which Islamic terrorists were responsible were outside J&K

Table 1.6 Number of terrorist incidents in India by terrorist group and year

	Terrorist group				
	Islamic	*Left-wing extremists*	*Northeast groups*	*Other groups*	*Total*
2004	21	9	19	59	108
	19.44	8.33	17.59	54.63	100
2005	33	14	26	73	146
	22.6	9.59	17.81	50	100
2006	24	30	35	77	166
	14.46	18	21.08	46	100
2007	14	17	51	68	150
	9.33	11.33	34	45.33	100
2008	53	168	96	218	535
	9.91	31.4	17.94	40.75	100
2009	10	402	99	161	672
	1.49	60	14.73	24	100
2010	9	527	50	77	663
	1.36	79.49	7.54	11.61	100
2011	9	422	82	132	645
	1.4	65.43	12.71	20.47	100
2012	24	249	100	240	613
	3.92	40.62	16.31	39.15	100
2013	50	243	137	264	694
	7.2	35.01	19.74	38.04	100
Total Congress: 2004–2013	**247**	**2081**	**695**	**1369**	**4392**
	5.6	*47.4*	*15.8*	*31.2*	*100*
2014	39	348	167	305	859
	4.54	40.51	19.44	35.51	100
2015	49	390	121	325	885
	5.54	44.07	13.67	36.72	100
2016	48	392	111	474	1025
	4.68	38.24	10.83	46.24	100
2017	93	341	166	365	965
	9.64	35	17.2	38	100
2018	143	288	62	395	888
	16.1	32.43	6.98	44.48	100
2019	62	251	22	287	622
	9.97	40.35	3.54	46.14	100
2020	36	175	32	207	450
	8	38.89	7.11	46	100
2021	21	95	9	109	234

(continued)

Table 1.6 (continued)

	Terrorist group				
	Islamic	*Left-wing extremists*	*Northeast groups*	*Other groups*	*Total*
	8.97	40.6	3.85	46.58	100
Total BJP 2014–(June) 2021	**491**	**2280**	**690**	**2467**	**5928**
	8.28	38.46	11.64	41.62	100
Total: 2004–(June) 2021	738	4361	1385	3836	10,320
	7.2	*42.3*	*13.4*	*37.1*	*100*

Figures in italics are percentages of row totals
Source Own calculations from the Global Terrorist Database

and 26.7% were in the RoI. One of the most notorious of these attacks was the attack in Mumbai 26 November 2008 when terrorists from the Deccan Mujahideen (a front for the *Lashkar-e-Taiba*) carried out a series of coordinated bombing and shooting attacks lasting four days; but equally infamous were the Mumbai train bombings of 2006, which killed 209 people, and for which the *Lashkar-e-Qahhar* (also a front for the *Lashkar-e-Taiba*) claimed responsibility, and the bombing in February 2010 of the German Bakery in Pune which caused 17 deaths and for which the *Indian Mujahideen* (also a front for the *Lashkar-e-Taiba*) claimed responsibility. During the subsequent period, 2014–2021, of BJP government, the proportion of incidents by Islamic terrorists carried out outside J&K shrunk to 6.3%. So, under the BJP government Islamic terrorists were largely restricted (restricted themselves?) to their home turf of J&K. Tables 1.13 and 1.14 of the Appendix lists incidents carried out by Islamic groups outside J&K under, respectively, Congress and BJP governments.

As Table 1.10 of the Appendix shows, most of the terrorist incidents for which Islamic terrorists took responsibility were, in fact, due to a small number of terrorist organisations. Of the 738 incidents over 2004–(June) 2021 that were attributed to Islamic terrorists: 225 were due to *Hizbul Mujahideen*, 198 were due to *Lashkar-e-Taiba*, 116 were due to *Jaish-e-Mohammed*, and 53 were due to the Indian Mujahideen (a front for the *Lashkar-e-Taiba*). If one adds to this number the eight incidents due

Table 1.7 Terrorist activity by group and region

Congress: 2004–2013					
Terrorists	*Jammu & Kashmir*	*Red Corridor*	*Northeast*	*Rest of India*	*Total*
Islamic	155	21	5	66	247
	62.75	*8.5*	*2.02*	*26.72*	*100*
Marxist	1	1885	69	126	2081
	0	*90.58*	*3*	*6.05*	*100*
Northeast	0	21	672	2	695
	0	*3.02*	*96.69*	*0.29*	*100*
Other	394	186	609	180	1369
	28.78	*13.59*	*44.49*	*13.15*	*100*
Total	550	2113	1355	374	4392
	12.52	*48.11*	*30.85*	*8.52*	*100*
BJP: 2014–(June) 2021					
Islamic	460	3	0	28	491
	93.69	*0.61*	*0*	*5.7*	*100*
Marxist	1	2014	71	194	2280
	0.04	*88.33*	*3*	*8.51*	*100*
Northeast	0	97	593	0	690
	0	*14.06*	*85.94*	*0*	*100*
Other	1081	441	528	417	2467
	43.82	*17.88*	*21.4*	*16.9*	*100*
Total	1542	2555	1192	639	5928
	26.01	*43.1*	*20.11*	*10.78*	*100*
	Congress + BJP: 2004–(June) 2021				
Islamic	615	24	5	94	738
	83.33	*3.25*	*0.68*	*12.74*	*100*
Marxist	2	3899	140	320	4361
	0.05	*89.41*	*3.21*	*7.34*	*100*
Northeast	0	118	1265	2	1385
	0	*8.52*	*91.34*	*0.14*	*100*
Other	1475	627	1137	597	3836
	38.45	16.35	29.64	15.56	100
Total	2092	4668	2547	1013	10,320
	20.27	*45.23*	*24.68*	*9.82*	*100*

Figures in italics are percentages of row totals
Source Own calculations from GTD

to the Deccan Mujahideen (also a front for the *Lashkar-e-Taiba*), then 81.3% of incidents by Islamic terrorists were due to just three groups: *Hizbul Mujahideen; Jaish-e-Mohammed; and Lashkar-e-Taiba.*

A feature of LWE terrorism is that many LWE incidents unclaimed by a specific LWE organisation and so it was up to others, like journalists or security forces, to attribute organisational responsibility. Table 1.11 shows that, of the 4361 incidents over 2004–(June) 2021 for which LWE were responsible, 2110 (51%) were attributed to the Communist Party of India—MaoistCPI (Maoist)). When specific attribution was not possible, a generic term, "Maoists" or "Naxalites" was used by journalists: thus, the GTD, which relies on news channels for its data, attributed 1946 of the 4361 LWE incidents (44%) to Maoists/Naxalites.[14]

Terrorist organisations from the Northeast restricted 92% of their activities (1265 incidents out of 1385) over 2004–(June) 2021 to the seven states which comprised this area. When they did stray, it was to North Bengal (Darjeeling, Kalimpong)—included in this book in the "Red Corridor"—mainly under the auspices of the *Gorkha Janmukti Morcha (GJM)* with contributions by the *Kamtapur Liberation Organization (KLO)* and the *Tritiya Prastuti Committee (TPC).*

Terrorists in the Northeast of India were numerous and fragmented: Table 1.12 of the Appendix identifies 97 separate groups responsible for 1385 incidents. There were, however, certain dominant groups: the United Liberation Front of Assam (319 incidents); the Garo National Liberation Army (169 incidents); The National Socialist Council of Nagaland and the National Socialist Council of Nagaland [Isak-Muivah faction] (192 incidents); and the National Democratic Front of Bodoland (133 incidents).

Although the United Liberation Front of Assam (ULFA) and the National Socialist Council of Nagaland (NSCN) want, respectively, a sovereign Assam and a sovereign Nagaland, independent of India, in recent years both organisations have been riven by factionalism. The NSCN has split into the majority Isak-Muivah (I-M) faction, which on 3 August 2015 signed a peace agreement with the Indian government, and the Khaplang faction which has rejected peace and, most notoriously, was responsible in June 2015 for the killing of 18 soldiers of the Indian Army in an ambush in the Chandel district of Manipur. In a similar vein,

[14] The term Naxalites derives from Naxalbari, the district in West Bengal where the first Maoist-inspired insurgency began in 1967.

the National Democratic Front for Bodoland, which seeks an independent Bodoland, is a breakaway faction from a "Progressive" group which was in talks with the Indian government.

The category "other" terrorist groups deserve comment. Table 1.7 shows that of the 10,320 incidents between 2004 and (June) 2021, 3836 (37.2%) were by "others". Of these 3836 incidents, the perpetrators in the respect of 3652 incidents (95.2%) were "unknown" in the sense that their affiliation could not be identified, even in broad terms like "Maoist" or "Islamic", by the news media (upon which the GTD depends for information).

1.8 Terrorist Targets

The GTD distinguished 22 types of terrorist targets which in this book were reorganised into the following six broad categories: (i) private persons and property;15F[15] (ii) business—businessmen, corporate officers, business establishments; (iii) government;16F[16] (iv) police—personnel (including prison officers) or installations (including prisons); (v) military—personnel, barracks, and equipment; and (vi) other targets.

As Table 1.8 shows, between 2004 and (June) 2021, the police were targeted in 38.5% of the 2069 incidents in J&K, and in 20.7% of the 4646 incidents in the "Red Corridor". By contrast, in the same period, the police were targets in only 8.9% of the 2529 incidents in Northeast and in 15.3% of 958 incidents in the RoI. In contrast to the police, the military were targeted mainly in J&K (in 17.0% of incidents) and in the Northeast, particularly in Manipur (in 10% of incidents).[17]

There were important differences between the periods of Congress and BJP governments in the targets chosen by terrorists in the different terrorist regions. In J&K, attacks on private persons and property fell from 26.3% of all attacks in 2004–2013 (Congress) to 16% in 2014–(June) 2021 (BJP) but attacks on the police and the military, as a proportion

[15] Attacks on individuals, the public, or attacks in public areas including markets, traffic intersections, commercial malls (Global Terrorism Database, 2019, p. 35).

[16] Any attack on government buildings (including courts), government members, including judges and prosecutors, (current or former), their convoys, political events, government sponsored institutions (Global Terrorism Database, 2019, p. 33).

[17] For example, on the 12 July 2018, 17 soldiers from the Indian Army were killed in Manipur in an attack involving an IED and rocket propelled grenades.

Table 1.8 Terrorist targets by region: 2004–(June) 2021

	Congress: 2004–2013				
	Jammu & Kashmir	*Red Corridor*	*Northeast*	*Rest of India*	*Total*
Private persons and property	142	566	422	125	142
	26.35	*26.88*	*31.35*	*34.63*	*26.35*
Business	16	193	154	39	16
	2.97	*9.16*	*11*	*10.8*	*2.97*
Government	88	350	228	55	88
	16.33	*16.62*	*16.94*	*15.24*	*16.33*
Police	158	444	140	54	158
	29.31	*21*	*10.4*	*14.96*	*29.31*
Military	79	47	99	3	79
	14.66	*2.23*	*7.36*	*0.83*	*14.66*
Other	56	506	303	85	56
	10.39	*24.03*	*22.51*	*23.55*	*10.39*
Total	539	2106	1346	361	539
	100	*100*	*100*	*100*	*100*
	BJP: 2014–(June) 2021				
Private persons and property	630	299	166	1340	630
	16.01	*24.8*	*25.27*	*27.81*	*16.01*
Business	55	360	214	51	55
	3.59	*14.17*	*18.09*	*8.54*	*3.59*
Government	133	257	151	89	133
	8.69	*10*	*12.76*	*14.91*	*8.69*
Police	638	519	86	93	638
	41.7	*20.43*	*7.27*	*15.58*	*41.7*
Military	273	178	155	10	273
	17.84	*7.01*	*13.1*	*1.68*	*17.84*
Other	186	596	278	188	186
	12.16	*23.46*	*23.5*	*31.49*	*12.16*
Total	1530	2540	1183	597	1530
	100	*100*	*100*	*100*	*100*
	Congress + BJP: 2004–(June) 2021				
Private persons and property	387	1196	721	291	2595
	18.7	*25.74*	*28.51*	*30.38*	*25.44*
Business	71	553	368	90	1082
	3.43	*11.9*	*15*	*9.39*	*10.61*
Government	221	607	379	144	1351

(continued)

Table 1.8 (continued)

	Congress: 2004–2013				
	Jammu & Kashmir	*Red Corridor*	*Northeast*	*Rest of India*	*Total*
	10.68	*13.07*	*14.99*	*15.03*	*13.24*
Police	796	963	226	147	2132
	38.47	*20.73*	*8.94*	*15.34*	*20.9*
Military	352	225	254	13	844
	17.01	*4.84*	*10.04*	*1.36*	*8.27*
Other	242	1102	581	273	2198
	11.7	*23.72*	*22.97*	*28.5*	*21.54*
Total	2069	4646	2529	958	10,202
	100	*100*	*100*	*100*	*100*

Figures in italics are percentages of column totals
Source Own calculations from GTD

of total attacks, rose from, respectively, 29.3% and 14.7% in 2004–2013 to 41.7% and 17.8% in 2014–(June) 2021. Similarly, in the Northeast, attacks on private persons and property, the government, and the police fell from, respectively, 31.4%, 16.9% and 10.4% of all attacks in 2004–2013 (Congress) to 25.3%, 12.8%, and 7.3% in 2014–(June) 2021 (BJP). The counterpart to this was that attacks on the military rose from 7.4% of all attacks in 2004–2013 (Congress) to 13.1% in 2014–(June) 2021 (BJP).

1.9 Terrorist Weapons

The GTD distinguished 13 types of terrorist weapons as the *primary* types of attack, and these were reorganised in this book into the following five broad categories: (i) Firearms; (ii) Explosives; (iii) Incendiary devices; (iv) Melee18F[18]; and (v) Other. As Table 1.9 shows, between 2004 and (June) 2021, 87.5% of attacks in J&K, 71% in the Red Corridor, 84.8% in the Northeast, and 77.8% in RoI involved either firearms or explosives. However, although firearms and explosives were the most popular weapons of attack the balance between the two varied by region. In J&K

[18] Melee is defined in the GTD as a weapon—targeting people rather than property—that does not involve a projectile.

there was an almost equal division between firearms (used in 44.8% of total attacks) and explosives (used in 42.7% of total attacks) while in the Red Corridor and in the northeast the balance favoured explosives. In the Red Corridor, firearms and explosives were used in, respectively, 29.5% and 41.5% of all attacks while in the Northeast firearms and explosives were used in, respectively, 29.5% and 55.3% of all attacks.

There were, however, some striking differences in the pattern of weapons usage between the Congress and the BJP regimes. During the Congress government of 2004–2013, 35.6% of attacks in the Red Corridor used firearms and 35% used explosives; during the BJP government of 2014–(June) 2021, this proportion fell to 24% for firearms and rose to 46.9% for explosives. The use of explosives fell from 48% under the Congress to 40.7% under the BJP and this was paralleled by a rise in the use of incendiary devices from 1.1% to 7.7% under the BJP. In the RoI, the use of firearms rose from 21.9% under the Congress to 32.1% under the BJP while the use of explosives fell from 56.7% under the Congress to35.8% under the BJP.

1.10 The Plan of the Book

In presenting the topic of the political economy aspects of terrorism in India, the book comes in two parts. Part 1, comprising Chapters 2, 3, and 4 introduces the reader to the whys and the wherefores of the conflicts: What were the grievances? What were the demands for redress? What was the means for getting redress? What was the official reaction to grievances/demands/methods? These three chapters introduced many of the pertinent issues which underpinned the unrests. For example, the "stolen election" of 1976 in Jammu and Kashmir in Chapter 2; the system of land tenure in Naxalbari in Chapter 3, which sparked the left-wing extremist movement; in Chapter 4, the flowering of the bamboo tree in the state of Mizoram which triggered a famine that led to insurgency in the state. Contained in these chapters are maps that illustrate the geographical areas of unrest.

Part 2 of the book (Chapters 5 and 6) is concerned with quantitative analysis in the context of political economy. As discussed earlier, circumstances in India provide a natural experiment for studying inter-party-in-government differences in the effectiveness of dealing with terrorists by bifurcating the period 2004–2021 into "Congress" and "BJP" sub-periods.

Table 1.9 Weapons of attack by region

	Congress: 2004–2013				
	Jammu & Kashmir	*Red Corridor*	*Northeast*	*Rest of India*	*Total*
Firearms	242	752	392	82	1468
	44	*35.59*	*28.93*	*21.93*	*33.42*
Explosives	266	741	776	212	1995
	48	*35.07*	*57.27*	*56.68*	*45.42*
Incendiary Devices	6	277	70	34	387
	1.09	*13.11*	*5.17*	*9.09*	*8.81*
Melee	19	146	9	29	203
	3.45	*6.91*	*0.66*	*7.75*	*4.62*
Other	17	197	108	17	339
	3.09	*9.32*	*7.97*	*4.55*	*7.72*
Total	550	2113	1355	374	4392
	100	*100*	*100*	*100*	*100*
	BJP: 2014–(June) 2021				
Firearms	696	622	358	205	1881
	45.14	*24.34*	*30.03*	*32.08*	*31.73*
Explosives	627	1197	633	229	2686
	40.66	*46.85*	*53.1*	*35.84*	*45.31*
Incendiary Devices	119	327	59	106	611
	7.72	*12.8*	*4.95*	*16.59*	*10.31*
Melee	44	196	22	55	317
	2.85	*8*	*2*	*8.61*	*5*
Other	56	213	120	44	433
	3.63	*8.34*	*10.07*	*6.89*	*7.3*
Total	1542	2555	1192	639	5928
	100	*100*	*100*	*100*	*100*
	Congress + BJP: 2004–(June) 2021				
Firearms	938	1374	750	287	3349
	44.84	*29.43*	*29.45*	*28.33*	*32.45*
Explosives	893	1938	1409	441	4681
	42.69	*41.52*	*55.32*	*43.53*	*45.36*
Incendiary Devices	125	604	129	140	998
	5.98	*13*	*5*	*13.82*	*10*
Melee	63	342	31	84	520
	3	*7*	*1*	*8.29*	*5*
Other	73	410	228	61	772

(continued)

Table 1.9 (continued)

	Congress: 2004–2013				
	Jammu & Kashmir	*Red Corridor*	*Northeast*	*Rest of India*	*Total*
	3.49	*8.78*	*8.95*	*6.02*	*7.48*
Total	2092	4668	2547	1013	10,320
	100	*100*	*100*	*100*	*100*

Figures in italics are percentages of column totals
Source Own calculations from GTD

Chapter 5 examines fatalities resulting from terrorist activity, both of non-terrorists and of terrorists. It begins by defining a measure of government effectiveness in dealing with terrorism—the kill-ratio or, following an incident, the ratio of terrorists to non-terrorists killed (Hultman, 2007). This can be interpreted as the price of terrorism and the object of government is to deter terrorism by raising its price. The chapter then uses a novel decomposition method to analyse the contribution of sub-regional kill-ratios to the *overall* kill-ratio in a terrorist region. Lastly, this chapter develops the concept of the *Equally Distributed Equivalent Fatality Rate*. This incorporates society's *aversion to inequality* in the distribution of fatalities across incidents which leads it to shun terrorist incidents that cause many fatalities.

Chapter 6 explores the likelihood of terrorist incidents, in the three main zones of terrorist activity in India, of being successful. It uses a logit model, which is a statistical model that predicts the probability of a binary outcome (in this case, whether a terrorist incident was successful or not) after controlling for several factors like: the targets chosen by terrorists, their weapons, and their zones of operation. This method is used in conjunction with statistical testing using z-values which are used to determine if the difference in probabilities between different scenarios (e.g. Congress vs. BJP) was statistically significant.

The statistical model has two innovative features. First, it uses an interactive model to allow the BJP/Congress effects to be different for different components of the determining variables—for example, in the context of terrorist groups, there may have no difference between the parties in dealing with Islamic groups but a significant difference in dealing with left-wing extremists. Second, recognising that terrorist incidents differ in several aspects—region, assault type, terrorist group—it uses the "method of recycled proportions" to isolate the effects of political party on the number of fatalities and on the predicted probability of a terrorist attack being "successful". Both these innovations are described in detail in Chapter 6. Chapter 7 concludes the book with some final thoughts.

Appendix: List of Terrorist Groups by Broad Category

See Tables 1.10, 1.11, 1.12, 1.13, and 1.14.

Table 1.10 Islamic terrorists

Terrorist groups	*Number of incidents*	*Percentage of total*
Al-Arifeen	2	0.27
Al-Badr	7	0.95
Al-Fajr	1	0
Al-Madina	1	0.14
Al-Mansoorian	13	1.76
Al-Nasireen Group	3	0.41
Al-Nasirin (India)	1	0.14
Al-Shuda Brigade	4	0.54
Al-Umar Mujahideen	4	1
Al-Ummah	4	0.54
Ansar Ghazwat-ul-Hind	5	0.68
Deccan Mujahideen	8	1.08
Harakat ul-Mujahidin (HuM)	1	0.14
Harkatul Jihad-e-Islami	9	1.22
Hizbul Mujahideen (HM)	225	30.49
Indian Mujahideen	53	7.18
Islamic Front	4	0.54
Islamic Movement of Kashmir	2	0.27
Jaish-e-Mohammad (JeM)	116	15.72
Jamiat ul-Mujahedin (JuM)	4	0.54
Jammu and Kashmir Islamic Front	2	0.27
Khorasan Chapter of the Islamic State	13	1.76
Lashkar-e-Islam (India)	13	1.76
Lashkar-e-Taiba (LeT)	198	26.83
Mahaz-e-Inquilab	3	0.41
Muslim extremists	10	1.36
Quit Kashmir Movement (QKM)	1	0.14
Save Kashmir Movement	2	0.27
Students Islamic Movement of India (SIMI).	10	1.36
Tehrik al-Mojahedin	14	1.9
Tehrik-e-Galba Islam	2	0.27
Tehrik-e-Hurriyat (TeH)	1	0.14
United Jihad Council	2	0.27
Total	738	100

Source Own calculations from GTD

Table 1.11 Left-wing extremists

Terrorist groups	*Number of incidents*	*Percentage of total*
Bengali Sangram Mukti Bahini	1	0.02
Communist Party of India Maoist (CP.	2110	48
Communist Party of India- Marxist	10	0.23
Communist Party of India- Marxist-Len.	6	0.14
Jharkhand Bachao Aandolan	1	0.02
Jharkhand Janmukti Parishad (JJP)	14	0.32
Jharkhand Kranti Raksha Dal (Utari Ch.	1	0.02
Jharkhand Liberation Tigers (JLT)	7	0
Jharkhand Prastuti Committee (JPC)	4	0.09
Jharkhand Sangharsh Jan Mukti Morcha	2	0.05
Maoist Communist Center (MCC	8	0.18
Maoist Communist Party of Manipur	3	0.07
Maoists	1918	43.98
Naxalites	28	0.64
New People's Army (NPA)	1	0.02
Pathalgadi Movement	4	0.09
People's Committee against Police Atr.	22	0.5
People's Liberation Army (India	79	1.81
People's Liberation Front of India	84	1.93
People's Revolutionary Party of Kangl.	32	0.73
People's Revolutionary Party of Kangl.	11	0.25
People's United Liberation Front (PULF)	7	0.16
People's War Group (PWG)	3	0.07
Popular Front of India	1	0.02
Popular Front of India (PFI)	1	0.02
Revolutionary Communist Centre (RCC)	1	0.02
Terai Janatantrik Party	1	0.02
Thadou People's Liberation Army (TPLA)	1	0.02
Total	4361	100

Source Own calculations from GTD

Table 1.12 Northeast terrorists

Terrorist groups	*Number of incidents*	*Percentage of total*
A'chik Matgrik Elite Force (AMEF)	6	0.43
Achik Matgrik Army (AMA)	1	0.07
Achik National Cooperative Army (ANCA)	4	0
Achik National Liberation Army (ANLA)	4	0.29
Achik National Volunteer Council-B (A.	9	0.65
Achik Songna An'pachakgipa Kotok (ASAK)	18	1.3
Achik Tiger Force	1	0.07
Adivasi Cobra Militants of Assam (ACMA)	1	0.07
Adivasi National Liberation Army (ANLA)	6	0
Adivasi People's Army (APA)	3	0.22
All (Baksa District) B.F.D.N Sangodan	2	0.14
All Assam Revolutionary Army (AARA)	1	0.07
All Kamatapur Liberation Force	1	0.07
All Tripura Tiger Force (ATTF)	2	0.14
Arakan Army (AA)	1	0.07
Arakan Rohingya Salvation Army (ARSA)	1	0.07
Bangladesh Tiger Force	1	0.07
Barak Valley Tiger Force (BVTF)	1	0.07
Birsa Commando Force (BCF)	1	0.07
Black Widows	12	0.87
Bodo Liberation Tigers (BLT)	2	0.14
Bodo People's Front (BPF)	1	0.07
Bru Democratic Front of Mizoram (BDFM)	1	0.07
Bru National Liberation Front (BNLF)	3	0.22
Coordination Committee (CORCOM)	22	1.59
Dima Halao Daoga (DHD)	19	1.37
Dima Hasao National Army	1	0.07
Garo National Liberation Army	169	12.2
Gorkha Janmukti Morcha (GJM)	67	4.84
Gorkha Liberation Army (GLA)	9	0.65
Hill Tiger Force (HTF)	4	0.29
Hmar People's Convention-Democracy (H.	6	0.43

(continued)

Table 1.12 (continued)

Terrorist groups	*Number of incidents*	*Percentage of total*
Hynniewtrep National Liberation Counc.	13	0.94
Indigenous People's Front of Tripura	1	0.07
Kamtapur Liberation Organization (KLO)	13	0.94
Kanglei Yawol Kanna Lup (KYKL)	7	0.51
Kangleipak Communist Party (KCP)	42	3.03
Karbi Longri National Liberation Fron.	2	0.14
Karbi Longri North Cachar Liberation.	15	1.08
Karbi People's Liberation Tigers (KPLT)	20	1.44
Karbi Tribe	1	0.07
Khasi Students Union	10	0.72
Kuki Independent Organization (KIO/KIA)	1	0.07
Kuki Liberation Army (KLA)	3	0.22
Kuki National Army (KNA)	3	0.22
Kuki National Front (KNF)	16	1.16
Kuki National Liberation Front (KNLF)	4	0.29
Kuki Revolutionary Army (KRA)	6	0.43
Kuki Tribal Militants	8	0.58
Kuki Unification Frontal Organization.	1	0.07
Liberation of Achik Elite Force (LAEF)	1	0.07
Manipur Naga People's Army (MNPA)	11	0.79
Manipur Nationalist Revolutionary Par.	1	0.07
Moran Tiger Force (MTF)	2	0.14
Muslim United Liberation Tigers of As.	1	0.07
Naga National Council (NNC)	2	0.14
Naga People	1	0.07
Naga People's Council (NPC)	1	0.07
Naga extremists	4	0.29
National Democratic Front of Bodoland.	133	9.6
National Liberation Council of Taniland	1	0.07
National Liberation Force of Bengalis.	4	0.29
National Liberation Front of Tripura	35	2.53
National Revolutionary Front of Manip.	2	0.14
National Santhali Liberation Army (NS.	2	0.14

(continued)

Table 1.12 (continued)

Terrorist groups	*Number of incidents*	*Percentage of total*
National Socialist Council of Nagaland	102	7.36
National Socialist Council of Nagaland.	70	5.05
National Socialist Council of Nagaland.	3	0.22
National Socialist Council of Nagaland.	3	0.22
National Socialist Council of Nagaland.	2	0.14
Nikhil Bharat Bangali Udbastu Samanna.	1	0.07
Rabha National Security Force	1	0.07
Tiwa Liberation Army	1	0.07
Tribal Revolutionary Army (TRA)	1	0.07
Tribesmen	6	0.43
Tritiya Prastuti Committee (TPC)	28	2.02
United Achik Liberation Army (UALA)	3	0.22
United Achik National Front (UANF)	1	0.07
United Bengali Liberation Front (UBLF)	1	0.07
United Democratic Liberation Army (UD.	11	0.79
United Democratic Terai Liberation Fr.	1	0.07
United Garo Security Force (UGSF)	1	0.07
United Gorkha People's Organization (.	1	0.07
United Karbi	1	0.07
United Kuki Liberation Front (UKLF) -.	3	0.22
United Liberation Front of Assam (ULFA)	319	23.03
United Liberation Front of Barak Vall.	2	0.14
United National Liberation Front (UNLF)	39	2.82
United National Liberation Front of W.	1	0.07
United People's Democratic Solidarity.	2	0.14
United Reformation Protest of India	1	0.07
United Revolutionary Front	6	0.43
United Tribal Liberation Army (UTLA)	4	0.29
Volunteers of Innocent People of Naga.	2	0.14
Yimchunger Liberation Front (YLF)	1	0.07
Zeliangrong United Front	18	1.3
Zomi Revolutionary Army (ZRA)	2	0.14
Total	1385	100

Source: Own calculations from GTD

Table 1.13 List of incidents outside Jammu & Kashmir by Islamic terrorists: 2004–2013

Terrorist group	*State*	*Year*	*Month*
Tehrik-e-Galba Islam	Andhra Pradesh	2009	5
Tehrik-e-Galba Islam	Andhra Pradesh	2010	5
Harkatul Jihad-e-Islami	Andhra Pradesh	2007	5
Lashkar-e-Taiba	Andhra Pradesh	2013	2
Lashkar-e-Taiba	Andhra Pradesh	2005	8
Lashkar-e-Taiba (LeT)	Andhra Pradesh	2013	2
Indian Mujahideen	Bihar	2013	10
Indian Mujahideen	Bihar	2013	10
Indian Mujahideen	Bihar	2013	10
Indian Mujahideen	Bihar	2013	7
Indian Mujahideen	Bihar	2013	7
Indian Mujahideen	Bihar	2013	7
Indian Mujahideen	Bihar	2013	10
Indian Mujahideen	Bihar	2013	10
Indian Mujahideen	Bihar	2013	10
Indian Mujahideen	Bihar	2013	10
Indian Mujahideen	Bihar	2013	10
Indian Mujahideen	Bihar	2013	7
Indian Mujahideen	Bihar	2013	10
Indian Mujahideen	Bihar	2013	10
Indian Mujahideen	Bihar	2013	7
Mahaz-e-Inquilab	Delhi	2005	10
Indian Mujahideen	Delhi	2008	9
Lashkar-e-Taiba (LeT)	Delhi	2006	4
Indian Mujahideen	Delhi	2008	9

(continued)

Table 1.13 (continued)

Terrorist group	*State*	*Year*	*Month*
Indian Mujahideen	Delhi	2008	9
Indian Mujahideen	Delhi	2008	9
Mahaz-e-Inquilab	Delhi	2005	10
Indian Mujahideen	Delhi	2008	9
Mahaz-e-Inquilab	Delhi	2005	10
Harkatul Jihad-e-Islami	Delhi	2011	9
Lashkar-e-Taiba (LeT)	Delhi	2007	4
Indian Mujahideen	Delhi	2010	9
Indian Mujahideen	Delhi	2008	9
Lashkar-e-Taiba (LeT)	Delhi	2005	10
Lashkar-e-Taiba (LeT)	Delhi	2012	2
Lashkar-e-Taiba (LeT)	Delhi	2006	12
Indian Mujahideen	Delhi	2008	9
Indian Mujahideen	Gujarat	2008	7
Indian Mujahideen	Gujarat	2008	7
Indian Mujahideen	Gujarat	2008	7
Indian Mujahideen	Gujarat	2008	7
Indian Mujahideen	Gujarat	2008	7
Indian Mujahideen	Gujarat	2008	7
Indian Mujahideen	Gujarat	2008	7
Indian Mujahideen	Gujarat	2008	7
Indian Mujahideen	Gujarat	2008	7
Indian Mujahideen	Gujarat	2008	7
Indian Mujahideen	Gujarat	2008	7
Indian Mujahideen	Gujarat	2008	7
Deccan Mujahideen	Gujarat	2008	11
Students' Islamic Movement of India (SIMI)	Gujarat	2009	6

Terrorist group	*State*	*Year*	*Month*
Indian Mujahideen	Gujarat	2008	7
Indian Mujahideen	Gujarat	2008	7
Indian Mujahideen	Gujarat	2008	7
Indian Mujahideen	Gujarat	2008	7
Indian Mujahideen	Gujarat	2008	7
Lashkar-e-Taiba (LeT)	Karnataka	2005	12
Hizbul Mujahideen (HM)	Karnataka	2010	4
Al-Ummah	Karnataka	2013	4
Deccan Mujahideen	Maharashtra	2008	11
Deccan Mujahideen	Maharashtra	2008	11
Indian Mujahideen	Maharashtra	2012	8
Deccan Mujahideen	Maharashtra	2008	11
Indian Mujahideen	Maharashtra	2011	7
Indian Mujahideen	Maharashtra	2012	8
Lashkar-e-Taiba (LeT)	Maharashtra	2006	7
Deccan Mujahideen	Maharashtra	2008	11
Deccan Mujahideen	Maharashtra	2008	11
Indian Mujahideen	Maharashtra	2012	8
Indian Mujahideen	Maharashtra	2011	7
Indian Mujahideen	Maharashtra	2010	2
Indian Mujahideen	Maharashtra	2012	8
Deccan Mujahideen	Maharashtra	2008	11
Deccan Mujahideen	Maharashtra	2008	11
Indian Mujahideen	Maharashtra	2012	8
Indian Mujahideen	Maharashtra	2011	7
Indian Mujahideen	Maharashtra	2012	8
Indian Mujahideen	Rajasthan	2008	5
Lashkar-e-Taiba (LeT)	Rajasthan	2007	10

(continued)

Table 1.13 (continued)

Terrorist group	*State*	*Year*	*Month*
Al-Ummah	Tamil Nadu	2013	7
Al-Ummah	Tamil Nadu	2013	7
Harkatul Jihad-e-Islami	Tripura	2008	9
Harkatul Jihad-e-Islami	Tripura	2008	9
Harkatul Jihad-e-Islami	Tripura	2008	9
Harkatul Jihad-e-Islami	Tripura	2008	9
Harkatul Jihad-e-Islami	Tripura	2008	9
Lashkar-e-Taiba (LeT)	Uttar Pradesh	2005	7
Lashkar-e-Taiba (LeT)	Uttar Pradesh	2008	1
Indian Mujahideen	Uttar Pradesh	2010	12
Harkatul Jihad-e-Islami	Uttar Pradesh	2007	5
Students' Islamic Movement of India (SIMI)	Uttar Pradesh	2010	4

Source Own calculations from GTD

Table 1.14 List of Incidents outside Jammu & Kashmir by Islamic terrorists: 2014–(June) 2021

Terrorist group	*State*	*Year*	*Month*
Students' Islamic Movement of India (SIMI)	Haryana	2016	1
Students' Islamic Movement of India (SIMI)	Jharkhand	2015	8
Students Islamic Movement of India (SIMI)	Karnataka	2014	12
Students Islamic Movement of India (SIMI)	Karnataka	2015	11
Khorasan Chapter of the Islamic State	Kerala	2017	3
Khorasan Chapter of the Islamic State	Madhya Pradesh	2017	3
Students' Islamic Movement of India (SIMI)	Maharashtra	2015	9
Hizbul Mujahideen (HM)	Maharashtra	2014	7
Lashkar-e-Taiba (LeT)	Punjab	2015	7
Lashkar-e-Taiba (LeT)	Punjab	2015	7
Lashkar-e-Taiba (LeT)	Punjab	2015	7
Lashkar-e-Taiba (LeT)	Punjab	2015	7
Lashkar-e-Taiba (LeT)	Punjab	2015	7
Lashkar-e-Taiba (LeT)	Punjab	2015	7
Lashkar-e-Taiba (LeT)	Punjab	2015	7
United Jihad Council	Punjab	2016	1
Students' Islamic Movement of India (SIMI)	Tamil Nadu	2014	5
Al-Ummah	Tamil Nadu	2014	6
Students' Islamic Movement of India (SIMI)	Tamil Nadu	2014	5
Muslim extremists	Tamil Nadu	2017	3
Muslim extremists	Tamil Nadu	2016	9
Muslim extremists	Tamil Nadu	2016	9
Khorasan Chapter of the Islamic State	Uttar Pradesh	2019	10
Khorasan Chapter of the Islamic State	Uttar Pradesh	2017	3
Indian Mujahideen	Uttar Pradesh	2017	8
Khorasan Chapter of the Islamic State	Uttar Pradesh	2017	3
Jaish-e-Mohammad (JeM)	Uttar Pradesh	2019	2
Khorasan Chapter of the Islamic State	Uttar Pradesh	2017	3
Students' Islamic Movement of India (SIMI)	Uttaranchal	2014	12
Muslim extremists	West Bengal	2017	5

Source Own calculations from GTD

References

Borooah, V. K. (2008). "Deprivation Violence and Conflict", An Analyis of Naxalite Activity in the Districts of India. *International Journal of Conflict and Violence, 2*, 317–333.

Card, D. & Krueger, A. (2000). Minimum Wages and Employment: A Case Study of the Fast-Food Industry in New Jersey and Pennsylvania. *American Economic Review 84*, 772–793.

Global Terrorism Database. (2019). *Codebook: Inclusion Criteria and Variables*. University of Maryland.

Hoffman, B. (1998). *Inside Terrorism*. Columbia University Press.

Hultman, L. (2007). 'Battle Losses and Rebel Violence: Raising the Costs for Fighting.' *Terrorism and Political Violence, 19*, 205–222.

Fair (2014). *Fighting to the End: The Pakistan Army's Way of War*. Oxford University Press: Oxford.

Lafree, G., & Dugan, L. (2007). Introducing the Global Terrorism Database. *Terrorism and Political Violence, 19*, 181–204.

Lafree, G., Dugan, L., & Miller, E. (2015). *Putting Terrorism in Context: Lessons From the Global Terrorism Database*. Routledge.

Piazza, J. A. (2009). Is Islamist Terrorism More Dangerous? An Empirical Study of Group Ideology Organization, and Goal Structure. *Terrorism and Political Violence, 21*, 62–88.

Rosenzweig, M. R., & Wolpin, K. I. (2000). Natural Natural Experiments in Economics, *Journal of Economic Literature 38*, 827–874.

Second Administrative Reforms Commission. (2008). *Combatting Terrorism: Protecting by Righteousness*. Government of India.

Silke, A. (2003). Becoming a Terrorist. In A. Silke (Ed.), *Terrorists, Victims, and Society: Psychological Perspectives on Terrorism and its Consequences* (pp. 29–54). Wiley.

CHAPTER 2

Jammu & Kashmir: To Have and to Hold

2.1 Background: British India and the Princely States

At the time of its partition in 1947 into the two new independent countries ("Dominions") of India and Pakistan, British India contained 562 princely states—that is states with a hereditary ruler—which were formally outside the purview of British administration in India.[1] These states covered 40% of the area of British India and contained 23% of its population (Map 2.1). So much so, that it would have been impossible to traverse the length of India without passing through at least one of these princely states (Zubrzycki, 2023). The rulers of these states were conferred with the title of Maharaja or Raja (if Hindu) or Nawab (if Muslim)—for example, the Maharaja of Kashmir or the Nawab of Junagadh; in an exceptional case, the ruler of Hyderabad was known as the Nizam of Hyderabad.

Although these states were independent, they functioned under the paramountcy of the Crown which exercised its control through the presence of its officers (under the aegis of the Indian Political Service) in the

[1] The number of states (562) was the used by the Sir Harcourt Buttler Committee of 1927 to investigate and clarify the relationship between the paramount power of the British Raj in India, and the rulers of Princely States.

V. K. Borooah, *The Political Economy of Terrorism*,
https://doi.org/10.1007/978-3-032-08553-5_2

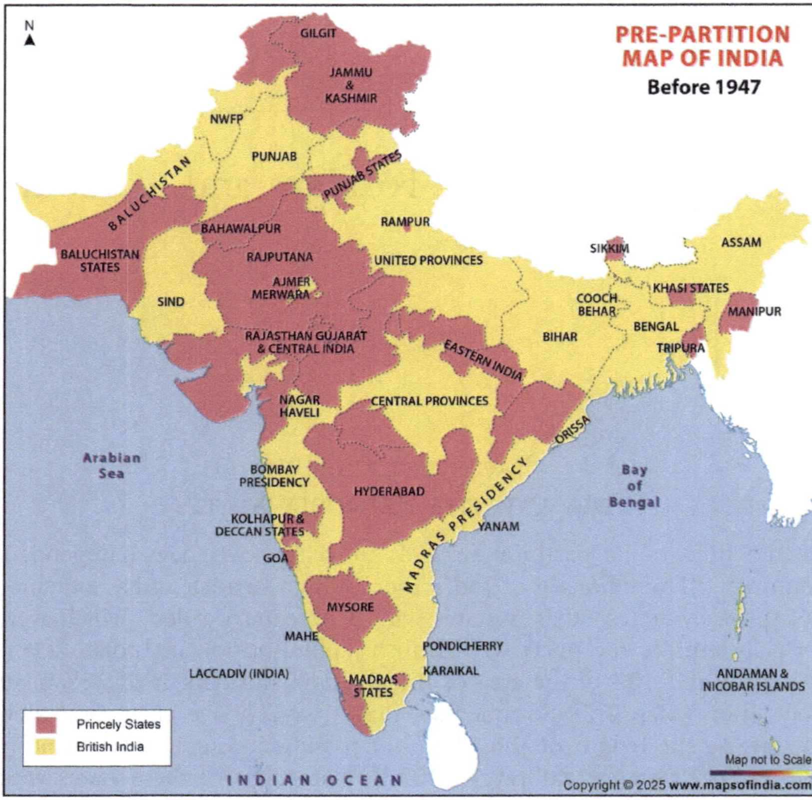

Map 2.1 Princely states in India (*Source* Maps of India)

states. These were termed "Residents" (in the larger states) and "Political Agents" (in the smaller states) and they "advised" the states' rulers on matters of policy and acted to prevent, or at least to curb, any of their behavioural excesses. This control was, however, very light: the Residents and Political Agents were advised by their Instructions Manual that "unless misrule reaches a pitch which violates the elementary laws of civilisation, the Imperial Government will usually prefer to take no overt measures for enforcing reform".[2]

The policy of recognising the princely states as independent entities was a departure from the earlier East India Company policy of annexing the native states and incorporating them into British India. This was based on the "doctrine of lapse" which allowed the Company to take over a state if its ruler died without a male heir. The most vigorous exponent of this policy was Lord Dalhousie, the Governor-General of India from 1848 to 1856, who during his tenure annexed nearly a dozen states, *inter alia* Satara, Jhansi, Nagpur, Tanjore, and, most famously of all, on 7 February 1856, Oudh (*Awadh*). After the unsuccessful Mutiny (First War of Independence) of 1857, the Crown took over the administration of India and the policy of annexation was abandoned in the belief that an important factor contributing to the Mutiny was—as the policy of annexation embodied—riding roughshod over native sentiments. Instead, a patchwork quilt of native states, both large and small, all in a subordinate relationship with the Crown which provided them guaranteed protection against internal unrest but which, otherwise, left them to do pretty much as they pleased.

In order to establish a hierarchy among the Princely states, the Imperial Government devised a system of hereditary "gun salutes" with 149 of the 562 states being awarded the honour of gun salutes: 21—"hereditary" gun salutes for Hyderabad, Kashmir, Mysore, Gwalior, and Baroda; 19 for Bhopal, Indore, Kolhapur, Travancore, and Udaipur; 17–11 salutes for a clutch of 77 states—including Patiala, Jaipur, Jodhpur (17 salutes), Dholpur, Dungarpur, Jaisalmer, (15 salutes)—and states like Sangli, Bhor, Chhota Udaipur bringing up the rear with 9 salutes. By contrast, the Imperial Majesty and the Viceroy of India were due, respectively, 101- and 31-gun salutes.[3]

The princely states were a mixed bag. There were states like Travancore and Baroda in which the Maharaja's rule was benevolent and enlightened. Under Baroda's ruler, Gaekwar Sayajirao, child marriage and bigamy were

[2] Manual of Instructions to Officers of the Political Department of the Government of India, p. xiii Accessed December 15, 2025 from https://www.qdl.qa/en/archive/81055/vdc_100073939522.0x000021).

[3] For a full list, Accessed December 15, 2025 fromhttps://en.wikipedia.org/wiki/Salute_state#:~:text=Apart%20from%20these%2C%20no%20other,and%20the%20Maharana%20of%20Udaipur.

made illegal, school education was both free and compulsory for all children in the early 1900s. Travancore, under the guidance of its Dewan, Ramaswami Iyer who ruled on behalf of the tutelary deity, Sri Padmanabha, had a literacy rate of 47% which was three times the literacy rate of British India and, in 1936, it opened its temples to the "untouchable" castes which, all over India, were debarred from visiting temple premises (Zubrzycki, 2023). The other princely states, however, were less enlightened. Chudgar (1929) described the typical ruler as:

> While they talk of their rights, they show not the slightest regard for the elementary rights of their subjects. While they plead for justice for themselves, they deny it to their people. They talk of being trustees of their people, and yet waste all money drawn from them in reckless extravagance without any sense of responsibility. (p. 215)

At partition, these states were given the option of joining either India or Pakistan or to remain as separate entities. These options were made laid out in an address, on 25th July 1947, by the newly appointed Viceroy, Lord Mountbatten to the Chamber of Princes (COP). Formed in 1921, the COP comprised the 108 states permitted at least 11-gun salutes, with an additional 12 members representing the other states, and it was the closest that the native rulers had to an institution which would represent their collective views.[4] At COP's well attended meeting of July 1947, though with Hyderabad's Nizam, Travancore's Chief Minister (*Dewan*), Indore's Maharaja and Bhopal's Nawab as prominent absentees—Mountbatten informed them that they would be given instruments of accession to sign, choosing between the two Dominions, with independence as the third option. Accession would only involve defence, foreign affairs, and communications and in every other respect their sovereignty would remain untouched.

His offer contained a threat and a caveat. The threat was that sanctions would be imposed on any state which, by choosing independence, refused to accede. The caveat was the expectation that geographic realities would play a major role in the states' decision as to which Dominion they would

[4] Though Hyderabad, Mysore, and Baroda refused to join, and Cochin, Jaipur, Indore, Travancore, and Udaipur would not attend its meetings. Attendance at its annual meetings rarely exceeded forty (Zubrzycki, 2023).

accede and, under this expectation, most of the states were "irretrievably linked with the Dominion of India" (Philips, 1962).

After Mountbatten's address to the COP, some states considered going independent but, after a meeting, on 28 July 1947, at the Viceregal Palance with the triumvirate of Mountbatten, Sardar Vallabhbhai Patel—the Home Minister in the pre-Independence interim government sworn in on 2 September 1946—and Patel's able and trusted aide, the civil servant, V.P. Menon, most were persuaded that independence was a mirage and that they were better off becoming part of the Dominion of India that was to be born on 15 August 1947.[5]

There remained, however, three holdouts: the Dewan of Travancore, the Nizam of Hyderabad, and the Maharaja of Kashmir were adamant that their states would seek independence in preference to joining either India or Pakistan. Travancore was easily settled: after a failed assassination attempt on his life by a member of the Kerala Socialist Party, the Dewan of Travancore—in the face of a warning from the Congress Party that, in the event of Travancore independence, India would not assist it against communist insurrection—agreed to accede to India, an event that was formally consummated on 30 July 1947.

Hyderabad, however, proved a tougher nut to crack. The Nizam of Hyderabad, Mir Osman Ali Shah, with his coterie of mostly Muslim civil servants, ruled a Hindu-majority state which was the largest and the richest of all the princely states covering an area of 215,000 square kilometres with 17 districts. In June 1947, in response to the British plan for the partition of the country, the Nizam of Hyderabad announced that Hyderabad would accede to neither India nor Pakistan but, instead, would be an independent country.

A Standstill Agreement, to preserve the status quo, which would have allowed Hyderabad and India's new government to negotiate a settlement beyond 15 August 1947, the date of Indian independence, was proposed and due to be signed on October 1947. This, however, was sabotaged by Qasim Razvi, the leader of the Muslim party *Majlis-e-Ittehad-ul-Muslimeen (MIM)*, which represented the militant views of Muslims in Hyderabad. Prior to the signing, the MIM organised a massive demonstration in the city of Hyderabad which surrounded the residences of the

[5] The Interim Government was headed by the Viceroy, Lord Mountbatten, with *inter alia* Nehru (Congress) as Minister for External Affairs, Vallabhbhai Patel (Congress) as Home Miniter, and Liaqat Ali Khan (Muslim League) as Minister for Finance.

Prime Minister of Hyderabad, the Nawab of Chattari, and of Sir Walter Mockton, the Nizam's constitutional adviser and reviled their role in "Hyderabad's betrayal" (Hyder, 2012). This Agreement was finally signed in November 1947 and under its terms, the Government of India (GoI, hereafter) would not, from the date of signing, exercise any authority over Hyderabad for a year.

Over the course of this "standstill year", the Nizam and his coterie made strenuous efforts to strengthen Hyderabad's prospects for independence. An important part of this was to bolster the size of a paramilitary force, set up by the MIM called the *Razakars*, which had become the armed wing of the party. The *Razakars* brutally put down an armed insurrection by Left-Wing Extremists and their peasant sympathisers, primarily in the districts of Nalgonda and Warangal, against the feudal rule of large landowners (Rao, 2012, p. 284) and killed those Muslims, such as the journalist Shoebullah Khan, who welcomed the merger of Hyderabad with India. At the same time Hyderabad made overtures to Pakistan. As the MIM leader, Qasim Razvi, expressed it, "we must use the time under standstill to reason with them but always from a position of strength-...that is why Razakars are necessary! We have a strong case in law; we have inalienable rights; we have powerful allies! We must put our trust in Allah and show we are prepared to resist" (as quoted in Hyder, 2012, p. 24).

In the face of these provocations during the "standstill year", the Indian government decided to use its Army—in an operation euphemistically termed "police action"—and annex Hyderabad. The military operation began on 13 September 1948 was over by 18 September: on that date, Hyderabad surrendered and became formally a part of India. And, putting all these complexities in the shade, are the many twists and turns of the "Kashmir question" which is the subject of the subsequent sections.

2.2 Jammu & Kashmir: The Beginning

When speaking of Jammu & Kashmir, one should most accurately be referring to it as the collective of three parts: (i) Jammu; (ii) Kashmir; and (iii) Ladakh. This three-part geographical entity is, hereafter, referred to as Jammu and Kashmir (J&K) as shown in Map 2.3. Jammu is the predominantly Hindu region in the south of J&K (with districts: Jammu, Kathua, Samba, Poonch, Rajouri, Udhampur, Reasi, Ramban, Doda, and Kishtwar); Kashmir is the predominantly Muslim valley to its north (with districts: Srinagar, Anantnag, Pulwama, Kupwara, Shopian, Ganderbal, Bandipora, Baramulla, Budgam, and Kulgam); and Ladakh is the sparsely populated region to the east of the Kashmir valley (districts: Leh, dominated by Buddhists, and Kargil, dominated by Shia Muslims, in eastern and western Ladakh, respectively).[6] Collectively, the population of J&K is split between two-thirds Muslim and one-third Hindu with a scattering of Sikhs and Buddhists, the latter mostly in Ladakh. This distinction is important because the Maharaja of J&K was a Hindu, with Jammu town as the state's capital, ruling over a population which was majority Muslim (Anand, 1964)

Prior to the rule of the Hindu Maharajas, from 1846 till 1947, J&K was a fiefdom of the Sikh kingdom of Ranjit Singh. After Ranjit Singh's defeat in the Anglo-Sikh war of 1846, during which Gulab Singh actively assisted the British, he was, in reward for his loyalty, awarded the state of J&K—comprising Jammu, the Kashmir Valley, Gilgit-Baltistan and Ladakh—on very favourable terms, and was enthroned as the Maharaja of J&K.

According to Article III of the Treaty of 16 March 1846, Gulab Singh was allowed to purchase the state of J&K for "the sum of Rupees fifty lakhs to be paid on the ratification of this Treaty and twenty-five lakhs on or before the first October of the current year, AD 1846" (Akbar, 2002, p. 64). Thus began the line of *Dogra* (which was Gulab Singh's Rajput sub-caste) kings that ruled J&K for the next century until Indian independence. Gulab Singh (1846–1856) was succeeded by Ranbir Singh (1856–1885), who was followed by Pratap Singh (1885–1925), with Hari Singh (1925–1952) as the last Maharaja of J&K before Indian independence. The Treaty of 1846 gave the Dogra dynasty not just *sovereignty* over but also *ownership* of the state of J&K.

A feature of Dogra rule in J&K was the poor living conditions of its Muslim population. Sir Albion Rajkumar Banerjee, who was appointed in 1927 by the last Maharaja, Hari Singh, as the first and only Prime Minister of J&K, resigned in 1929 in protest at conditions in the state with the damning observation:

> Jammu and Kashmir state is labouring under many disadvantages, with a large Mohammedan population absolutely illiterate, labouring under

[6] Though the GoI plans to reconfigure Ladakh with five districts: Sham, Nubra, Changthang, Zanskar, and Drass.

> poverty and very low economic conditions of living in the villages and practically governed like dumb driven cattle. There is no touch between the government and the people, no suitable opportunity for representing grievances... The administration has at present no or little sympathy with people's wants and grievances. (Geelani, 2006, p. 33)

Another feature of Dogra rule was that the small minority of Kashmiri *Pandits* (Hindu *Brahmins*)—about 5% of J&K's population—exercised inordinate influence in the administration and were also disproportionately wealthy. Though *Pandits* and *Dogras* practised different forms of "Hinduism", many *Pandits* were employed as debt collectors and landlords, functioning as the public face of Dogra exploitation (Kallepalli, 2024).

Two further areas in which Pandits dominated J&K were in the shawl industry and in government jobs. European demand for Cashmere (Pashmina) shawls in the late nineteenth century had led to a booming industry in J&K, offering the state's merchant class an opportunity to vie, in terms of wealth, with its landowners. Under Maharaja Ranbir Singh, a government department, called the *Daghshawl*, exercised control over the manufacture of shawls. The department had about 200 employees and was responsible for certifying that shawls were suitable for export. The head of this department, called the *Daroga,* was an office of considerable power and influence and this was a hereditary position within the ambit of a Pandit family descended from Birbal Dhar.[7]

The Pandits also had a stranglehold over government jobs, and this became an increasing source of resentment for the growing number of Muslim youths returning to J&K equipped with degrees from Aligarh and Lahore. In fact, Mohammed Abdullah—who later, as Sheikh Abdullah, became a giant of J&K politics—obtained a Master's degree in Chemistry from Aligarh Muslim University contemporaneously with a *Pandit* student who received the same qualification, but from Benares Hindu University; to Abdullah's chagrin, on their return to J&K, the latter was appointed a college lecturer while Abdullah could only get a temporary school-teacher's position.

After Mountbatten's address to the COP on 25 July 1947, Hari Singh, Maharaja of J&K, faced the same choices as the other rulers of the princely states: accede to India or to Pakistan, or remain independent.

[7] See Ahmad (2005) and Devdas (2019)

Pakistan pinned its hopes of obtaining J&K on the experience of the princely state of Junagadh which had a Muslim ruler (the Nawab of Junagadh) ruling over an overwhelmingly Hindu population. Despite this, the Nawab announced that he would be acceding to Pakistan. The resulting uproar from Junagadh's population, after this announcement, aided by a blockade of the state by India, led the Nawab and his entourage to flee to Pakistan and Junagadh acceded to India. J&K was the mirror image of Junagadh: A Hindu ruler with a majority Muslim population: if Junagadh could go to India, why shouldn't J&K come to Pakistan?

India, on the other hand, had two factors in its favour. First, unlike Pakistan, it did not have a state religion. So, while a majority Hindu state, like Junagadh, could not be expected to accede to Muslim Pakistan, there was no reason why a Muslim majority state, like J&K, should not accede to secular India. The second factor in India's favour was that Kashmir's most popular and prominent politician, Sheikh Abdullah, did not favour Kashmir's accession to Pakistan and leaned towards joining India. In a statement to a press conference on 6 March 1948 he stated that: "we have decided to work with and die for India ...we made our decision in 1944 when we resisted the advances of Mr. Jinnah. Our refusal was categorical"; and, on 29 September 1948, at another press conference: "We have burnt our boats. There is no place in Kashmir for a theocratic state" (as quoted in Akbar, 2002, p. 137).

On his return to J&K in 1930, after obtaining a Master's degree in chemistry from Aligarh Muslim University, Sheikh Abdullah did a stint as a schoolteacher at Srinagar Government High School but shortly thereafter he immersed himself entirely in the politics of the state by forming, in October 1932, a new political party, the Jammu and Kashmir Muslim Conference, of which he became the first President. In the September 1934 elections to the state's *Praja Sabha* (legislative assembly)—which had been forced upon the Maharaja by the Glancy Commission of 1932 to investigate Muslim grievances in J&K—Sheikh Abdullah's Muslim Conference won 16 of the 21 seats reserved for Muslims. In a subsequent election in 1938, it won all 19 Muslim seats.[8]

Over the past few years, Sheikh Abdullah had been shifting his initial Muslim perspective on J&K's affairs to a vision which included all those

[8] The *Praja Sabha* had 75 members with 33 elected representatives of whom 21were reserved for Muslims, 10 for Hindus, and two for Sikhs.

who lived in J&K, irrespective of their religion. This revived the historical concept of *Kashmiriyat,* originating from the great ruler of Kashmir, Zayn al-Abidin (1395–1470). This emphasised the cultural commonality—in terms of food, art, clothing, and language—of the people of J&K, notwithstanding differences in their religions, and it represented a political culture of inclusiveness and equality amid diversity. In the wake of this change in Sheikh Abdullah's views, his party's name was altered, on 11 June 1939, from the Jammu and Kashmir *Muslim Conference* to the Jammu and Kashmir *National Conference* (hereafter, simply NC).[9]

Sheikh Abdullah, and by extension the NC, was bitterly opposed to continuance of Dogra rule in J&K. In a Memorandum sent to the three-man Cabinet Mission which arrived in India on 24 March 1946 to consult with political leaders on India's constitutional future, Sheikh Abdullah argued that the *Dogras* had no legitimacy in J&K since "no sale deed can condemn four million men and women to the servitude of an autocrat when the will to live under his rule is no longer there" (cited in Lone, 2024). This was the beginning of the NCs, and Sheikh Abdullah's, *Quit Kashmir* movement which, after months of disruption in J&K, culminated in his arrest on 20 May 1946 followed, on 10 September 1946, by his conviction for sedition with a concomitant sentence of three years imprisonment.

But, in the face of this India or Pakistan choice, Hari Singh had another idea which rode roughshod over any aspirations that the NC might have had for a democratic J&K: he wanted an independent J&K with himself as its ruler which would, as he envisaged it, make J&K "the Switzerland of the East". Meetings with Lord Mountbatten in Srinagar between 19 and 22 June 1947 failed to make Hari Singh commit to either India or Pakistan. Instead, he offered to sign standstill agreements with both countries, suggesting to representatives of both the Indian and Pakistani Dominions, through telegrams sent on 12 August 1947, that "*existing arrangements should continue pending settlement of details*". This offer was accepted by Pakistan, but not by India which wanted more time to examine its implications.[10]

[9] This did not command the universal support of Muslims in the party. In 1941, Chaudhury Ghulam Abbas left the NC to revive the old Muslim Conference which became an affiliate of Jinnah's Muslim League.

[10] There have been suggestions that while Nehru, perhaps because of his Kashmiri heritage, was keen on J&K joining India, Vallabhbhai Patel was ambivalent about the

Pakistan used the time offered by its standstill agreement to prepare an attack on J&K which began on 22 October 1947 when 5000 tribals from Pakistan's North-West Frontier Province invaded J&K.[11] As Hodson (1969) noted, the timing of the invasion was well calculated to place the defence of Kashmir from India at a disadvantage: winter was beginning to close in upon the passes and, if the invaders could capture Srinagar airfield, Indian troops would have to take the arduous and hazardous land route to J&K.

In response to the Maharaja's plea to India for help against the invaders, Mountbatten, who as Governor-General, was chairing the Government's Defence Committee Meeting held over 22–25 October 1947, declared that: "it would be quite improper to move Indian troops into what was, at the moment, an independent country. … If it were true that the Maharajah was now anxious to accede to India, then Jammu and Kashmir would become part of Indian territory. This was the only basis on which Indian troops could be sent to the rescue of the State from further pillaging by the aggressors" (Menon, 1956, p. 399). On 25 October 1947, Menon flew to Jammu and returned the next day with Hari Singh's signature on an Instrument of Accession to India combined with the Maharaja's commitment "to set up an interim government at once and to ask Sheikh Abdullah to carry the responsibilities in this emergency with Mehr Chand Mahajan, his Prime Minister" (Menon, 1956, p. 400). After some discussion, the Defence Committee accepted J&K's accession to India on 26 October 1947, *subject to the proviso that a plebiscite should be held in the State when the law-and-order situation allowed.*

Then India began an audacious defence of J&K against its foreign marauders. In the early hours of the morning of 27 October over a hundred civilian aircraft and Royal Indian Air Force (RIAF) planes were mobilised to fly troops, equipment, and supplies to Srinagar. Their

wisdom of having a large Muslim-majority state within a newly independent India. Consequently, the Patel-Menon combine, in dealing with Hari Singh, dragged their feet and did not engage in the arm-twisting that they had employed on other princely states. If they had done so, J&K might have acceded much earlier (Akbar, 2002, p. 101).

[11] Mr. Liaqat Ali Khan, Prime Minister of Pakistan, did not deny knowledge of the movement of tribals from the North-West Frontier Province (and beyond) into Kashmir, but said that any attempt by Pakistan authorities to interfere with the movement of tribesmen in defence of their fellow-Muslims would have precipitated trouble with the rest of the tribes on the Frontier (Hodson, 1969, p. 447).

orders were to secure Srinagar airfield, to assist the Kashmir Government (assumed to be a popular administration under Sheikh Abdullah) in maintaining law and order in Srinagar, and if possible to drive away any tribesmen who might have entered the city. By the end of the month three more battalions of the Indian Army had reached Srinagar and the military position had been stabilised (Hodson, 1969).

In the story of the Indian defence of J&K, nothing was more remarkable than the speed and efficiency with which troops were flown to Srinagar on 27 October 1947. It was an airlift which won the admiration of Lord Mountbatten, and it changed the course of history in J&K. The Indian Army was able to liberate the Kashmir Valley, Jammu, and Ladakh from invading forces and the Indian army came close to taking the Muzaffarabad-Poonch-Mirpur belt, which today lies within Pakistan, but, at this point, Prime Minister Nehru chose to refer the issue to the United Nations (UN) for mediation and resolution.[12]

If India had been hoping for an unequivocal condemnation of Pakistan's actions by the UN they were disappointed. Following Nehru's petition, the United Nations Security Council (UNSC) passed Resolution 47, which set out three conditions for the resolution of the conflict in Jammu and Kashmir. Firstly, both Pakistan and India should agree to establish a ceasefire. Secondly, Pakistan should withdraw all its troops from J&K and India must reduce the number of its number of troops to the minimum needed for preserving law and order. Thirdly, there needed to be a plebiscite, supervised by the United Nations, to determine the wishes of the people of J&K as to whether they desired to be part of India or of Pakistan.

Of these three conditions, only the first was implemented by a "ceasefire line"—established through the Karachi Agreement, between Military Representatives of India and Pakistan, signed on 27 July 1949, and supervised by the Truce Subcommittee of the United Nations Committee for India and Pakistan (UNCIP). This line divided the princely state of J&K into two parts: Pakistan Occupied Kashmir (PoK) comprising the districts of Mirpur, Muzaffarabad, and a part of Poonch with, Gilgit-Baltistan, which was administered separately from PoK, also part of Pakistan; on the other hand, Ladakh along with the Jammu and the Kashmir Valley

[12] EFAS (2020, p. 3). The idea of referring the issue to the UN was Mountbatten's who overcame Nehru's initial objections to the idea. On 20 December 1947, the Indian Cabinet decided to appeal to the UN accusing Pakistan of being the invader.

were in India (see Maps. 2.2 and 2.3). Hereafter in this chapter, Jammu and Kashmir (J&K) refers to that part of the erstwhile princely state which belongs to India.

Sheikh Abdullah was appointed Prime Minister of J&K on 5 March 1948 and, after winning the 1951 elections to the J&K Constituent Assembly, he became its first elected Prime Minister. After his election as Prime Minister in 1951, Sheikh Abdullah set in motion a sweeping programme of land reforms in J&K, the like of which had never been seen before—though it had often been promised—in the rest of India. Bose (2021, p. 52) provides the details. Of the 2.2 million acres of private farmland, almost all was owned by 396 big landlords and 2347 medium-sized landlords who rented to landless peasants. After the reforms, 1 million acres were expropriated, *without compensation*, making landowners of 700,000 erstwhile serfs. As the next chapter shows, had similar reforms been carried out in other parts of India, the left-wing armed insurrections of the 1960s in Andhra Pradesh, Bihar, Chhattisgarh, Jharkhand, Orissa, and West Bengal might never have occurred.

Map 2.2 Jammu & Kashmir showing line of control and Pakistan occupied Kashmir (PoK)

Map 2.3 District Map of Jammu and Kashmir (*Source* Maps of India)

2.3 Jammu & Kashmir's Special Status

After, accession to India, J&K was awarded special status by the Indian Constitution through Articles 370 and 35A. Article 370, adopted in 1949, provided J&K autonomy over its internal affairs, with the GoI retaining control over foreign affairs, defence, communication, and currency. This granted J&K the right to its own constitution and flag, and to pass its own laws. The executive head of government would be known as "Prime Minister" and not, as in the other Indian states, as "Chief Minister" and the Head of State would be known as *Sadr-i-Riyasat* and not, as in the other Indian states, as "Governor". Article 35A, adopted in 1954, reserved for "permanent residents", defined those residents who had been issued a permanent resident certificate, of J&K: the right to buy land and property, to obtain employment in local government, and to be awarded local scholarships in education.

It is apposite at this stage to examine Pakistan's attitude towards that part of the J&K princely state—PoK (population 4.5 million) and Gilgit-Baltistan (population 1.8 million)—which came to it. Responsibility for the administration of Gilgit-Baltistan was transferred to Pakistan's central government, without any reference to the wishes of its people, so that the part of the princely state which accrued to Pakistan was split into two separate entities. As a result of the 1963 Sino-Pak border agreement, Pakistan ceded an area of 5300 square kilometres in Northern Kashmir to China.

Under its 1974 interim constitution, PoK has its own legislature (unicameral with 53 seats) and executive (in the form of a Prime Minister and Head of State). However, PoK is controlled by a Kashmir Council, based in Islamabad, headed by the Prime Minister of Pakistan. While the Interim Constitution grants PoK the right to form its own government, the Kashmir Council retains legislative competence over the affairs of PoK and can dismiss any elected government thereby destroying any semblance of autonomy for the region. Furthermore, the interim constitution states that: no person or political party in PoK is permitted to propagate against, or take part in activities prejudicial or detrimental to, the ideology of the State's accession to Pakistan; no one can assume office unless they take the oath of Jammu & Kashmir's accession to Pakistan and no one can be appointed to any government job unless they express loyalty "to the concept of Jammu & Kashmir's accession to Pakistan" (EFAS, 2020).

Thus, unlike India's treatment of J&K, according to its constitutionally guaranteed special status and autonomy, Pakistan's attitude towards PoK was central control with minimum autonomy and unquestioning acceptance of accession.

2.3.1 The Erosion of J&K's Special Status

However, as Bose (2021) points out, the force of Article 370 was eroded by the GoI from its inception. Protests about the special treatment accorded to J&K, and a concomitant demand for full integration of the state with the rest of India, were spearheaded by the *Praja Parishad* Party—formed in 1947 by ex-officials of the Maharaja with its rallying cry, *Ek Vidhaan, Ek Nishaan, Ek Pradhan* (one constitution, one flag, one leader)—in Jammu. These protests, which had the support of Buddhist leaders from Ladakh, climaxed in May 1953 with the visit of Shyama Prasad Mukherjee, President of the Bhartiya Jan Sangh—the precursor of India's ruling party today, the Bhartiya Janata Party (BJP)—to J&K. The Prime Minister, Sheikh Abdullah, and his National Congress government were in confrontational mode in responding to the demand for "full integration". A report of the party's Working Committee recommended a plebiscite but now with a third option—India, Pakistan, *or independence*. On 9 August 1953, Sheikh Abdullah was arrested under the J&K Public Security Act, thus beginning a 22-year period of incarceration, with brief spells of freedom, which only ended in 1975. He was also dismissed as J&K's Prime Minister by J&K's *Sadr-i-Riyasat*, the 22-year-old son of Hari Singh, Karan Singh, who then invited Bakshi Ghulam Mohammed to form a new government as Prime Minister.

The dilution of Article 370 began from that moment. First, a constitutional order by the President of India in 1954 extended the GoI's legislative reach over J&K to most subjects, not just those specified by Article 370: foreign affairs, defence, and communications. Second, India's Supreme Court was awarded full authority in J&K. Third, the constitutionally guaranteed fundamental rights of Indian citizens were extended to residents of J&K. By Article 370, all these changes needed the consent of the J&K government, and this was readily forthcoming from a compliant Bakshi Ghulam Mohammed.

The J&K Constituent Assembly—formed after elections to it in September/October 1951 which resulted in all its 75 members being from the NC—approved a draft constitution for the state (this came force on 26 January 1957) which began by asserting that "the state of Jammu and Kashmir is and shall be an integral part of the Union of India". This was on the heels of Prime Minister Nehru declaring to the Indian parliament in March 1956 that a "plebiscite was now beside the point" (Bose, 2021, p. 66). Thereafter, the Constituent Assembly dissolved itself and it was replaced by a Legislative Assembly through elections held in March 1957.

J&K's special status was diluted further after 1963. In December 1964, the GoI extended the scope of Articles 356 and 357 of the Indian Constitution to J&K. This empowered the GoI to dismiss an elected state government and to impose "President's rule", that is rule by the GoI. In March 1965, the title of Prime Minister of J&K was replaced, as in other states, with "Chief Minister" and the title of *Sadr-i-Riyasat* was replaced, again as in other states, with "Governor". In 1967, the practice by the J&K legislature nominating members to the Indian parliament was discontinued and replaced by direct elections from J&K constituencies.

On 5 August 2019, all pretence at "special status" for J&K was dropped entirely. By an Order of the President of India, all the provisions of the Indian Constitution were made to apply to the State *without any special provisions*. This implied that the State's separate Constitution stood inoperative, including the privileges granted by Article 370—which existed till then, albeit in watered down form—and Article 35A. The removal of privileges under Article 35A meant that ownership of land and property, and employment in government jobs, in J&K was no longer restricted to persons who were permanent residents of J&K but was open to all Indian citizens.

Alongside these changes, the status of J&K was downgraded from that of a full state of the Indian Union to two union territories: the J&K Reorganisation Act which took effect from 31 October 2019, bifurcated the existing state of J&K into the Union Territory of Jammu and Kashmir and the Union Territory of Ladakh.[13] The J&K Union Territory contained 14 million people (8 million in the Kashmir Valley and 6 million in the Jammu region) while Ladakh had a population of only 30,000.

With the addition of J&K and Ladakh, India has now eight union territories and 28 states, after the departure of J&K. An ingrained part of

[13] The eight Union territories in India are directly ruled by the GoI (that is, the central government), while its 28 states have a separate government for administrative purposes.

India's political culture is the aspiration of union territories to be "promoted" to a state and, since independence, several have managed this: Arunachal Pradesh; Goa; Himachal Pradesh; Manipur; Mizoram; Nagaland; and Tripura. Full statehood confers both prestige and the power to legislate on several areas which fall within the purview of the states (the "state list"). The case of the erstwhile state of J&K is, however, the first in which a state has been *demoted* to union territory status.

Union territories are either directly ruled by the GoI (that is, the central government)—Andaman & Nicobar Islands, Chandigarh, Dadra and Nagar Haveli and Daman and Diu, Lakshadweep—or they have elected legislatures with restricted powers, and strong oversight by a Lieutenant Governor, functioning as little more than municipal councils—Puducherry and Delhi. Ladakh joins the list of union territories of the first type while J&K is now a union territory of the second type. After these changes, India's attitude towards J&K has converged with that of Pakistan's towards PoK: both J&K and PoK were a part, like any other part, of their respective countries, and were certainly not due any "special status".

2.4 Election Irregularities in Jammu & Kashmir

While India went to the polls in the General Election of 1951, J&K elected a 75-seat Constituent Assembly (with 43 seats from the Kashmir Valley, 30 from Jammu, and two from Ladakh) over September/October 1951. But, unlike the free, fair, and contested Indian elections, all 75 seats were "won" by Sheikh Abdullah's NC in what was, in essence, a non-election: candidates from opposition parties either had their nomination papers rejected or withdrew, or were forced to withdraw, their candidature.[14]

The election irregularities that had characterised the elections to the Constituent Assembly in 1951, continued in the 1957 elections to J&K Assembly. Elections to 30 seats in the Kashmir Valley, "won" by the NC, were unopposed and the NC "won" another 10 seats in which the nomination papers of opposition candidates were rejected. All in all, only 28 of the 75 Assembly seats were contested: 20 from Jammu and eight from

[14] The *Praja Parishad Party* tried to field candidates from 28 of the 30 Jammu seats: 13 were disqualified and the other 15 withdrew in protest; the two non-NC candidates that tried to stand from the Kashmir Valley were forced to withdraw (Bose, 2021).

the Kashmir Valley. The result of the 1957 elections was that the NC held 68 of the 75 seats in the J&K Assembly and Bakshi Ghulam Mohammed continued as Prime Minister. The results from the 1962 elections told a similar story: the NC won 70 of the 75 seats, with only 39 of the 75 seats being contested—11 in the Kashmir Valley, and 28 in Jammu. Thirty NC candidates, including Bakshi Ghulam Mohammed, were returned unopposed, and another ten NC candidates were elected after their opponents' nomination papers were declared invalid.

The NC's attitude to elections was an extension of its authoritarian nature—the elections to the J&K Constituent Assembly in 1951 and the subsequent elections to the J&K Assembly of 1957 and 1962 all revealed a "win at all costs" mentality which pre-empted as many contests as possible before elections by getting opposing candidates to withdraw. This was combined with a ruthlessness towards those who disagreed with the NC's ruling clique: after Sheikh Abdullah's arrest, 33 other NC leaders who supported him were also arrested between 9 and 10 August 1953 under the J&K Public Security Act and in 1954, a left-wing Indian party, the *Praja Socialist Party*—not be confused with the *Praja Parishad Party* discussed earlier—was violently prevented from setting up an office in Srinagar. As Bose (2003) observed, Bakhshi's regime was notorious for two attributes: rampant corruption and the liberal use of police and gangs of professional thugs against any sign of opposition. By 1963, Bakshi Ghulam Mohammed had become an embarrassment with his strong-arm electoral tactics giving Indian democracy a bad name. He was asked by the GoI to step down and was replaced as Prime Minister by one of his cabinet ministers, Khwaja Shamsuddin.[15]

In the meanwhile, the NC had split into two factions headed respectively by Bakshi Ghulam Mohammed and Ghulam Mohammed Sadiq. After Bakshi's ouster, the Sadiq faction took control of the NC and, on 3 January 1965, the NC announced it would dissolve itself and merge with India's ruling Congress Party as its J&K outpost. In February 1964, after the uproar in the Kashmir Valley following the theft of a hair from the Prophet's beard from Srinagar's Hazratbal shrine on 27 December 1963 (which, as it happened, was returned safely by 4 January 1964), Khwaja Shamsuddin was replaced as Prime Minister by (the soon to be Congress party member) G.M. Sadiq. The first crisis that Sadiq faced was

[15] Bose (2003).

a no-confidence motion by his great rival Bakshi Ghulam Mohammed and his supporters. Sadiq's response was typical of his authoritarian NC antecedents: Bakshi and six of his supporters were arrested and imprisoned under the draconian Defence of India Rules for "endangering national security".[16]

In the 1967 elections to the J&K Assembly, 39 seats were uncontested and, of these, 22 accrued to ex-NC/Congress candidates of the Sadiq faction. It was also in the 1967 elections that, for the first time, members to the Indian Parliament (the *Lok Sabha*) were directly elected from six J&K constituencies (earlier they had been nominated by the J&K Assembly): five of the six seats were won by the Congress amidst allegations of widespread electoral irregularities.

Election irregularities in J&K were deemed necessary because otherwise, in the words of Bazaz (1967, p. 157), "if free elections are held—even as free as in other Indian States—it may be taken for granted that so long as the present conditions prevail the majority of seats will be captured by those unfriendly to India".

An example of electoral suppression is the treatment of the *Plebiscite Front* (PF), a new party launched on 10 August 1955 by loyal supporters of Sheikh Abdullah responding to the fact that the NC had been hijacked by his opponents—Bakshi Ghulam Mohammed, G.M. Sadiq, and Mir Qasim. This party, as its name implied, demanded that a free and fair plebiscite to finally solve the accession dispute. In December 1970, the PF, which had previously boycotted elections, announced that it would contest the 1971 Indian Parliamentary elections and the 1972 J&K Assembly elections.

This rang alarm bells among the NC politicians in J&K. The PF had proved itself to be one of the most popular political organisations in J&K and one of Sheikh Abdullah's principal opponents, the then Prime Minister Mir Qasim, admitted retrospectively, that "if the elections were free and fair, the Front's victory was a foregone conclusion".[17] On 12 January, the GoI declared the PF to be an unlawful organisation under the Unlawful Activities (Prevention) Act because the PF had asserted a claim to determine whether Jammu and Kashmir will remain a part of

[16] This act, passed during the First World War, granted the executive wide powers of preventive detention, internment without trial, and restrictions on writing, speech, and movement.

[17] Qasim (1992, p. 132).

India" (Bose, 2003, p. 76). On 9 January 1971, an Externment Order was passed on Sheikh Abdullah while he was in Delhi, preventing his entry into J&K, but this was lifted in June 1972 when he returned to J&K.

Politics in J&K were completely upturned with the "Delhi Accord" between Sheikh and Indira Gandhi in November.[18] By the terms of this accord, Sheikh Abdullah and the Plebiscite Front confirmed their support for Indian sovereignty over Kashmir and gave up their demand for a plebiscite; the *quid pro quo* was autonomy and self-government under Article 370 but *without any requirement that the Article's erosion (since its inception in 1949) be reversed.*[19] After this agreement, Mir Qasim (who, on G.M. Sadiq's death in 1971, had succeeded him as Chief Minister of J&K) stepped down and was replaced by Sheikh Abdullah who then dissolved the Plebiscite Front and, with himself as leader, reestablished the NC.[20]

The 1977 elections to the J&K Assembly held in June, which followed the "Delhi Accord", are widely considered the first free and fair elections J&K had known since its creation in 1948 (Puri, 2022). Sheikh Abdullah's NC won 47 of the 76 seats, and the Janata Party and the Congress won, respectively, 13 and 11 seats. On the positive side, the presence of the NC, the Janata Party, and the Congress as electoral competitors in J&K, with the Congress and the Janata Party dominating in Jammu and the NC in the Kashmir Valley, injected much needed political competition into the state's politics. On the negative side, an important aspect of political discourse in J&K—the determination of the state's future through a plebiscite—was lost, now that both the major political parties in the state

[18] The interlocutors in this were Mirza Afzal Beg and G. Parthasarthi from, respectively, the J&K and Indian sides.

[19] All of Sheikh Abdullah's proposals in respect of these were rejected as were his proposal that the Congress and the Plebiscite Front merge in J&K. On the other hand, Sheikh Abdullah turned down the Congress' invitation for him to join the party (Baloria, 2019).

[20] The timeline of Sheikh Abdullah's many periods of alternating incarceration and freedom is as follows: (i) arrested on 9 August 1953; (ii) released on 8 January 1958; (iii) rearrested on 30 April 1958 on "Kashmir Conspiracy Case" charges; (iv) released on 8 April 1964; (v) rearrested on 8 May 1964; (vi) released on 2 January 1968; (vi) Externment order on 8 January 1971 on Sheikh Abdullah, while he was Delhi, preventing his entry into J&K; (vii) Externment order lifted in June 1972 and Sheikh Abdullah returned to J&K; and (viii) Takes over, in 1975, from Mir Qasim as Chief Minister J&K.

were agreed that J&K was irrevocably a part of India. This was a gap that was sought to be filled by other parties, both existing and new.

Sheikh Abdullah died on 8 September 1982 and was succeeded by his son Farooq Abdullah, who left his medical practice in England—presaging Bashar al-Assad, who succeeded his father in Syria—to become a Member of the Indian Parliament and then Chief Minister of J&K much to the chagrin of Sheikh Abdullah's son-in-law, Ghulam Mohammad Shah (hereafter, G.M. Shah) who regarded himself as the Sheikh's rightful heir and Farooq as a parvenu.

Unfortunately, Farooq Abdullah, not content to operate in the shadow of Indira Gandhi and her Congress party, sought to carve a more independent role for himself by fostering relationships with the Indian opposition parties. This boded badly for him: although he decisively won the 1984 elections to the J&K Legislative Assembly, in June 1984, twelve of his deputies were persuaded to defect from his party and, along with another Independent, to join hands with the Congress deputies to form a government with G.M. Shah as the Chief Minister. This change was facilitated by the new Governor, Jagmohan Malhotra (known by the mononym, Jagmohan) who, after taking office in April 1984—following his predecessor's, the less compliant B.K. Nehru, transfer as Governor of Gujarat—dismissed Farooq Abdullah, denied him a test of support by way of a 'floor count', and refused his appeal for fresh elections.[21]

Shah lasted 21 months until an outbreak of violence against Hindus in J&K led the GoI to invoke Article 356 to dismiss his government in March 1986, on the grounds that law and order had broken down,[22] and to run the state through "Governor's Rule" with Jagmohan, as the Governor of J&K, exercising supreme executive authority.[23] This lasted for six months (till November 1986) after which it would have had to be renewed by a vote in the Indian Parliament. When Farooq Abdullah

[21] For details of the machinations underlying these events see Widmalm (1997).

[22] The "law and order breakdown" referred to the riots in the Anantnag district of J&K targeting Hindu families and places of worship. These riots followed the Babri Masjid mosque in Ayodhya—the birthplace of the Hindu deity, *Ram*—being allowed by the GoI in February 1986, when Rajiv Gandhi was Prime Minister, to open as a place of worship for Hindus.

[23] Under Article 92 of the J&K constitution, Governor's Rule implies absolute power that, unlike President's Rule in other states, is not accountable to the Indian Parliament (Puri, 2008, p. 97).

ended his flirtation with Indian opposition parties and reprised his role as understudy to the Congress party in J&K, the Congress withdrew its support for G.M. Shah and allowed Farooq Abdullah to reclaim the Chief Ministership in November 1986, pending elections in March 1987.[24]

2.4.1 A Stolen Election?

Following the free and fair 1977 elections, the results of the 1987 election to the J&K Assembly raised several questions, many of which related to the election's integrity. The main parties contesting were: Farooq Abdullah's NC, the Congress, and the Muslim United Front (MUF), a coalition of Islamic parties that had come together in 1987 and was generally expected to do well at the polls.[25] J&K voters went to the polls on 23 March 1987 and, after counting began, it became apparent that MUF was on track to win 15–20 seats in the 76 seat Assembly. However, when the results were finalised it turned out that the Congress-NC combine won 87% of the available 76 seats (with the NC winning 40 and the Congress securing 26) on the back of the 53% of the popular vote in J&K, while the Independents, with 35% of the vote share, obtained eight seats, of which four were won by MUF candidates. The J&K elections were conducted, as they were in all of India, under the first-past-the-post (FPTP) system under which the candidate obtaining a plurality of votes was declared the winner. As a result of this, the FPTP system is characterised by (sometimes considerable) imbalance between vote and seat shares: in the 2014 Lok Sabha elections, for example, the BJP won 282 seats with 31% of the popular vote while the Congress with 19.1% of the vote could only manage 44 seats. So, the observed imbalance in the 1987 J&K Assembly elections *could* be explained by vagaries of the electoral system.

The matter might have rested there where it not for several reported instances of "vote-rigging"", many of which are detailed in Badhwar (1987). As Widmalm (1997, p. 1021) wrote, "The exact extent of rigging

[24] When Farooq was asked why he needed the Congress's support at all, when he had won a comfortable majority in the state, he replied, "The Congress commands the centre. In a state like Kashmir, if I want to implement programmes to fight poverty and disease and run a government, I must stay on the right side of the centre. That is a hard political reality that I have come to accept" (Donthi, 2016).

[25] The pro-Pakistan Jama'at-i-Islami was part of this as was the Popular Front led by Abdul Ghani Lone.

remains difficult to assess, but an anonymous source at the Indian Intelligence Bureau claims that approximately 13 seats may have been lost by the MUF because of electoral malpractice. The same source comments that such electoral hijinks were quite unnecessary since the political opposition could never have won a majority of seats even in a free and fair election. Electoral rules, fragmented opposition, and strength of the Congress–NC combine made the cartel almost unbeatable".

None of the complaints of electoral tampering were investigated by any of the public institutions responsible for dispensing justice—not by the GoI, not by the J&K High Court, not by the Electoral Commission whose role it was to oversee the elections. On the contrary, it became commonplace to categorise protest as "anti-national" and to respond to it with ferocity with police opening fire on protesting crowds and arresting opposition candidates. It is widely agreed that the repression of the popular will in 1987 played a part in setting off the waves of militancy that flooded the state in the years that followed.[26] Many of those who joined the militancy were MUF supporters who saw armed revolt as the only way forward.[27] As Abdul Ghani Lone expressed it: "It was this [the 1987 elections] that motivated the young generation to say, 'to hell with the democratic process and all that this is about' and they said 'let's go for the armed struggle'" (as quoted in Widmalm, 1997, p. 1021).

Before, however, one regards this explanation for the unrest that followed the 1987 elections to the J&K Assembly as the *only* explanation, one should also consider alternative, supplementary, interpretations. Farooq Abdullah attributed the rising discontent to the fact that the GoI was niggardly in disbursing funds to J&K relative to the generosity it displayed towards other states: 70% of the aid that J&K received was in the form of grants and 30% was issued as loans, in contrast to other hill states for which 90% was grants and only 10% was loans (Puri, 2008, p. 88).

[26] A study of the views and perceptions of militant separatists made by a team of Indian Army psychiatrists and psychologists, which revealed that violence was seen mainly as a means to fight a corrupt system and justified by "a deep sense of alienation" rather than by Islamic fundamentalism or notions of holy war (Widmalm, 1997, p. 1022).

[27] The MUF leader Muhammad Yusuf Shah, who "lost" from Amirakadal constituency in Srinagar, would take on the name Sayeed Salahuddin, and rise to head the Hizbul Mujahideen. His election manager from 1987, Yasin Malik, would go on to head the Jammu and Kashmir Liberation Front, a Kashmiri nationalist organisation.

Another source of discontent according to Farooq Abdullah was that there was widespread discrimination against Muslims who failed to get jobs because these had become the preserve of Kashmiri Pandits and Dogras: where will 2 lakh [200,000] unemployed Kashmiri youth go? He asked plaintively.[28] This feeling was echoed by others who argued that the Pandits and the Dogras belonged to the traditional elite in J&K and, like the upper castes all over India, they were overrepresented in banks, private companies, and salaried jobs in the public sector (Widmalm, 1997, p. 1024). Though, in the absence of corroborating evidence, there is little reason to believe that the unrest which gripped J&K *immediately after the elections* was caused by long-term fiscal and social factors. Indeed, in this case, post hoc *ergo propter hoc* might be a reasonable conclusion.

2.5 The Uprising in Jammu and Kashmir

The post-1987 election uprisings in J&K began innocuously enough. On 10 June 1988, there were demonstrations in Srinagar to protest a rise in electricity prices in the face of erratic power supplies. The police opened fire on these protestors killing three and the government dubbed these demonstrations as 'anti-national'. There then followed a spate of demonstrations over the next few months of a decidedly mixed bag nature: (i) anti-India and pro-Pakistan demonstrations in 1988 and 1989: India's Independence Day was met with black flags and a state-wide strike was called on 26 January 1989, India's Republic Day; (ii) Pro-Pakistan demonstrations in 1988: Pakistan's Independence Day (14 August) was celebrated and, on 17 August, a demonstration in the Valley condoled the death of Pakistani President, Zia-ul-Huq; (iii) Commemorative demonstrations: on 5 February to commemorate the hanging of Maqbool Butt convicted of murder of an Indian diplomat and on 5 April to commemorate the death in police custody of Shabir Shah (iv) Pro-Islamist demonstrations (on 13 February against Salman Rushdie's). But all these demonstrations, airing a diversity of grievances, met with the same harsh response from the authorities and usually involved police firing on unarmed crowds (Puri, 2008).

[28] *The Times of India*, New Delhi, 4 November 1988.

The insurrection took hold in 1990 under the banner of the pro-independence Jammu and Kashmir Liberation Front (JKLF), an organisation that was formed in PoK in 1965 with Amanullah Khan and Maqbool Butt (see point (iii), above). This was a movement which sought independence for J&K in its entirety and thus was in disfavour with both the Indian and Pakistani governments. The JKLF became infamous for taking hostages: in December 1989, Rubaiya Sayeed, the daughter of the Indian Home Minister, Mufti Mohammed Sayeed—who was a prominent Congress politician from J&K—was kidnapped, and to secure her release, the GoI released five JKLF activists that it had jailed.

On 19 January 1990, Farooq Abdullah's government, elected on the back of the back of the infamous 1987 election, was dismissed, on the charge that law and order had broken down in J&K. Jagmohan, who had left his post in July 1989 after a five-year stint as Governor, returned as Governor and the state once again came under "Governor's Rule". There then followed a wave of demonstrations, each calling for *Azadi* (freedom) from India. They were confronted by battalions of the Central Reserve Police Force (CRPF)—which was a paramilitary force under the command of the GoI—and a bloodbath followed. The CRPF fired upon crowds of demonstrators (in the three days between 21 and 23 January 1990, 300 demonstrators were shot dead in Srinagar) and engaged in armed confrontation with militants of the JKLF.[29] Between 1990 and 2002, 16,000 militants and 4600 Indian security personnel were killed (Bose, 2021, p. 98).

All this came with human rights abuses on both sides. Government security forces killed a large number of unarmed civilians, conducted warrantless house-to-house searches, seized youths, beat protestors, and destroyed whole neighbourhoods (Goldston & Grossman, 1991). A favourite tactic of Indian security forces was Cordon-and-Search Operations—tactic employed earlier in the Naga and Mizo hills and against left-wing extremists in central India. This involved surrounding a neighbourhood (or *mohalla*) or a cluster of villages, assembling all the men in an open space and asking paid informants, who were hooded to hide their identities, to identify from this assemblage those who were militants. The identified men were taken away for interrogation and were often never seen again. The Association of Parents of Disappeared Persons (APDP)

[29] Bose (2021, p. 105).

estimates that there are over 8000 missing persons and these disappearances only gathered pace with the Armed Forces Special Powers Act (AFSPA) imposed in J&K in September 1990 (Osuri & Fatima, 2018).

On the militants' side, the first political killing was in Srinagar, on 21 August 1989, when a block president of the NC was shot dead; thereafter, the first Kashmiri Pandit, Jia Lal Taploo, a BJP leader was killed and, on 14 September 1989, Neel Kanth Ganjoo, the judge who had sentenced the JKLF founder, Maqbool Bhatt, to death was assassinated. The human rights body, Human Rights Watch said that J&K militants had flagrantly violated international rules of war by summarily executing numerous civil servants and suspected government informers, throwing explosive devices at buses and government buildings, sowing terror through death threats and assassinating members of the minority Hindu community and Muslims thought to be insufficiently supportive of the insurgency.[30] Puri (2008, p. 92) also observed that, as the character of militancy in J&K changed from an inclusive, secular, pro-Azadi stance, encompassing both PoK and Indian J&K, embracing both Hindus and Muslims, to a pro-Pakistani and pro-Islamic position, militants became more brutal and fanatical.

2.6 Pakistan's Proxy War in J&K

One of the features about unrest in J&K is that, notwithstanding Pakistan's bellicosity about sovereignty over the territory, the Pakistan army has been extremely reluctant to engage *directly* in combat with the Indian army. Instead, a time-honoured Pakistani tactic in J&K has been, and continues to be, to seek groups which would fight Indian forces on its behalf but without officially involving Pakistani forces. These "proxy wars", in which third parties fought on Pakistan's behalf, began in 1948 when, as discussed above, tribesmen from the NWFP invaded J&K with the Pakistani government asking religious scholars to declare the incursion as a *jihad* (a war in defence of Islam) and the marauders as *mujahideen* (those who undertake *jihad*).[31]

The next proxy war in J&K occurred when Pakistan launched Operation Gibraltar in 1965 under the aegis of which approximately 30,000

[30] Goldston and Grossman (1991, p. 155).

[31] Haqqani (2005).

irregulars from PoK, under the command of Pakistani army officers of the rank of major, crossed the LoC in August 1965 with a view to rousing the local population to rebel against the Indian "occupation". It was Pakistan's hope that India would be sufficiently enfeebled by Nehru's death in 1964, and its decisive defeat by China in the 1962 Sino-Indian war, to pave the way for the operation's success. However, no local support from the J&K populace was forthcoming and with an Indian counterattack, aimed at sovereign Pakistan territory, Operation Gibraltar turned out to be a damp squib.

The next war with India in 1971—which did not involve J&K—resulted in a decisive defeat for the Pakistani army and the breakup of Pakistan into two parts—Pakistan and Bangladesh. This defeat and breakup deepened Pakistan's desire for revenge against India but this was leavened by the recognition that, given India's military strength it was unlikely to come through conventional warfare. This left proxy warfare as the only practical means by which Pakistan could exact vengeance. Given Pakistan's perception of Hindu India as an existentialist threat to Pakistan, proxy warfare in J&K was given a religious gloss in Pakistan by legitimising the idea that liberating J&K Hindu colonialists was *jihad*.

The most recent major conflagration between India and Pakistan was the war in Kargil (The Kargil War). This was a reprise of the infiltration and attack on J&K in 1948 by Pakistani tribesmen. This time, in the winter of 1998–1999, soldiers of the Pakistani army's Northern Light Infantry crossed the LoC from Gilgit-Baltistan into Kargil and set up 140 posts along a 110-mile stretch, at altitudes of over 15,000 feet, overlooking the valleys below. This incursion was undetected by Indian security forces until an Indian reconnaissance patrol, in summer 1999, was ambushed and its members killed.

Then began the Indian fightback, led by Atal Bihari Vajpayee's caretaker government—a consequence of him losing a vote of confidence in April 1999 by a single vote—pending fresh elections. From June 1999, Indian forces pulverised the Pakistanis by land and air—and with the Pakistanis forced to preserve the fiction that this was a spontaneous uprising by Kashmiri freedom fighters, unable to retaliate—the war was soon over. The Pakistanis were pressured into retreating from the LoC by the United States, the sanctity of the LoC was affirmed, as was the importance of settling the dispute through bilateral negotiations between India and Pakistan.[32]

These proxy wars were orchestrated by the Pakistan Army's Inter-Services Intelligence (ISI). Pakistan's external intelligence agency. The ISI and Military Intelligence (MI) are the two military intelligence services in Pakistan, and they are complemented by two civilian agencies—the Intelligence Bureau and the police's Special Branch. Of these agencies, the ISI is disproportionately powerful, and, within its sprawling structure, it is its directorate S (or S-wing) that is of relevance to this chapter because it is this directorate that is responsible for external operations and for working with non-state proxies (Tankel, 2014).

2.6.1 Pakistan's Funding of Militant Groups in J&K

In addition to setting off major conflagrations—the incursions of 1948, Operation Gibraltar in 1965, the Kargil war in 1999—the ISI was also responsible for funding, training, and facilitating the activities of a host of militant organisations in J&K. When the insurrection in J&K began in 1990, the JKLF was the only militant organisation in the state and the usual practice of its members was to slip across the LoC into PoK, receive training, funds and arms from Pakistani sources, and then renter J&K to carry out terrorist activities. At that time, there were very few non-Kashmiris involved in militancy and over 90% of militants killed by Indian security forces were local to J&K (Bose, 2021, p. 121).

There was, however, a tension between the Pakistani authorities who trained and funded the JKLF and the JKLF itself. For the former, the accession of PoK to Pakistan was irrevocable and, indeed, as pointed out earlier in this chapter, no person or political party in PoK was permitted to propagate against, or take part in activities prejudicial or detrimental to, the ideology of the State's accession to Pakistan. On the other hand, the core ideology of the JKLF comprised seeking an independent J&K, encompassing *both* PoK and Indian J&K, which was inclusive and secular embracing both Hindus and Muslims.[33]

[32] See Bose (2021, p. 154) and The Kargil Review Committee Report (1999).

[33] The founder of the JFLK, Amanullah Khan's book *Free Kashmir* sought a united, neutral, secular, and federal republic of J&K.

This contradiction caused the relationship between the two sides to unravel in the early 1990s as the Pakistani funders sought militant groups whose views cleaved more closely to Pakistan's requirements: pro-Islamic rather than secular, and pro-Pakistan rather than pro-independence. The second phase of the J&K began when Pakistan found such clients first by encouraging JKLF members to defect from the parent body and form splinter organisations and, second, by building proxy forces in J&K which would fight Pakistan's war in J&K.

The chosen proxy was Hizbul Mujahideen (HUM)—meaning Party of Holy Fighters—which was formed as the military arm in J&K of the fundamentalist Sunni organisation Jama'at-i-Islami (JI)—meaning Society of Islan—which, in fact, had contested seats in the 1987 election to the J&K Assembly. The leader of HUM was Sayeed Salahuddin who, under his real name, Muhammad Yusuf Shah, had "lost" the 1987 elections from the Amirakadal constituency in Srinagar for which, in a twist of irony, Yasin Malik, one of the future leaders of the JKLF, was his election manager.

The Jama'at-i-Islami is said to have set up the HUM at the behest of the ISI, to counter the JKLF and many of the early HUM cadres were former JKLF members. In contrast to the JKLF's demand for an independent J&K in its entirety (that is, Indian J&K and PoK, collectively), the aim of HUM was the integration of (Indian) J&K with Pakistan in tandem with the Islamisation of J&K. The organisation had its headquarters in Muzaffarabad (the capital of PoK) and, consistent with the desires of the ISI, attacked both Indian security forces and members of the pro-independence JKLF.

By 1993, HUM was paramount in militant activities in J&K. The main leaders of JKLF had been killed—Asfaq Wani was killed in March 1990, Yasin Malik was wounded and captured in August 1990, and Hamid Sheikh was captured and subsequently killed in November 1992. After his release from prison on bail in May 1994, Yasin Malik—the sole surviving leader of the JKLF in J&K—declared an indefinite ceasefire with the Indian government after three hundred of its activists had been killed, many because of information supplied by the HUM. This ceasefire was not acceptable to JKLF's PoK branch and the JKLF split into pro- and anti-ceasefire factions, with Yasin Malik and Amanullah Khan as their respective leaders.

By 1994, according to Bose (2021), the JKLF was on its last legs. In an echo of outcomes in Nagaland (described in Chapter 4), it had become riddled with factionalism, and this spawned several splinter groups of 'freedom fighters': the *Jaanbaaz* Force, the *Jehad* Force, the *al-Barq*, the *Lashkar-e-Islam*. The eclipse of the JKLF was paralleled by the ascendancy of the HUM which was now the dominant militant force in J&K. The HUM now, through a programme of targeted assassinations of prominent J&K citizens, allied to efforts to instil Sunni orthodoxy on the Sufi traditions of Kashmiri Muslims, unleashed a wave of terror in the state.[34]

In an effort to combat HUM, the Indian security forces, much as they did with the *Salwa Judum* in Chhattisgarh (see Chapter 3) and with the Surrendered ULFA (SULFA) in Assam (see Chapter 4), began recruiting a force of auxiliaries (termed the "renegades" or, in local parlance, "*Ikhwanis*") from those JFLK militants who wished to stop being 'freedom fighters' and to seek instead a steady income as 'Special Police Officers' in India's security infrastructure. The Ikhwan-ul-Muslimeen was formed by Mohammad Yusuf Parray (aka Kuka Parray) and, by early 1994, the group sided with the Indian forces to fight the militants backed by the Pakistani government. Besides Ikhwan, another group was operated by Javed Ahmad Shah (who had the backing of the state police's Special Operations Group, see below) and a third by Liaqat Khan in the Anantnag district). Depending on where they lived, many of the *Ikhwanis* were attached as auxiliaries of the counter-insurgency units of the Indian Army's *Rashtriya Rifles* (National Rifles) operating in various parts of J&K (Bose, 2021).

Also, consistent with Indian security practices in the "Red Corridor" of Central India, described in Chapter 3, a specialist 2300-strong counter-insurgency unit, drawn from personnel of the J&K police force and named the Special Operations Group (SOG), was formed in March 1994.[35] The role of the SOG was to conduct anti-insurgency operations either by itself or jointly with other security forces and thereby "involve the passive J&K police force in anti-terrorist activities and give a local face to these operations". The rewards for belonging to this group are reported to be several:

[34] Among others, Maulvi Farooq, the *Mirwaiz* (chief preacher) of the Northern Valley, in May 1990; Maulana Masodi in December 1990; Dr Abul Guru in April 1993; Qazi Nissar, the *Mirwaiz* of the southern part of the Kashmir valley in June 1994.

[35] Similar units in mainland India were the *Greyhounds*, created in 1985 by the Andhra Pradesh government as an elite force drawn from within the Andhra police, the *Jharkhand Jaguars*, a Special Task Force for the eradication of left-wing terrorism in the state of Jharkhand, and a *Special Operations Group* which is a similar force to combat Naxalite violence in Orissa.

a bonus of ₹3500 ($400)–₹50,000 ($570) for every militant killed—with payments also being made for arrests of militants and of arms caches seized—and out-of-turn promotions (Peer, 2002).

A combination of the *Ikhwani* auxiliaries of the *Rashtriya Rifles* and the SOG of the J&K police fought a ferocious Kashmiri-on-Kashmiri internecine conflict with the HUM in the 1990s and the GoI felt sufficiently emboldened by its success in neutralising militant activity to hold the elections, which had been due in 1992 but which had been postponed due to the security situation, in September 1996. On an overall turnout of 54% of eligible voters, Farooq Abdullah's NC won 57 of the total of 86 seats and he became Chief Minister again after an interregnum of over six years.

2.6.2 The ISI"s Change in Strategy in the New Millennium: The Rise of Fedayeen Attacks in J&K

The overall aim of the ISI was, and is, to make remaining in J&K such a burden for the Indian government that it would be tempted to abandon the area. However, fighting proxy wars using indigenous militants had, from the ISI's point of view two disadvantages: first, the aims of the sponsored militant groups, as with the JKLF, might not align with those of the Pakistan government; second, even when ISI-militant aims did align, as with the HUM, the growing efficiency of Indian security forces meant that indigenous militants could be hunted down. In a highly publicised encounter on 8 July 2016, Burhan Wani, the flamboyant leader of the HUM was killed in a gun battle with a joint team of the SOG of the J&K police and the *Rashtriya Rifles*. This then led to a change in the ISI's strategy for proxy warfare in J&K: henceforth, its support for indigenous militants declined and it began to promote militant activity in J&K by non-Kashmiris, either Pakistani nationals or nationals of other Islamic countries, many of whom had been battle-hardened in the crucible of the Afghan jihad..

2.6.3 Changes in the Form of the Insurrection: Martyrdom Attacks

This led to a change in the form of the insurrection from armed clashes between *groups* of militants (JKLF, HUM) and Indian security forces to one in which militants, usually operating in groups of 3 or 4 *pairs* (usually a combination of native and non-native Kashmiris), forced their way into a targeted site and took up attack positions, firing on Indian soldiers and lobbing grenades, with the intention of killing as many soldiers as possible before being killed themselves. Since the terrorists carried an adequate supply of ammunition and rations, these battles lasted between 24 and72 hours. During the first decade of the twenty-first century, *fedayeen* (Arabic for "those who sacrifice themselves") or suicide attacks had become an increasingly common mode of attack by Islamic militants, and this was reflected in the war in J&K.[36]

The rise of the *fedayeen* in J&K eclipsed the prominence of the earlier militant groups (the JKLF and then the HUM) in the state as these were replaced in the ISI's favour by two *fedayeen* groups, the *Lashkar-e-Taiba* (Army of the Pious, LeT), led by Hafiz Saeed with Zaki-ur-Rehman Lakhvi as operational commander and the *Jaish-e-Mohammad* (Army of Mohammad, JeM) led by Maulana Azhur. There is some suggestion that the ISI sponsored JeM to check the LeT's growing power (Tankel, 2014, p. 64). The *fedayeen* attacks unleashed a wave of killings in J&K, both of members of the Indian security forces and of unarmed civilians. Many of these incidents are detailed in the South Asian Terror Portal's, *Major Incidents of Terrorist Violence in Jammu and Kashmir*.[37] But, among these, two events standout for targeting civilian institutions.

In the first of these, on 1 October 2001, three terrorists, after detonating a car bomb outside the gates of the J&K Assembly in Srinagar, broke into its compound and engaged in a shoot-out with its security staff which resulted in 38, in addition to the three terrorists, dead and 60 persons injured. The second, and more egregious, attack was on the India Parliament building in New Delhi on 13 December 2001 by five members

[36] The roots of suicide attacks lie in a martyrdom culture in the Middle East and in Pakistan which extols the martyr (or *shaheed*) who are prepared give up their lives fighting for a cause and who had the full support of their families. Fair (2008) surveyed 141 Pakistani families whose male members had become *shaheed* (martyrs) in Kashmir and Afghanistan and observed (p. 60) that "Pakistan, like Palestine and other theatres for Islamist conflict, has a rich martyrdom culture wherein the community confers an important status to families of *shaheed*." She argues that, contrary to popular belief, Pakistani terrorists operating in Kashmir and Afghanistan, and their households, were well educated by Pakistani standards. So, in terms of equipment, there was evidence that Islamic *jihadists* operating in India were sufficiently well educated and motivated to readily absorb the high quality of training they received.

[37] https://www.satp.org/satporgtp/countries/india/states/jandk/data_sheets/majori ncidents.htm.

of the *JeM* group. In the gunfight between the terrorists and Indian security officers, all five terrorists were killed along with six police officers from Delhi, two officers from parliamentary security, and a gardener. Following the attack, four alleged "masterminds" behind the atrocity were put on trial of whom one, Afzal Guru, was eventually convicted, sentenced to death and, on 9 February 2013, hanged in Delhi's Tihar Jail after his petition for mercy had been rejected by the President of India.

On 14 February 2019, a suicide bomber, affiliated to the *JeM* group, mounted a vehicle-based attack on a convoy of vehicles carrying Indian security personnel on the Jammu Srinagar National Highway at Lethpora in the Pulwama district of Jammu and Kashmir (hereafter, J&K) in India: 40 members of India's Central Reserve Police Force, along with the bomber, were killed. What was significant about this attack was not that it happened—it was after all, the latest in deadly litany of such bombings in J&K. This attack stood out for the carnage that it inflicted—the 16 suicide attacks between 2005 and 2018 in J&K had resulted in 67 deaths whereas, in Pulwama, a single attack had killed 41 people.[38] But it was even more remarkable for the response it elicited from Prime Minister Modi's Bhartiya Janata Party (BJP) government.

On 26 February, twelve days after the Pulwama attack, fighter jets of the Indian Air Force flew 50 miles across the LoC (the de facto international border between India and Pakistan) and bombed, what was alleged to be, a JeM training camp near Balakot in Pakistan's Khyber-Pakhtunkhwa province. Since this was the first time since the Indo-Pakistan war of 1971 that the Indian Airforce had conducted airstrikes in Pakistan this muscular response by the BJP government was a radical departure from the more muted responses of earlier governments and it signalled a willingness on the part of the Modi government to risk war, if necessary, in order to punish both terrorist groups and their sponsor.

[38] The death toll refers to the total of security personnel and terrorists killed. Of the 16 suicide attacks in J&K between 2015 and 2018, six were in 2015, four in 2016, four in 2017, and two in 2018. https://www.satp.org/satporgtp/countries/india/states/jandk/data_sheets/Suicide_attacks_Jammu_Kashmir_2015.htm (accessed 28 March 2018).

2.6.4 Changes in the Targets of the Terrorism: Attacks on Hindus

The second change that occurred in the new millennial was that terrorists were increasingly targeting Hindus. Many of these attacks, though not all, took the form of attacks on Hindu pilgrims to the cave of Amarnath, which was sacred to the god Shiva and where he revealed the secrets of immortality and creation to his consort, the goddess Parvati. On 2 August 2000, LeT terrorists killed 32 people in the vicinity of Amarnath: 21 pilgrims, seven local Muslims, and four Indian security personnel. In July 2001, another attack killed 13 people of whom eight were pilgrims. On 10 May 2001, LeT terrorists killed seven Hindus in the erstwhile district of Doda (today's Kishtwar) and on 15 July 2001, they killed a further 15 Hindus. And, on 10 July 2017, eight Hindus on their way to Amarnath were murdered by LeT terrorists.[39]

It seemed that the abrogation of Article 370 in August 2019 had resulted in the restoration of normalcy in J&K with only 127 fatalities in 2024 compared to 283 in 2019 and 321 in 2020. Consequently, the number of tourists to J&K reached a peak of 23.6 million in 2024 much to the delight of residents in the Kashmir valley where every family is, directly or indirectly, dependent on the tourist trade for its livelihood.[40] This illusion was shattered on 22 April 2025 when 26 tourists were shot dead by gunmen in an attack near Pahalgam.

2.7 The Expansion of Political Representation and Unlikely Coalitions

On 12 January 1971, the GoI had declared the Plebiscite Front (PF), formed by Sheikh Abdullah's supporters, to be an unlawful organisation under the Unlawful Activities (Prevention) Act because "the PF had asserted a claim to determine whether Jammu and Kashmir will remain a part of India" (Bose, 2003, p. 76). Consequently, the only views that could be aired at the ballot box were pro-Indian views, either by the Congress Party or by the NC and electoral competition was reduced to contests between these two parties.

[39] Several killings of Hindus also followed the abrogation, on 5 August 2019, of J&K's special status (Chowdhary, 2022).

[40] https://indianexpress.com/article/opinion/columns/after-pahalgam-patience-and-precision-must-guide-the-way-forward-9961878/.

The 2002 elections in J&K introduced a third political party. Mufti Mohamed Sayed, a prominent Congress politician and former Union Home Minister, whose daughter had been kidnapped by terrorists in December 1989, founded the Jammu and Kashmir People's Democratic Party (PDP) in 1999 which—unlike the NC which was opposed to the separatist political agenda—sought to bring the separatist discourse into the mainstream of J&K politics. The precursor to the PDP was the *All Parties Hurriyat Conference* (APHC) founded in 1993 as an alliance of pro-freedom Kashmiri freedom organisations.

The introduction of the PDP meant that electoral politics in the Kashmir valley, hitherto dominated by the NC, became more competitive. Disappointment with the willingness of the NC to address represent Kashmiri identity politics had led to disillusion among Muslims in J&K with the electoral process and the formation of the PDP went a long way to ameliorating this. The PDP was concerned with "governance"—the quotidian problems faced by people in respect of employment, infrastructure, development—and left alone issues of "conflict resolution" relating to the status of J&K within India. The consequence of this was that, after 2002, elections in J&K were seen as being conducted in a free and fair manner (Chowdhary, 2015): indeed, for the first time during the 2002 elections, electronic voting machines were used in counting votes in J&K The consequence of the 2002 election was that the PDP formed the government in J&K in coalition with the Congress with the Mufti as Chief Minister of J&K for the first three years and Congress's Ghulam Nabi Azad for the next three.[41] This coalition government did not last its full term because, in response to the Amarnath land controversy, the PDP withdrew its support for its coalition partner before Azad could complete his three years as Chief Minister.[42]

[41] Although the NC, with Omar Addullah, Sheikh Abdullah's grandson as leader, emerged as the single largest party (with 28 seats) it could not command a majority.

[42] On 26 May 2008, the government of India and the state government of Jammu and Kashmir reached an agreement to transfer 100 acres of forest land to the Shri Amarnath Shrine Board (SASB) to set up shelters and facilities for Hindu pilgrims. This move was opposed by the people of Kashmir valley, who interpreted this as a permanent transfer of land to outsiders, following strong and sustained protests about this transfer, the J&K State government reversed the decision to transfer land. As a result, Hindus in the Jammu region launched counter-agitations and blocked the valley till 31 August 2008, when the agreement was signed between the group leading the Jammu agitation and J&K governor

The elections of 2008, saw the formation of a new coalition government between the NC and the Congress with Omar Abdullah—Farooq Abdullah's son and Sheikh Abdullah's grandson—of the NC as Chief Minister. The remarkable feature of the 2008 elections to the J&K Assembly was that turnout rose to 61.5% from the 43.7% turnout in the 2002 elections and that constituencies like Anantnag and Pulwama (which had turnouts in 2002, in response to a call to boycott the polls, of respectively, 7.2% and 18.1%) saw their turnouts rise to, respectively, 41.2% and 40.8% respectively. The emergence of the PDP as a party giving voice to separatists in J&K appeared to have dealt a decisive blow to the politics of electoral boycott which, hitherto, had been a pervasive feature of J&K elections.

The 2008 coalition of the NC and the Congress faced a turbulent future with several unsettling incidents acting as road bumps. First, the legacy of the Amarnath land controversy injected a regional divide into J&K politics pitting Hindus from Jammu against Muslims from Kashmir—the Muslims from the Valley were against the transfer of land while Hindus from Jammu were for it. Following that was the rape and murder, in May 2009, of two young girls—Ayesha and her sister-in-law, Nelofar—in Shopian allegedly, by almost universal public belief, by the Indian security forces; a month later, was the alleged harassment and abuse of a woman by the police in Baramulla when she went to seek the release of her husband from police detention. On 11 June 2010, two police personnel in Srinagar allegedly killed17-year old Tufail Mattoo as he walked home from a tutoring session for school. More than 120 people were killed in the violent protests following his death. In all these cases, the public reaction was one of deep distrust in the impartiality of the forces of law and order (Mattoo, 2009).

The coalition government limped on till the 2014 elections when a seemingly sea change occurred in the J&K political landscape: the NC was knocked off its perch as J&K's dominant party and ceded first position to the PDP which won 28 seats in J&K (twenty-five and three seats from, respectively, the Kashmir and Jammu regions) and second position to the BJP (25 seats, all from the Jammu region). The NC itself came third winning only 15 seats (twelve and three seats from, respectively, the Kashmir and Jammu regions). The outcome of this election was a

N. N. Vohra's appointed panel. Under the terms of the agreement the SASB would make *temporary* use of 100 acres of land during the yatra period every year (Wasi, 2009).

coalition government between the PDF and BJP with Mufti Mohammad Sayeed of the PDF as chief minister for the full term of six years and Nirmal Kumar Singh of the BJP as Deputy Chief Minister.

The two coalition partners could not have been more different. The BJP represented the interests of Hindus in Jammu, the PDP the interests of Muslims in Kashmir. The BJP viewed the Azadi movement as a manifestation of Pakistan's proxy war in J&K; the PDP saw the Azadi movement as a legitimate expression of people's concerns and one that needed to be incorporated into the political process. Since its formation in 1951, the BJP had maintained a hardline stance on the Kashmir issue and has stood for the repeal of Article 370 of India's constitution which granted special autonomous status to the state. In sharp contrast to the BJP, the PDP has been seen as a pro-Kashmir party. Critics accuse it of peddling "soft separatism" revolving around reconciliation with Pakistan and separatist groups fighting against Indian rule in Kashmir.

Because of these factors, the PDP-BJP coalition government, formed on 1 March 2015, collapsed under the weight of its own contradictions. The death of the Chief Minister, Mufti Mohammed Sayeed, on 7 January 2016, of natural causes, meant that disagreements arose between the two partners on the way forward and it was not till 4 April 2016 that the Mufti's daughter and chosen successor, Mehbooba Mufti, could be sworn in as Chief Minister. On 19 June 2018, the BJP said the three-year alliance with the PDP had become "untenable" in the wake of increasing violence in the state. The state then formally came under President's rule which lasted till the next elected government which followed the elections in 2024 to the J&K Assembly.

The 2024 elections to the J&K Assembly saw several new parties enter the electoral contest. The logic of these parties—like the *Apni Party* or the Democratic Progressive Azad Party—was that with the abrogation of Article 370, traditional parties like the NC or the PDP, which were based on autonomy for J&K had lost their *raison d'être* and there was space for parties to articulate other concerns. The most visible political grouping was the traditional coalition of the Congress and the NC. The Congress was dominant in the Jammu region where it was in direct competition with the BJP while the NC vied for influence with the PDP in the Kashmir valley. The PDP had, however, fallen on hard times after the death of its founder, Mufti Mohammed Sayeed, and his daughter's tenure as Chief Minister, as part of a BJP coalition had not been successful and had been followed by the GoI imposing a prolonged period of President's rule.

In the event, after the 2024 elections in J&K, a Congress-NC government was elected, on the back of an overall turnout of nearly 64%—compared to the 65.5% turnout in the 2014 election—with the NC winning 42 seats (35 from Kashmir and seven from Jammu) and the Congress winning six seats (five from Kashmir and one from Jammu). The two winners of the election were the NC and the BJP which won, respectively, 42 and 29 seats of the 90 seats in the Assembly with all the BJP wins coming from Jammu. The results of the 2024 elections thus reemphasised the electoral divisions within J&K—the BJP was dominant in Hindu-majority Jammu while the NC was dominant in Muslim-majority Kashmir.

2.8 Concluding Thoughts on Jammu and Kashmir

Earlier in this chapter it was suggested that Vallabhbhai Patel and V.P. Menon, the two architects of the accession of the erstwhile princely states to the newly independent union of India, might have been ambivalent about the accession of J&K to India, particularly about the wisdom of having a large Muslim-majority state within a newly independent India and all the problems that it might entail. Consequently, the Patel-Menon combine, in dealing with Maharajah Hari Singh, dragged their feet and did not engage in the vigorous arm-twisting that they had employed on rulers of the other princely states. For example, when, in 1947, a representatives of the Kashmir government sought a lead from the States Ministry on the choice between India and Pakistan, he was brushed off by V.P. Menon saying that the Government of India could give no guidance on the matter and that if a formal proposal for accession was received it would be considered in the light of all the relevant factors (Hodson, 1969, pp. 443–444).

On the other hand, the sentimentalist in Nehru saw Kashmir as his ancestral home—though the earliest recorded ancestor of the Nehru family moved from Kashmir to Delhi in 1716; the idealist in Nehru saw in Kashmir an opportunity to burnish his secularist credentials; and the politician in Nehru saw in Kashmir an opportunity to be seen as an international statesman, by "peacefully" incorporating a Muslim majority state into a newly independent India. In this tussle between Patel's "realism" and Nehru's "sentimentality", the latter won: but who is to say that it was not a poisoned chalice that Nehru offered his countrymen?

There then followed a series of errors on the military, diplomatic, and political front. Militarily, there is the suggestion that in 1948, the Indian army came close to taking the Muzaffarabad-Poonch-Mirpur belt, which today lies within PoK, but before it could do that, Nehru chose to refer the issue to the United Nations (UN) for mediation and resolution. In military terms this was a mistake since the Poonch-Rajouri area became a major source of infiltration for insurgents.

On the diplomatic front, if India had been hoping for an unequivocal condemnation of Pakistan's actions by the UN it was disappointed. Following India's petition, the United Nations Security Council passed Resolution 47, which set out three conditions for the resolution of the conflict in Jammu and Kashmir. Firstly, both Pakistan and India should agree to establish a ceasefire. Secondly, Pakistan should withdraw all its troops from J&K and India must reduce the number of its number of troops to the minimum needed for preserving law and order. *Thirdly, there needed to be a plebiscite, supervised by the United Nations, to determine the wishes of the people of J&K as to whether they desired to be part of India or of Pakistan.* Even though, to date, only the first of these conditions has been fulfilled, referring the dispute to the UN unnecessarily internationalised an issue which should only have been of bilateral concern.

On the political front, giving J&K a "nation-within-a-nation" status through the special privileges it enjoyed under Article 370 and Article 35A was an act of folly. J&K was awarded autonomy over its internal affairs, with the GoI retaining control over foreign affairs, defence, communication, and currency. Accompanying this autonomy, were juvenile ego-boosting trinkets and baubles like a separate constitution and flag for J&K and grandiose description of public offices—Prime Minister instead of Chief Minister; *Sadar-i-Riyasat* instead of Governor. Then there was Article 35A under which only permanent residents of J&K could hold property and public jobs in the state. In effect, J&K was persuaded to remain part of India by having these carrots dangled before it.

In addition to all these mistakes, Nehru's friendship with Sheikh Abdullah led him to ignore the latter's authoritarian bent and his unwillingness to brook dissent. The signs were evident in the elections to the J&K's Constituent Assembly in 1951 when *all* 75 seats in the Assembly were "won" by Sheikh Abdullah's NC in what, essentially, was a non-election: candidates from opposition parties either had their nomination papers rejected or withdrew, or were forced to withdraw, their candidature. This electoral cynicism was carried over to subsequent elections—the 1957 and 1962 elections which returned Bakshi Ghulam Mohammed as Chief Minister of J&K and the 1987 election, which is generally regarded as the catalyst for the troubles of the 1990s in J&K, which had Farooq Abdullah return as Chief Minister.

The authoritarianism was not confined to elected politicians in J&K—it emanated from the GoI. As Farooq Abdullah said "The Congress commands the centre. In a state like Kashmir, if I want to implement programmes to fight poverty and disease and run a government, I must stay on the right side of the centre. That is a hard political reality that I have come to accept" (Donthi, 2016). The authoritarianism of the GoI was accompanied by a political amorality which thought nothing of violating norms of political behaviour: governments that had become inconvenient were dismissed at will by engineering defections with the willing cooperation of the GoI appointed Governor.

There was also the unsavoury feature of dynastic politics in J&K: Sheikh Abdullah was succeeded by his son Farooq Abdullah (passing over his son-in-law, G.M. Shah) who was succeeded by his son, Omar Abdullah. In effect, the people of J&K, except for brief interludes, have known no chief ministers other than those provided by the Abdullah family.

The best thing that India's BJP government has done is to remove J&K's special status and to reduce it just another state. The fact that it was downgraded to a Union Territory meant one that the major campaigning point of all the political parties in the 2024 Assembly elections was the restoration of J&K's status as a full state of the Union which made a change from, as in previous elections, demanding *azadi*.

Lastly, there is the issue of proxy warfare which the Pakistan Army conducts in J&K through a range of militant groups, accompanied by stout denials by Pakistan of any involvement, in the face of compelling evidence to the contrary, whenever its proxies are challenged by Indian security forces. In line with this thinking, a "Kashmir cell" within ISI is assigned the task of recruiting, training, and arming Kashmir militants. Indeed, Pakistan's Bureau of National Reconstruction argued that the solution to Pakistan's military problems lay in irregular warfare: "the essence of irregular warfare is to deny the enemy any target and to keep attacking him at unexpected places" (Haqqani, p. 46).

So how should India counter Pakistan's proclivity for proxy warfare? First, it must recognise that Pakistan has elevated the conflict in J&K to the status of *jihad*. This means that the ideology of Islam with its cult of martyrdom, referred to earlier, provides an endless supply of *jihadis* seeking paradise through the barrel of an AK-47 rifle. Second, it must recognise that the Pakistan-sponsored *jihadis* operate using sophisticated tools of warfare. Third, it must recognise, as it surely does, that the *jihadis* have well-established bases in Pakistan from where they emerge. For example, the LeT in headquartered in a 15-acre estate in Mudrike, about an hour's drive from Lahore equipped with every kind of facility (Tankel, 2014) while JeM occupies an 18-acre estate in Bahawalpur in Pakistan which, as aerial pictures show, has several buildings.[43]

There is little doubt that India is in a state of permanent war with Pakistan over Jammu and Kashmir. The problem for India is that Pakistan, through its proxies, gets to choose the times and targets of its attacks and India simply reacts. By adopting a more pro-active role, India, using its superior economic and military strength, could and should make Pakistan pay a heavier price for its addiction to proxy warfare.

References

Ahmad, P. (2005). Shawl Industry and Institution of Daghshawl in Kashmir (1846–1947). *Proceedings of the Indian History Congress, 66*, 809–817.

Akbar, M. J. (2002). *Kashmir: Behind the Vale*. Roli Books.

Anand, A. S. (1964). Kashmir's Accession to India. *Journal of the Indian Law Institute, 6*, 69–86.

Badhwar, I. (1987, April 15). A Tarnished Triumph. *India Today*.

Baloria, A. (2019). Return of Sheikh Abdullah to Power. *Proceedings of the Indian History Congress, 80*, 1136–1142.

Bazaz, P. N. (1967). *Kashmir in Crucible*. Pamposh Publications.

Bose, S. (2003). *Kashmir: Roots of Conflict, Paths to Peace*. Harvard University Press.

Bose, S. (2021). *Kashmir at the Crossroads: Inside a 21st Century Conflict*. Yale University Press.

Chowdhary, R. (2015). Democratic Process in the Context of Separatism and Political Divergence: An Analysis of the 2014 Assembly Elections in Jammu and Kashmir. *Studies in Indian Politics, 3*, 1–15.

[43] https://www.youtube.com/watch?v=DtpdrHViEGA.

Chowdhary, R. (2022). On Targeted Killings in Kashmir. *Economic and Political Weekly, 57*, 8.

Chudgar, P. L. (1929). *Indian Princes Under British Protection: A Study of Their Personal Rule, Their Constitutional Position and Their Future*. Willams and Norgate Ltd. Accessed December 15, 2025 from https://archive.org/details/dli.ministry.03143/page/n5/mode/2up.

Devdas, D. (2019), *The Story of Kashmir*. David Devdas.

Donthi, P. (2016, March 23). How Mufti Mohammad Sayeed Shaped the 1987 Elections of Kashmir. *The Caravan: A Journal of Politics & Culture*.

EFAS. (2020). *Ethnic, Cultural and Religious Diversity in Jammu and Kashmir Perceptions on Unity, and Discord*. European Foundation for South Asian Studies.

Fair, C. C. (2008). 'Who Are Pakistan's Militants and Their Families?' *Terrorism and Political Violence, 20*, 49–65.

Geelani, S. B. (2006). *Kashmir, Kashmiris, and Kashmiriyat*. In *Manufacturing Terrorism: Kashmiri Encounters with Media and the Law* (p. 33). Promilla and Co.

Goldston, J. A., & Grossman, P. (1991). *Kashmir Under Siege*. Human Rights Watch.

Haqqani, H. (2005). *Pakistan: Between Mosque and Military*. Carnegie Endowment for International Peace.

Hodson, H. V. (1969). *The Great Divide: Britain, India, and Pakistan*. Hutchinson. Accessed December 15, 2025 from https://archive.org/details/dli.pahar.3371/page/451/mode/2up.

Hyder, M. (2012). *October Coup: A Memoir of the Struggle for Hyderabad*. Roli Books.

Kallepalli, N. (2024). *To Understand India, Listen to the Pandits of Kashmir*. Pulitzer Center. Accessed December 15, 2025 from https://pulitzercenter.org/stories/understand-india-listen-pandits-kashmir

Lone, M. B. (2024). The Quit Kashmir Movement 1946. *Research Journal of Humanities and Social Sciences, 15*, 156–160.

Mattoo, A. (2009). Kashmir After Shopian. *Economic and Political Weekly, 64*, 39–43.

Menon, V. P. (1956). *The Story of the Integration of the Indian States*. Macmillan.

Osuri, G., & Fatima, I. (2018). *A Provisional Biography of a Journey Towards Justice for the Enforced Disappeared*. Accessed December 15, 2025 from https://apdpkashmir.com/ebmedia/sitename_eb/wp-content/uploads/2020/02/APDP-biography-02-02-2020.pdf

Peer, B. (2002, October 31). SOG: Good Guys or Bad Guys? *The Redriff Special*. Accessed December 15, 2025 from https://www.rediff.com/news/2002/oct/31spec.htm

Philips, C. H. (1962). *The Evolution of India and Pakistan, 1858 to 1947: Select Documents*. Oxford University Press.
Puri, B. (2008). *Kashmir: Insurgency and After*. Orient Black Swan.
Puri, R. (2022). Kashmir in the Twenty-First Century: Democracy Identity and Elections. *Webster Review of International History, 2*, 24–32.
Qasim, M. (1992). *My Life and Times*. Allied Publishers.
Rao, P. R. (2012). *History and Culture of Andhra Pradesh: From the Earliest Times to 1991.* Sterling Publishers.
Tankel, S. (2014). *Storming the World Stage: The Story of Lashkar-e-Taiba*. Oxford University Press.
The, Kargil, Review Committee Report. (1999). *From Surprise to Reckoning*. Sage Publications.
Wasi, A. B. (2009). Elections in Indian Held Kashmir and the Kashmir Dispute. *Policy Perspectives, 6*, 149–165.
Widmalm, S. (1997). The Rise and Fall of Democracy in Jammu and Kashmir. *Asian Survey, 37*, 1005–1030.
Zubrzycki, J. (2023). *Dethroned: The Downfall of India's Princely States*. C. Hurst and Co.

CHAPTER 3

Red Salute: Left-Wing Extremism in India

3.1 Introduction

Left-Wing Extremism is a doctrine which aims to capture power through armed insurrection accompanied by the mobilisation of a population. It is derived from the teachings of Mao Zedong which asserted that, in an essentially rural country [like China], revolution must begin in the countryside: "every Communist must grasp the truth, political power grows out of the barrel of a gun" and "encircle the cities from the countryside" (Griffith, 1961; Mohanty, 2015; Weili & Yingli, 1992). It plays upon the grievances of the rural dispossessed in respect of economic and social inequalities, in large part resulting from exploitation by landowners and money lenders ("class enemies"), by promising them a more equitable and prosperous future. This future is to be secured through the violent overthrow of "class enemies", which would be led by Party cadres and supported by most of the population. In India, adherents of this doctrine comprise those persons who act on the belief that:

> Contemporary Indian society is semi-colonial and semi-feudal under neo-colonial form of indirect rule, exploitation, and control.... The life of the peasant masses is shattered continuously by the exploitation and oppression by the gangs of local tyrants, the evil gentry, intermediaries, the police, the courts and by a long hierarchy of government officials-all of whom act as loyal agents of imperialism, feudalism, and comprador bureaucrat capitalism, and by the feudal dictum of various kinds. All these have made

V. K. Borooah, *The Political Economy of Terrorism*,
https://doi.org/10.1007/978-3-032-08553-5_3

> the life of the peasant intolerable. (*Strategy and Tactics of the Indian Revolution*, 2004, pp. 7–8)

The corollary to this situation is that the Indian state and its agents must be overthrown through armed insurrection by India's dispossessed against their oppressors in the shape of large landowners, moneylenders, bureaucrats, and members of the security forces. This movement adopts, without apology or qualification, the ideas and methods of the Chinese revolutionary leader, Mao Zedong. These activities, in independent India, originated in Naxalbari in North Bengal (discussed in the next section). Hence in this book, the terms *Left-Wing Extremists (LWE)*, *Maoists*, and *Naxalites* are used interchangeably to mean persons who subscribe to, and are prepared to act upon, the ideology and methods of Mao Zedong to lead and organise armed insurrection by the peasantry.

The LWE movement in India can be traced back to the communist-led peasants' revolt in Telangana (in the erstwhile state of Hyderabad) from 1946–1951. In the more contemporary setting of an established Indian Republic, it can be divided into four phases: first, from 1967 to 1975; second, from 1980–1990; third, from 1990 to 2009, fourth, from 2009 onwards.

The first phase began in Naxalbari (Map 3.1)—which also provided the generic name for LWE activities in India—in West Bengal and then spread to: the districts of Midnapur and Birbhum in that state; the districts of Muzaffarpur in Bihar; the districts of Dhanbad, Ranchi, and West Singhbhum (then in Bihar, now in Jharkhand); the district of Lakhimpur in Uttar Pradesh; in Orissa, the districts of Koraput and Ganjam (bordering Andhra Pradesh) and the Mayurbhanj district (bordering West Bengal) and the districts of Srikakulam, Warangal, and Khammam in (erstwhile) Andhra Pradesh (Map 3.2).[1]

This phase came to a juddering halt in the wake of a successful military operation, codenamed, "Operation Steeplechase", conducted between 1 July to 15 August 1971 against Naxalites in West Bengal, Bihar, and Orissa. By early 1972, all the top Naxalite leaders (including Kanu Sanyal) had been arrested; the party theoretician and its leading light, Charu Majumdar, was arrested on 16 July of that year and died in police custody a fortnight later. The movement was in disarray.

[1] For details of this phase see Singh (2006).

Map 3.1 Districts of West Bengal (*Source* Maps of India)

Map 3.2 Map of Andhra Pradesh and Telangana (*Source* Wikimedia Commons)

The second phase occurred from the late 1970s, after the lifting of Indira Gandhi's Emergency following her defeat in the Indian General election of March 1977. The Home Minister of the newly formed Janata government, Charan Singh, agreed to release all the Naxalite prisoners who had been in jail for more than five years, awaiting trial. In exchange, the political arm of the Naxalites, the Communist Party of India (Marxist-Leninist)—CPI (M-L) agreed to field candidates—three in West Bengal, one in Bihar, and one in Punjab— in the forthcoming Assembly Elections and to support the Communist Party of India (Marxist), the CPI (M), in West Bengal (where it was the party of government) and elsewhere.

During this phase, the Naxalites splintered into several factions but they also succeeding in extending their hold over the country. Of the different Naxalite factions, the following, listed by Singh (2006), were significant: the People's War Group (PWG), Maoist Communist Centre (MCC), CPI (M-L) Liberation Group, CPI (M-L) Party Unity, CPI (M-L) Ramachandran faction, CPI (M-L) Jan Shakti, CPI (M-L)New Democracy, Kerala Communist Party, CPI (M-L) Red Flag, and the Communist Organisation of India (M-L).

In terms of territory, collectively, as Banerjee (2009) has noted, Naxalite influence extended to some 160 districts in India spread over 10 states, covering 400,000 square kilometres (or one-eighth of India's land mass). This area was twice the size of the other theatres of insurgency in India—the Northeast and Jammu and Kashmir.

The third phase occurred when, on 21 September 2004, the leaders of the various Naxalite factions met and agreed to form a single party—the Communist Party of India (Maoist), hereafter CPI (Maoist)—which would guide Naxalite activity in India. The CPI (Maoist) was formed through a coming together of the two largest Naxalite groups —the PWG and the MCC. The agenda of this single party was set out in a document, *Strategy and Tactics of the Indian Revolution*, discussed in some detail in a subsequent section of this chapter.[2]

The fourth and current phase of Naxalite activities began with more military operations by the GoI and state governments. The centrepiece of these was "Operation Green Hunt" but the government also supplemented it with additional operations—the counterinsurgency force, called the *Salwa Judum*, in south Chhattisgarh; "Operation Hill Vijay" in Jharkhand's *Giridih* district and "Operation Sarbanda" in Jharkhand's *West Singhbhum* District.

The main theatre of war against Naxalite activity, in the past 10 years, has been in the mineral-rich, and tribal-inhabited districts of Bastar and Dantewada in Chhattisgarh. Here issues of injustices in agriculture, which dominated Naxalite discourse in other regions, were displaced by attempts by mining companies to acquire tribal land to access the mineral wealth that lay beneath it.

This chapter examines three geographical areas of left-wing extremist activity: Naxalbari in West Bengal, the font head of left-wing extremist

[2] See also Ahluwalia (2012) for a discussion of this document.

activity in independent India; Srikakulam and Khammam (in erstwhile Andhra Pradesh), which signalled the spread of Naxalite activity into South India which, it should be said, already had a tradition of armed insurrection under the rule of the Nizam of Hyderabad; and the districts of Bastar and Dantewada in Chhattisgarh which in the past decade has become the focal area for LWE activity.

Then the chapter examines changes to the structure and organisation of communists in India in the wake of Naxalbari, culminating in 2004 in the merger of the Naxalite factions into a single entity, the CPI (Maoist). This new party issued an important document, *Strategy and Tactics of the Indian Revolution,* which is discussed at some length in a subsequent section.

Lastly, it addresses the question of what the government has done to address the issue of Naxalite activity. There has, most obviously, been a military response encapsulated in various military operations, and this chapter discusses these. In addition, the GoI and the state governments have tried to address some of the basic issues in rural India which have provided fertile ground for Naxalites. To this end, in October 2006, a left-wing extremist division was established within the GoI's Ministry of Home Affairs aimed at capacity building within the affected states.

3.2 Naxalbari: The Beginning

The Left-Wing Extremist (LWE) movement in post-independent India was sparked in *Naxalbari*—an administrative block, under the jurisdiction of the Naxalbari Police Station, of the Siliguri subdivision of Darjeeling district in the state of West Bengal—when, on 3 March 1967, three sharecroppers—Lappa Kishan, Sangu Kishan, and Ratia Kishan—backed by about 150 supporters belonging to the Communist Party of India (Marxist), hereafter CPI (M), raided the granary of the local *jotedar* (landlords who rented out land to peasants in exchange for a portion, usually half, of the harvested crop) and made away with 300 maunds (1200 kilograms) of paddy (Singh, 2006).

Although the CPI (M)—which was a breakaway from the original parent body, the Moscow-supporting Communist Party of India (CPI)—was aligned with China, it did not overtly support armed action by India's peasantry, à la Mao Zedong in China, because in the aftermath of the India-China border war of 1962, and because of China's support for India's traditional enemy, Pakistan, it was sensitive to the charge of being regarded as "anti-national". The CPI(M) members in West Bengal, however, contained a "Siliguri group"—of which Charu Mazumdar, Kanu Sanyal, and Jangal Santhal were leading members—which had no such inhibitions and which, contrary to the CPI(M) party line, advocated armed revolt against the established agrarian order in West Bengal.

Charu Majumdar set out the aims of the Siliguri group for a peasant uprising succinctly: "How can the struggle to preserve the crops be conducted? (1) Organise armed forces in every village. (2) [Arrange] so that these forces can collect as much arms as they can and fix secret places to keep the arms. (3) Fix places for hiding the crops. (4) Besides armed units, small bands of peasants should be formed to keep guard, maintain communications, and other work. (5) Every unit will have to be given political education and political propaganda should certainly be carried on. It should be remembered that it is only the political propaganda campaign that can make this struggle more wide-spread and strengthen the fighting spirit of the peasant" (Majumdar, 1965).

The general background to peasant discontent in India—including *Naxalbari* and its neighbouring blocks of *Phansidewa* and *Kharibari* which, collectively, covered about 780 square kilometres and was populated in the most part by tribals: Santhals, Rajbanshis, and Oraons—was a sharecropping scheme (*bhagchash* arrangement) whereby landowners leased their land to cultivators (known as *bargadars*) on an annual basis in return for half the harvest. The demand in Naxalbari was—as it was in the earlier peasant uprisings of 1946 in United Bengal and of 1946–1951 in Telangana—was that the sharecropper be allowed to retain two-thirds of the harvest instead of surrendering half.

Overlaying the issue of harvest retention were issues relating to security of tenure and personal consumption loans made by landowners to their sharecroppers. According to the West Bengal Land Reforms Act of 1955, all sharecroppers had the right to permanently cultivate the land they had leased and, indeed, pass on these rights to their heirs if they honoured their obligations to landowners: that is, paid their share of the harvest; did not leave the land uncultivated or used it for non-agricultural purposes; cultivated it personally with the assistance of family members. Subject to these constraints, landowners could only evict their tenants by claiming that they needed the land for their personal cultivation. The "personal cultivation" caveat was, however, routinely used by landowners to evict tenants.

They were assisted in these evictions by the fact that tenants had to register their tenancy with government authorities and, with limited education, to jump the bureaucratic hurdles required to do so. Most ominously for the sharecroppers, the West Bengal Land Reforms Act of 1955 required that all disputes between the landowner and the sharecropper relating to the delivery of the produce, or the eviction of the sharecropper, would be decided "by such officer or authority as the State Government may appoint". In the context of rural India where corruption was endemic (Borooah, 2016) this immediately advantaged landowners, with their financial muscle, in any dispute resolved by government officials.

A further complication arose because sharecroppers had often to borrow money from landowners for non-agricultural purposes like medical expenses or expenditure incurred for weddings. Access to this line of credit depended upon the landowners' goodwill which could sour if sharecroppers claimed their legal rights by registering their holding or engaging in any formal disputes with the owners.

Following the incident at Naxalbari on 3 March 1967, a "Peasant Committee" (*Krishak Sabha*) was established in the Darjeeling region under the leadership of three members of the CPI(M-L): Charu Mazumdar, Kanu Sanyal, and Jangal Santhan. This Committee demanded that all landholdings of the *jotedars* be confiscated by the government and redistributed among peasants who were members of the Peasant Committee. After the formation of this Committee, there were nearly 100 incidents of peasant violence reported to police between March and May 1967 (Singh, 2006).

This in turn invited retaliation by *jotedars* leading to a highly publicised incident in which, on 23 May 1967, a sharecropper Bigul Kishan was assaulted by a *jotedar* and his servants. In his own words:

> I used to grow crops in the fields of Ishwar Tirkey. I had gone to take control of that land in accordance with the decision by the Krishak Sabha. But the goons of the landlord attacked me in the fields of Lahari Bura. They nearly crushed my head. They also took away my plough and oxen. In protest, peasants under the leadership of Prahlad Singh and Muzibur Rahman attacked the house of the landlord. The police came and arrested many on charges of rioting.[3]

[3] Afroz (2017, p. 50).

On the heels of this incident, on 24 May 1967, a party of police officers confronted a group of about 1000 armed peasants which resulted in the death of a police inspector, Somal Wangde of the Naxalbari police station. The next day, on May 25, at Bengai Jot village near Naxalbari, the police opened fire on a crowd of mainly women protesters and killed nine persons, including six women and two children.[4]

These two incidents of 24 and 25 March 1967, sparked what has come to be known as the *Naxal* movement, and its protagonists termed *Naxalites*: indeed, these have become generic terms used synonymously in India with, respectively, Left-Wing Extremist movements and Left-Wing Extremists. The peasant agitation for better conditions for sharecroppers morphed into armed revolt which spread from the obscurity of *Naxalbari* (and its neighbouring blocks, *Phansidewa* and *Kharibari*) and threatened to engulf the entire state of West Bengal. According to official sources, between just 8 and 10 June, there were as many as 80 cases of lawlessness, 13 armed robberies (*dacoities*), two murders and one abduction; armed bands were reported to have been dispensing "justice" and collecting taxes (Banerjee, 1980). More specifically, on 10 June 1967, the house of a *jotedar*, Nagen Roy Choudhary was looted, and he was kidnapped and, subsequently, killed; the same day, the house of another *jotedar*, Jaiandan Singh was looted (Singh, 2006).

On 2 March 1967, West Bengal first non-Congress government was sworn into office with Ajoy Mukherjee, leader of the *Bangla Congress*, as Chief Minister and Jyoti Basu, one of the founding members of the CPI (M) and a member of its Politburo, as the deputy Chief minister. The United Front government, as it was known, and the Government of India (GoI), under the aegis of the Home Minister, Yashwantrao Chavan, agreed that a "reign of terror" had been unleased in state by the Naxalbari uprising and the violence associated with it and, on 5 July 1967, the United Front government ordered "police action" against the rebellion. This commenced on 12 July and, with a force of 1500 officers, was quickly able to quash the rebellion and arrest many of its leaders.

[4] *Frontline Magazine*, "1967: Naxalbari Movement", 12 August 2022, https://frontline.thehindu.com/politics/india-at-75-epochal-moments-1967-naxalbari-movement/article65721597.ece.

With that police action the uprising in Naxalbari was over: it lasted just 52 days.[5]

This police action was followed by a much larger joint operation by the army and the police, named "Operation Steeplechase", launched on 1 July by the GoI, with the cooperation of the governments of West Bengal (which came under President's Rule on 29 June 1971), Bihar, and Orissa, in the bordering districts of the three states which were particularly affected by Naxalite activity (see Map 3.2). The offending districts were: Midnapur, Purulia, Burdwan, and Birbhum in West Bengal; Singhbhum, Dhanbad, and Santhal Parganas in Bihar; Mayurbhanj in Orissa (Singh, 2006).

The broad strategy of this operation was to surround as large an area as possible and seal the routes of entry and exit. The Army formed the outer cordon and the Central Reserve Police Force (CRPF) the inner ring. Suspected Naxalites were arrested, illicit weapon, ammunition and explosives seized.67F[6] Within six weeks this operation, which ended on August 15, 1971, had snuffed out left-wing extremism in these states. Charu Majumdar was arrested on 6 July 1972 and died in police custody a few days later.

To understand the failure of Naxalbari, consider the fable of the frog: a frog is put into a pot of boiling water, will jump out of the pot; the same frog put in pot of comfortably warm water, which is then slowly brought to the boil, will not perceive the danger of being boiled alive until it is too late. This fable goes a long way to explain the failure of Naxalbari. Reformist governments are often in a hurry to go too far, too fast, and too soon with their reforms. West Bengal's United Front government, after coming to power in March 1967, also was in a hurry to implement land reforms, which were a central plank of its manifesto, and, in this, it overreached.

The Minister for Land Revenue in the new government, Harekrishna Konar, immediately after being sworn into office, announced that land would be quickly redistributed to peasants and suggested that peasants could be more militant in this regard by securing progress using force.

[5] The term 'police action' in India is a euphemism for assaults by well-armed, well-trained, and well-supported men belonging to the government's paramilitary forces: for example, Central Reserve Police Force Force, the Assam Rifles, the National Security Guard.

[6] https://tklvch.wordpress.com/tag/operation-steeplechase/.

The problem with overturning established, and lawful, property rights in a democratic society through executive fiat was that the force of law could be used to repel it. And, indeed, landlords flocked to the law courts to nullify the seizure of their land and *ipso facto* thwarted the policy of land redistribution. The Minister ruefully acknowledged that the government faced a spate of civil suits with thousands of cases, involving more than 200,000 acres, pending before the courts (Banerjee, 1984). The *jotedar* frog had jumped out of the boiling water of land reforms.

Instead, a more gradualist process of reform, by bringing the water slowly to the boil, would have been more effective. After all, as discussed above, the two central problems of West Bengal's peasant economy were firstly, the sharing of the harvest (it was half; the sharecroppers wanted it to be two-thirds) and secondly, security of tenure. The issue of ownership did not enter this equation. Existing legislation, under the West Bengal Land Reforms Act of 1955, passed by earlier Congress governments, would have allowed the two issues of sharing and tenure to be addressed without recourse to the shrill rhetoric of land seizures and redistribution.

The second problem was the enthusiasm of the 'Siliguri group' for armed revolt did not transfer to CPI (M) headquarters in Calcutta. The party was an important part of West Bengal's governing coalition, in which its leader was the Deputy Chief Minister, and they were not inclined to sacrifice the trappings of power in pursuit of some Maoist dream. Consequently, when the Chief Minister of West Bengal—whose party, the *Bangla Congress*, controlled West Bengal's Home Ministry—initiated police action against the *Naxalities*, the communists fell in behind him. So much so, that the CPI (M) termed the 'Siliguri group,' and those surrounding it, as 'counter revolutionaries,' infiltrated by agent provocateurs who could be CIA agents (Banerjee, 1984, p. 94).

Naxalbari failed, but, in failure it succeeded in many things: Firstly, the debate engendered by events in Naxalbari, and the ruthlessness with which they were crushed, altered irrevocably the structure of India's communist parties. Secondly, after a pause, armed revolt, spread from the miniscule Naxalbari region to encompass several other parts of India until left-wing extremism became a subject of national concern; so much so that the then Prime Minister Manmohan Singh, addressing Chief Ministers at an Annual Security Conference on 20 December 2007, described

Naxalism as "the greatest internal security threat to our country".68F[7] Thirdly, it raised important questions of the appropriate governmental response to address law and order matters when they were intertwined with issues of social and economic deprivation—in other words, what the optimal mix of military and developmental action needed to dispel the dark clouds of left-wing extremism which darkened India. These matters are discussed in the remainder of this chapter.

3.3 Structural Changes in India's Communist Movement

The history of the communist movement in India is one of internecine conflict which in turn has splintered the previously monolithic organisation—*the* Communist Party of India (CPI)—into several factions, each peddling a different version of the communist ideology. The CPI, which was formed in Kanpur on 26 December 1925, took its inspiration from Russia and the October Revolution of 1917. Consequently, the emphasis in the CPI was on urban settings and on industrial labour rather than on the peasantry in India's villages. In addition, the CPI was ambivalent about armed revolt preferring, instead, to operate using trade union activity to organise labour. On the eve of India's independence in 1947, the CPI committed itself to working with Indian National Congress, which it recognised as the "main national democratic organisation", to secure an Indian Republic built on democratic foundations. In short, there was a comfortable and amicable relationship between the CPI's leaders and those of the Congress Party (Banerjee, 1984).

Ironically, for a party which embraced the urban, the first cracks in the CPI's complacency appeared with the 1946 uprising in the rural areas of Telangana in the erstwhile state of Hyderabad which, at the time of the uprising, was ruled by the Nizam of Hyderabad. In the 1940s, Telangana was the largest princely state in India with 17 districts and a population of about 17 million. The grievances of the Telangana peasantry mirrored those of later generations in Naxalbari and elsewhere: forced extractions of harvest and illegal evictions by landowners. In 1946 the peasants of Telangana, led by communists, revolted with the aim redressing these specific

[7] https://www.indiatoday.in/india/story/naxalism-greatest-threat-to-internal-security-pm-66750-2010-02-05.

issues but the revolt quickly morphed into an uprising to remove the regime of despotic feudalism embodied in the Nizam and his government.

By 1947, a guerrilla army of about 5000 was operating in Telangana and the peasantry in about 3000 villages, covering a population of three million, mostly in the three districts of Nalgonda, Warangal, and Khammam (see Map 3.2), succeeded in setting up 'gram-raj or village soviets. The landlords were driven away from the villages, their lands seized, and one million acres of land were redistributed among the peasantry (Banerjee, 1984).

The important date for the CPI was 13 September 1948 when the Indian Army, on the orders of the newly formed GoI overthrew the Nizam and, with his abdication on 17 December, Hyderabad was integrated into the Indian Union. The question before the CPI was whether, in these changed political circumstances, it should continue to support the Telangana agitation or to withdraw its support. The outcome of this debate within the CPI was that, in 1951, the party, bowing to the wishes of the GoI, formally withdrew its support on 21 October 1951 and asked its members in Telangana to surrender their arms.

The matter did not end there. General J.N. Chaudhuri, the military governor made a statement from Hyderabad, calling all "communists to surrender within a week, failing which they would be exterminated" (Sundarayya, 1972, pp. 195–196). The communist activists who continued with the insurrection were viewed as anti-national, whose desire was to overthrow the newly formed GoI, and were systematically hunted down (Mathews, 2011). Within weeks of the army action, landlords, who had fled their villages to escape the uprising, returned to reclaim their lands. The *status quo* had been restored.

At the 20th Congress of the Communist Party of the Soviet Union (CPSU) in February 1956, Nikita Khrushchev announced that armed insurrection was not an essential instrument for the transition from a capitalist to a socialist society and that this transition could equally well be achieved though the democratic process operating through the ballot box.69F[8] This was music to the ears of the "Right Wing" of the CPI who were in a cozy relationship with the Congress Party. Not so to the party's "Left Wing" who resented the inordinate influence of the Soviet

[8] Khrushchev reversed the Stalinist policy which assumed that a war with the capitalist West was inevitable and instead advocated a new policy of "peaceful coexistence." https://history.state.gov/milestones/1953-1960/khrushchev-20th-congress.

Union—and the concomitant neglect of their mentor, China—on the CPI's ideological direction. Matters came to a head shortly after the Indo-China border war of 1962, when the Leftists, at a meeting in Calcutta decided on 7 November 1964 (pointedly, the date of the Russian Revolution) to form a separate party—the Communist Party of India (Marxist), CPI(M)—with the Rightists retaining the original name, the Communist Party of India, CPI.

The CPI (M) was formed from the feeling among its members that the parent CPI had betrayed India's peasants by withdrawing its support to the Telangana uprising, deciding instead to cosy up to the ruling elites of the Congress party. The CPI(M) envisaged the formation of a "people's democracy based on a coalition of all genuinely anti-feudal and anti-imperialist forces headed by the working class" but it was careful to emphasise that it would try to achieve its objectives through peaceful means (Banerjee, 1984). Indeed, in explicit confirmation of its democratic credentials, a few years later the CPI(M) contested the 1967 elections to the Kerala and the West Bengal Assemblies: in Kerala it obtained an overwhelming majority, winning 113 out of 133 seats, and formed the government with E.M.S. Namboodiripad as Chief Minister; in West Bengal it became part of a coalition government with the CPI(M) leader, Jyoti Basu, as deputy Chief Minister.

The Naxalbari uprising, however, brought about a fresh charge from the "Siliguri group", which had spearheaded the uprising, that the "police action", ordered by the West Bengal government—of which the CPI (M) was a senior partner—which crushed the Naxalbari rebels was a betrayal of the proletariat cause and, in form and substance, no different from the suppression of the Telangana rebels. This led to another split in the communist movement with some members of the CPI(M) leaving to form a new party, the Communist Party of India (Marxist-Leninist) or CPI(M-L).

This party was headed by Charu Majumdar who set out his views in eight documents (Majumdar, 1965). Suffice it to say here that the new party was avowedly pro-China adopting as its slogan "China's Chairman is our Chairman. China's path is our path".0F[9] After Majumdar's death in 1972, the party splintered again but eventually the movement regrouped as two main entities: the People's War Group (PWG) and

[9] EFAS (2019).

the Maoist Communist Centre (MCCI). In 2004, these two groups merged into a single entity—the Communist Party of India (Maoist), CPI (Maoist)—and left-wing extremist activities in India took place under its banner.71F[10] Under the Unlawful Activities (Prevention) Act of 1967, the CPI (Maoist) is a proscribed terrorist organisation in India.

Both the PWG and the MCCI believed that class enemies should be eliminated, and that violence was necessary for securing the organisation's goals. However, the PWG adopted a Marxist-Leninist line while the MCCI veered towards Maoism. In the merger, a compromise was arrived at so that, the PWG Andhra Pradesh State Secretary asserted that, "Marxism-Leninism-Maoism will be the ideological basis guiding its (CPI (Maoist) 's) thinking in all spheres of its activities".[11]

3.3.1 Strategy and Tactics of the Indian Revolution

The principles under which the CPI (Maoist) would operate are set out in its document, *Strategy and Tactics of the Indian Revolution (STIR, 2004)*.73F[12] The aim of the Maoist movement is to achieve a "New Democratic Revolution" (NDR) by exploiting four contradictions in Indian society: (i) between feudalism and the masses; (ii) between imperialism and the Indian people; (iv) between capital and labour; and (iv) internal contradictions within the ruling classes. Of these, the Maoist analysis is that it is the first contradiction—between feudalism and the masses—that is the most important and should be addressed first (STIR, p. 9). Feudalism derives from a landlord class which extracts surplus from peasants at punitive rates and evicts them from their tenancies if they protest and try to negotiate better terms. Feudalism is buttressed by "comprador bourgeoise bureaucrats" (CBB)—civil service, police, army—that support and nourish the landlord class. The Indian state is thus a joint dictatorship of the landlord classes and CBB and these, therefore, should be the prime targets of the NDR; indeed, its first task should be the overthrow of these entities (STIR, p. 17).

[10] For details of the shifting sands of Maoist alliances in India see South Asia Terrorism Portal, "Communist Party of India-Maoist (CPI (Maoist)) all its formations and front organizations." https://satp.org/terrorist-profile/india/communist-party-of-india-maoist-cpi-maoist-all-its-formations-and-front-organizations.

[11] See earlier footnote.

[12] https://archive.org/details/strategy-tactics-of-the-indian-revolution2/mode/2up.

This is to be achieved through **protracted warfare**, adopting and adapting the Maoist model of warfare. The document approvingly quotes Mao Zedong: "*The seizure of power by armed force, the settlement of the issue by war, is the central task and highest form of revolution. But while the principle remains the same (for all countries), its application by the Party of the proletariat finds expression in various ways according to the varying conditions*" (STIR, p. 19). Unlike the Russian model of revolution whose epicentre is in urban areas with the urban proletariat as its basis, that of the Maoist model lies in the countryside with the peasantry as its foundation. The size of the country means that it would be impossible to begin the revolution on all-India basis. Consequently, protracted warfare must begin in those regions that are more backward and where social contradictions are sharp.

To pursue protracted warfare successfully, the party must seek a *United Front* of all those who are opposed to the forces of feudalism—STIR quotes Lenin: "*In order to properly conduct the revolution towards victory, the Communist Party in every country must, without fail, utilise every smallest opportunity to gain a friend from among the people, however vacillating that friend may be, however unable he may be, however unreliable he may be and even however temporary that opportunity may be*" (STIR, p. 42).

The instrument for protracted warfare will be the People's Liberation Guerrilla Army (PLGA)—founded on 2 December 2000 and later becoming the armed wing of the CPI (Maoist). The PLGA comprises three forces, categorised as the main, the secondary and the base forces, and is controlled by the party's Central Military Commission which, in turn, is answerable only to CPI (Maoist)'s highest bodies: the Central Committee and the Polit Bureau.[13]

In terms of dispensing justice, the Maoists run their own courts (*Jan Adalat*) which tries persons accused of being deserters, collaborators and informants, or class enemies. Persons found guilty of such crimes are punished by members of a *dalam*—a fighting unit comprising 5–7 persons. The *dalams* act as a secondary fighting force to the main PLGA (Chenoy & Chenoy, 2010).

[13] https://organiser.org/2023/11/30/208644/bharat/cpi-maoist-plga-anniversary-know-all-about-the-extremist-armed-wing/

3.4 The Spread of Left-Wing Extremism in India

3.4.1 Srikakulam, Warangal, and Khammam

Almost contemporaneous with events in Naxalbari was an armed uprising in Srikakulam in Northern Andhra Pradesh (see Map 3.2). Srikakulam district, covering nearly 10,000 square kilometres, comprises two parts: the hilly and forested regions of the Eastern Ghat mountains extending north into Orissa; and the coastal plains. The area in question, covering nearly 800 square kilometres of mountainous territory, on the Andhra Pradesh side of its border with the state of Orissa, was inhabited by members of the *Savara* and *Jatapu* tribes who collectively were referred to as *Girijans* (Mohanty, 2015). This district, with a hilly terrain covered with dense forest, provided an ideal location for an armed uprising.

The crucial point about the *Girijans* was that they practised—as did the tribals of Northeast India, discussed in a subsequent chapter—*jhoom* or shifting cultivation. Under this system, patches of forest were cleared and then burnt after which seeds were sown with the ashes being used as fertiliser. After harvesting, the tribals moved on to fresh patch of forest where the process was repeated with the earlier patch allowed to remain fallow and to recover (Banerjee, 1984).

This practice brought the *Girijans* into conflict with the government which had begun to enforce laws relating to the preservation of forests. This disrupted the *Girijan's* traditional way of life based around the exploitation of forest land for their food and fuel needs. Furthermore, though the transfer of land from tribals to non-tribals was proscribed in the area, there were, nevertheless, clandestine transfers of ownership, and mortgages taken out against land, the collective effect of which was to reduce the *Girijans* from being cultivators of their own land to working as labourers for non-tribal landowners and/or becoming severely indebted to moneylenders.

This was the situation with the Girijans when a group of Communist, led by Vempatapu Satyanarayana, a schoolteacher, mobilised the *Girijans*, under the banner of the *Girijan Sangham* (Girijan Association), in 1959 to campaign for:

1. Restoration of the ownership of *Girijan* lands from non-*Girijan* landowners and moneylenders

2. The right to use forest (*banjar*) land, the lifting of the on the use of forest timber, and the right to cultivate waste land.
3. The right to use forest produce and a fair market price of such produce.
4. Better wages, the abolition of debt, reductions in the rate of interest and in the share extracted by landlords under sharecropping arrangements.

By 1967, many of these demands were conceded without recourse to violence (Singh, 2006).

Then on 31 October 1967 an event occurred which triggered the violence for which Srikakulam became known. A group of peasants were confronted by landlords at a place called Levidi and, in the subsequent clash, two peasants were shot dead. Following that incident, the *Girijans*, organised under communist leadership, began their armed insurrection in Srikakulam. Between early 1968 and late 1970, the movement had mobilised the entire tribal population of the area and carried out several attacks killing thirty-four landlords. The highwater mark being July 1969 when left-wing terrorists controlled nearly 300 villages out of 518 in the area (Mohanty, 2015).

The reason for the emphasis on killing—and, indeed, the brutality of these killings, described in Singh (2006)—was that, under the influence of Charu Majumdar, the annihilation of class enemies (or *khatam*, meaning "finish") was built into the rubric of the Srikakulam insurrection in a way that it was not in Naxalbari. Charu Mazumdar did not view the killing of a village landlord or moneylender simply as an act of murder, satisfying the oppressed peasant's desire for vengeance. Instead, the killing should be viewed as a means of also liquidating the political, economic, and social authority of the class enemy. In that sense, the killing transcended the victim and became a political act designed to demolish the system (Banerjee, 1984).

Simultaneously with Srikakulam, there were also armed uprisings in the districts of Warangal and Khammam in (now) Telangana, (then) Andhra Pradesh. This was led by Nagi Reddy and his group, the Revolutionary Communist Committee (RCC) of Andhra Pradesh. Like Srikakulam, the area in question was a long stretch of forest extending over the two districts—bounded in the north by the Godavari River and by the Bastar Hills which formed the boundary between the (then) Andhra Pradesh and (then) Madhya Pradesh and (now) Chhattisgarh—and which was inhabited by members of the Koya and the Gond tribes.

Although there were ideological differences between the two centres of Naxalite activity—Srikakulam and Warangal/Khammam—in Andhra Pradesh, with the latter placing more emphasis on legal and extra-legal methods and the former emphasising guerrilla warfare and the killing of class enemies, in practice the insurrection in Warangal/Khammam also proved to be a violent affair. The Committees for the two of the three operational areas in the districts declared that:[14]

> All the officers of forest department functioning in the forest areas should be chased away and lands fit for cultivation should be occupied; .. . tyrant landlords should be chased away from the villages and if necessary should be killed and their properties taken over and distributed to the people; ... To implement this programme the police atrocities should be resisted and in possible places the police should be ambushed and attacked. CID constables visiting villages to secure information should be killed. (Banerjee, 1984, p. 117)

and this was followed by a spate of killing of landlords, attacks on police stations, and the burning of landownership records and credit note.

In response the governments of Andhra Pradesh, Orissa, and Madhya Pradesh sent 12,000 armed policemen drawn from the Central Reserve Police Force and the Andhra Pradesh Special Police Force. According to police accounts, 1380 Naxalites were arrested and 93 killed. The Srikakulam movement suffered a grievous blow when Vempatapu Satyanarayana and Adibatla Kailasam, the two top leaders of the Srikakulam movement were shot dead by the police on 10 July 1970. Nagi Reddy and seven other leaders of the Warangal/Khammam movement were arrested in December 1969. With these losses of its top personnel, the Naxalite movement in (then) Andhra Pradesh subsided until it was resurrected many years later under the banner of the CPI (Maoist).

3.4.2 *Bastar and Dantewada in Chhattisgarh*

Following the failure of talks between the Communist Party of India (Maoist) and the Andhra government in October 2004, Chandrababu

[14] Area Committees for Mulugu and Khammam

Naidu as Chief Minister of the state launched an assault on Left-Wing Extremists in 2005 (particularly, in Rayalaseema, the Nallamala forest, and south Telangana) thus impelling many of the Naxalites in Andhra to seek sanctuary in the southern part of the state of Chhattisgarh, particularly in the districts of Dantewada and Bastar (Map 3.3).

Dantewada district used to be a Tehsil of Bastar district and, therefore, in terms of demography and tribal culture it is indistinguishable from Bastar: it is the southern part of the Bastar region and so the district is named as *Dakshin Bastar Dantewada* (South Bastar Dantewada). Nearly 70% of the population of the Bastar/Dantewada districts in tribal, mostly *Gonds*. The dominating geographical feature of the Bastar/Dantewada region is the *Dandakaranya* (in Sanskrit meaning the abode of the demon *Dandaka*) forest covering an area 92,000 square kilometres, centred in Bastar/Dantewada but extending into the states of Maharashtra in the west, Telangana in the south, and Orissa in the east.

The story of LWE activity in Bastar/Dantewada is both different from, but also similar to, the narrative in Andhra Pradesh and West Bengal. The similarity lies in the fact that the "oppressed group" in all three states were tribals (*Adivasis*) and that the regions of activity in all three states were heavily forested providing good cover for guerrilla activity. In the case of Bastar/Dantewada, this cover was provided by the Dandakaranya forest. In addition, Naxalbari offered easy escape into Nepal while the state of Orissa offered an escape route to left-wing extremists in Srikakulam, Andhra Pradesh. The difference is that in both West Bengal and Andhra Pradesh (and in Bihar/Jharkhand and Orissa) extremism had its roots in peasant-landowner-money lender tensions engendered by insecurity of tenure, unfair extraction of surplus, and usurious interest rates.

In Bastar/Dantewada there was an additional factor—the presence of valuable minerals under the land on which the tribal population of Bastar/Dantewada lived and from which they earned their living. Chhattisgarh is one of India's most mineral-rich states with 19% of its iron-ore deposits, 16.4% of its coal deposits and 37.7% of its tin deposits (Prasad, 2016). So, a further source of tension in Bastar/Dantewada—over and above those associated with landowner/tenant or creditor/debtor relations—was the effort by mining companies to displace *Adivasis* from their land to extract the minerals that lay beneath it.

Naxalities had had a presence in South Chhattisgarh since the 1980s but it was low-key and did not intrude on public consciousness. This, however, changed in 2005 when the movement migrated from Andhra

Map 3.3 District Map of Chhattisgarh (*Source* Maps of India)

Pradesh to the sanctuary of the Dandakaranya forest and its environs in Bastar/Dantewada. In response, the BJP government in the state, in tandem with the Congress-dominated United Front government in New Delhi, launched an assault on the LWE in the states which attempted to replicate many of the methods—the destruction of villages, and the herding of their inhabitants into camps from which they could be controlled—used in Nagaland and Mizoram in the 1960s (detailed in a subsequent chapter). The instrument for doing so was a counterinsurgency organisation called the *Salwa Judum* (meaning "Purification Hunt" in the *Gondi* dialect).

This was a largely informal organisation comprising about 6500 "Special Police Officers" (SPOs) drawn from local villagers. Many of the *Salwa Judum* were armed by the state with the intention that they would use these against the Naxalities: the government's rationale for this was that the *Salwa Judum* would bolster the official police force, offer security to those working in the mining industry in Bastar/Dantewada region but, at the same time, since members of the *Salwa Judum* did not hold any official positions, their actions would not implicate the government in any wrongdoing (Miklian, 2009). It was, to all intents and purposes, a vigilante group operating with tacit government patronage and support. Its purpose was to conscript villagers into its ranks, move entire villages to detention camps, and to engage in warfare with LWE (Ramasubbu, 2008).

The *Salwa Judum* experiment showed, however, that counterinsurgency in fighting terrorism had its limits and that, when pushed beyond this, it could lead to even fiercer resistance from the people it was supposed to counter. Vigilantes, escorted by security forces, went to villages, burning and looting, and forcibly moving villagers into one of the 23 camps that the *Salwa Judum* had established in South Chhattisgarh. Those who escaped the vigilantes and their camps, left their burning villages, and made a 260-kilometre journey on foot and sought sanctuary in the district of Khammam in neighbouring Andhra Pradesh. Sundar (2022) has a poignant description of one of these raids:

> The force went inside the houses and took whatever they could find—rice, money, jewellery. Then they set fire to the houses…by 11am all the seventy mud and thatch huts in the hamlet were burning. Then they lunched on the village chickens [they killed] and the rice they had looted. By the time lunch was over, it was two in the afternoon and time for the next village.

After the catalogue of human rights abuses engendered by these vigilantes became too grave to be ignored, the Indian Supreme Court, based on a petition filed by activists Nandini Sundar and others, declared, on 5 July 2011, the organisation to be illegal and ordered its immediate disbanding.

The Supreme Court judgement was, however, not without controversy. It contained a searing indictment of the "neoliberal" development model and accused the adherents of this model of causing civil war in Chhattisgarh and putting the country and its constitutional values in danger. Regarding the environment, neoliberalism was held responsible for "predatory forms of capitalism" and "the plunder and looting of the natural resources". In terms of the human and social cost, it generated "great misery and hopelessness" and led to "a regime of gross violations of human rights". Politically and morally, it leads to the "failure of the state" regarding its "constitutional responsibilities". Official rhetoric, which claimed that "such a development paradigm is necessary, and its consequences inevitable, is untenable". The ruling adds: "The constitution itself ... demands that the state shall strive, incessantly and consistently, to promote fraternity amongst all citizens". The judgement was so polemical that even the usually staid newspaper, the *Indian Express* claimed that the judgement had the intellectual depth of a postgraduate student from Jawaharlal Nehru University, a famously left-wing university in India (Desquesnes & Jaoul, 2012).

3.5 Government Attitude Towards Left-Wing Extremism in India

The Government of India's (GoI) attitude to left-wing extremism) (LWE) in India embraces two perspectives. The first is a military perspective which regards the violence associated with the LWE movement as a "law and order" problem needing to be squashed by force. Indeed, armed insurrection associated with the CPI (Maoist) party is, for the adherents of this view—many of whom hold positions in India's Home Ministry—the greatest single internal security threat facing the country. The solution is to confront this menace with force, to seek the surrender of those willing to relinquish Maoism, and to offer them incentives to do so, but to eliminate those who continue to hold out. This solution has been executed through various military operations—"Operation Steeplechase" in 1971 (discussed earlier), "Operation Green Hunt" (so dubbed by the media) in November 2009, under the aegis of the then Home Minister, P. Chidambaram of the Congress Party; and, most recently, "Operation Prahar" launched in 2017 under the aegis of the current Hone Minister, Amit Shah.76F[15] In addition to these main operations, there have also been local operations: "Operation Hill Vijay" to eradicate LWE from the Parasnath hills in Jharkhand's *Giridih* district; and "Operation Saranda" to eliminate Naxalites from the Saranda forests in Jharkhand's *West Singhbhum* district (Bagul, 2022).[16]

When the armed might of the Indian state operates at full throttle, it combines the Central Armed Police Forces, the state police forces, special paramilitary units and, in some cases—like Assam and Kashmir—the Army. Special paramilitary units have become a feature of India's counterinsurgency operations. The *Salwa Judum* in South Chhattisgarh has been discussed earlier. In addition, there are the *Greyhounds*, created in 1985 by the Andhra Pradesh government as an elite force drawn from within the Andhra police, the *Jharkhand Jaguars*, a Special Task Force for the eradication of LWE in the state of Jharkhand (Jain, 2013), and a *Special Operations Group* which is a similar force to combat Naxalite violence in Orissa (Behera, 2021).

Under "Operation Green Hunt", 80,000 paramilitaries, augmented by the state police forces, would be deployed in the key states of Jharkhand, Chhattisgarh, Bihar, Orissa, and West Bengal and these would be bolstered by 10 combat helicopters from the Indian Air Force. In 2013, a further 10,000 troops from the CRPF were moved to Chhattisgarh and Orissa. "Operation Prahar", launched in 2017, targeted South Chhattisgarh with forces from the CRPF and state police and its successes—287 Naxalites killed, including 14 top leaders; 1000 arrests; 837 surrenders in a single year—emboldened the Home Minister, Amit Shah, to declare on 15 December 2024 at award-giving ceremony in Raipur (the capital of Chhattisgarh) that, the state would be free of Naxalite activity by 31 March 2026.

In addition to employing troops, the GoI has also brought about some fundamental changes in the funding of counter-insurgency measures

[15] https://www.theweek.in/news/india/2024/04/25/operation-prahar-explained-everything-you-need-to-know-about-the-anti-naxal-op-bastar.html.

[16] https://deshgujarat.com/2016/04/11/five-forces-join-hands-for-operation-hill-vijay/ and https://avenuemail.in/anti-naxal-operation-launched-saranda/.

and the technology of operations. The 76 districts in the states identified by the GoI as affected by Naxalite activity—Andhra Pradesh, Bihar, Chhattisgarh, Jharkhand, Orissa, Telangana, and West Bengal—were, from February 2005, covered by the Security Related Expenditure (SRE) scheme under which the GoI reimbursed these states for all expenditure on security related items such as: ex-gratia grant paid to families of the victims of Naxalite violence; providing logistic and camp facilities to the Central Armed Police Forces (CAPF); amounts spent on special training given to State Police personnel; provision of insurance for State Police personnel involved in anti-Naxalite operations; lumpsum grants to Village Defence Committees for security related expenditure; lumpsum amounts per militants who surrendered; the hiring of vehicles including helicopters, weapons, or communication equipment not covered under the Police Modernization Scheme; transportation, communication, force mobility, training, and infrastructure development.[17]

Furthermore, inter-state coordination was improved after the National Investigation Agency (NIA), formed in 2008, was involved in investigations and collection of intelligence across the states.79F[18] Earlier each state's jurisdiction did not extend beyond its borders, but now Joint Task Forces between neighbouring states were set up for coordinated strategies to restrict cross border mobility by Naxalites (Ahlawat, 2024).

Another component of the war against Naxalites in particular, but against terrorism in general, was setting up Counter-Insurgency and Anti-terrorism Training Schools. Police personnel, in the 20 such schools in 2024, receive training from experts from the ministry of defence, central police organisations and the Bureau of Police Research and Development. In conjunction with this, the police forces were also modernised with the construction of secure police stations; improved police housing; and an emphasis on rapid mobility, modern weaponry, and communication equipment.

Every military operation against the Naxalites in India appeared, at the time, to have been a success leaving the extremists in disarray. Yet, they have risen out of the ashes of their defeats and continued to make

[17] Simon (2022, pp. 110–111) and South Asia Terror Portal https://www.satp.org/satporgtp/countries/india/maoist/documents/papers/SREnaxalite.pdf.

[18] The National Investigation Agency (NIA) is a specialized counter-terrorism law enforcement agency in India established to investigate and prosecute cases related to terrorism, insurgency, and crimes that have national or cross-border implications.

their presence felt in the Indian countryside. This suggests that while military operations against the Naxalites have delivered significant gains, these gains have evaporated with time and that is because, blinded by the military aspects of counterinsurgency, the central and the state governments never addressed, or did so only half-heartedly, the fundamental issues which bedevilled rural India, and which provided the foundational support for the Naxalites (Behera, 2021).

Banerjee (2009) provides a succinct but comprehensive account of these issues. While overt issues like land tenancy, security of tenure, extraction of surplus by landlords from sharecroppers, rural indebtedness to usurious moneylenders are the most visible areas of concern, lying at the heart of the problem is the absence of dignity (*izzat*) with which the peasantry in India —and particularly those who belonged to the untouchable castes or were tribals—were treated by the landowning classes. The essence of Naxalite politics was to mobilise poor peasants to assert their dignity by resisting the humiliations that the rural upper classes had heaped upon them.

Such humiliations are, of course, not confined to areas where Naxalites hold sway; indeed, one can say without exaggeration, that they are an all-India phenomenon and pervade both Naxalite and non-Naxalite areas. Sundar (2022) raises the important question of why certain districts in India are centres of Naxalite activity while other, similar, districts are free of left-wing extremism. For example, *Jhabua* district in west Madhya Pradesh and *Bastar/Dantewada* in Chhattisgarh have similar characteristics: both have a high proportion of tribals in their populations, and both have high poverty rates and low literacy rates. But *Jhabua* is free of Naxalite activity while *Bastar/Dantewada* is a hotbed of it. Sundar (2022) put forward several reasons for this, but an important one is that the origins of the Maoist revolutionary movement in India lay in the state of West Bengal from where it spread to adjoining states: Andhra Pradesh, Bihar, Chhattisgarh, Jharkhand, and Orissa.

So, an important aspect of fighting the Naxalite ideology is preventing its spread to other parts of India while, simultaneously, eroding its support in those parts of the country in which it is active. Banerjee (2009) suggests what these might be:

> If immediate economic and social benefits (like a plot of land, a home, higher returns from labour, improvement in civic facilities, schooling for their children, better medical services, end to casteist discrimination and

> oppression) are offered in their everyday life by any government—irrespective of its political hue—some Indian peasants may rather opt for that in exchange of a long-drawn-out armed struggle in pursuit of a distant ideological dream of a 'people's democratic state. (p. 263)

Borooah (2008) is a unique study which is a quantitative assessment of such the impact of welfare-enhancing policies on Naxalite activity. Using district data for India for 2007, his econometric results showed that, even after controlling for other variables, the probability of a district being Naxalite affected rose with an increase in its poverty rate and fell with a rise in its literacy rate. So, in confirmation of Banerjee's (2009) heuristic finding, cited above, one prong in an anti-Naxalite strategy would be to address the twin issues of poverty and illiteracy in India. As Borooah's (2008) work showed this might go a considerable way in ridding districts of Naxalite presence.

3.6 Conclusions

In the twelfth century BC, the Greeks left a large wooden horse, on a beach of the Sea of Marmara, as a "gift" for the Trojans. Opinion among the Trojans as to what to do with the horse was divided. Some, a minority, suspecting a trick, favoured burning it down. But the majority prevailed; the gift was accepted; the horse was pulled into the city.

China's "gift" to India is the thoughts and teachings of Mao Zedong which provide the intellectual sustenance for India's left-wing extremists. These thoughts and teachings constitute the wooden horse within which are contained comrades, uncritically loyal to China ("China's Chairman is our Chairman, China's path is our path"), eager to wage protracted warfare against the Indian state *from within India* while troops of the Chinese People's Army attack Indian forces *from outside India*.

The outcome is intended to be a pincer attack on the Indian state, from within and without. Those who think such apprehensions are fanciful should remember the glee with which the Chinese Communist Party welcomed the events of 1967 in Naxalbari. The People's Daily, in its editorial of 5 July 1967 wrote: "A peal of thunder crashed over the land of India... The absolutely correct thing has been done by the revolutionary group of the Indian Communist Party, and they have done it well. The Chinese people joyfully applaud this revolutionary storm of the Indian peasants in the Darjeeling area as do all Marxist-Leninists and revolutionary people of the whole world".[19]

Beware the Chinese bearing gifts. Heeding this injunction, the most effective defence against this potential double attack, is to destroy the horse and its contents. The Indian government has not been shy of attempting this. Starting with "Operation Steeplechase" in 1971 (described above) it proceeded to Operation "Green Hunt" (so dubbed by the media) in November 2009, under the aegis of the then Home Minister, P. Chidambaram of the Congress Party. With each operation, it appeared that the enemy had been fatally wounded.

But the Naxalite movement in India is a hydra-headed monster which, after decapitation, uses the fresh wound to grow two heads to replace the one that was lopped off. In Greek mythology, *Heracles*, in slaying this monster as part of his labours, had to enlist the aid of his nephew, *Iolaus*, who cauterised the wound to prevent new heads from appearing. And so, it must be with India's Naxalites. GoI's military actions must be supplemented by it applying an emollient balm to the wounds of rural India.

There is, however, a problem. Left-wing extremism thrives precisely because the wounds of rural India are open and bleeding. Close these wounds and staunch the bleeding and the rural population's support for extremist activity crumbles. Which is why, to demonstrate to people the ineffectiveness of the state, Naxalites often oppose the implementation of various developmental projects such as the construction of roads, rails, schools, and hospitals in areas in which they hold sway (Lynch, 2016).

Several activists who, after having visited Naxalite strongholds in the forests of Bastar/Dantewada in 2010 at the invitation of the insurgents, have written about the Naxalite movement in Chhattisgarh—Myrdal (2012), Navlakha (2012), Roy (2011)—are much more sympathetic to the Maoists than journalistic opinion in India. Rather than arguing that Naxalites presents an existentialist threat to the Indian state, these accounts, on the contrary, stress that it is the Indian state which is waging a war against the people of India, under the guise of a Maoist threat (Shah & Jain, 2017).

These starry-eyed views of "freedom fighters" in the jungle ignore, however, the brutality and the corruption which accompanies the Naxalite

[19] People's Daily Editorial https://www.marxists.org/subject/china/documents/peoples-daily/1967/07/05.htm reproduced in *Liberation* Vol. I, No. 1, November 1967.

movement. However, as Banerjee (2009)—himself an ex-Maoist—has written "the excesses committed by them [Maoists] in the course of their armed struggle threaten to erode their moral base" (p. 256). Their armed insurrection has brutalised the Maoists themselves, leading them to violate the human rights of those living in areas which they control. These violations involve: killing villagers suspected of being informers; murdering landlords, often in a most brutal fashion; extorting money from traders; destroying public transport and public infrastructure like roads, railways, and buildings. Thus, while purporting to give voice to the alienation of the deprived poor they alienate the very people they wish to support and whose support, in turn, they need.

References

Afroz, N. (2017). The Dream That Failed. *The Caravan Magazine*, 1 June 2017: 50–61. https://caravanmagazine.in/reportage/naxalbari-fifty-years-uprising

Ahlawat, D. (2024). Naxal Insurgency in India: Managing Conflict Through Empowerment. *International Journal of Criminology and Sociology, 13*, 1–14.

Ahluwalia, V. K. (2012). Strategy and Tactics of the Indian Maoists. *Strategic Analysis, 36*, 723–734.

Bagul, S. B. (2022). Maoist Insurgency and Human Security in India and Nepal. In I. A. Khan (Ed.), *Different Dimensions of Human Security and Governance* (pp. 22–32). Interdisciplinary Institute of Human Security & Governance.

Banerjee, S. (1980). *Once Upon a Time in Naxalbari*. India History Collective. https://indianhistorycollective.com/once-upon-a-time-in-naxalbari/

Banerjee, S. (1984), *India's Simmering Revolution: The Naxalite Uprising*. Zed Books. https://archive.org/details/indias-simmering-revolution-sumanta-banerjee-1984-sm/page/n57/mode/2up

Banerjee, S. (2009). Reflections of a One-Time Maoist. *Dialectical Anthropology, 33*, 253–269.

Behera, A. (2021). India's Security Response to the Maoist Insurgency. *Indian Studies Review, 2*, 1–16.

Borooah, V. K. (2008). "Deprivation, Violence and Conflict", An Analysis of Naxalite Activity in Districts in India. *International Journal of Conflict and Violence, 2*, 317–333.

Borooah, V. K. (2016). Deconstructing Corruption: A Study of Cash for Favours in Rural India. *Journal of South Asian Development, 11*, 1–37.

Chenoy, A. R., & Chenoy, K. A. M. (2010). *Maoist and Other Armed Conflicts*. Penguin Books India.

Desquesnes, N., & Jaoul, N. (2012, January). Furore Around a Judgement. *Le Monde diplomatique*. https://mondediplo.com/Furore-around-a-judgment

EFAS. (2019). *A Historical Introduction to Naxalism in India*. European Foundation for South Asian Studies.

Griffith, S. B. [Translator] (1961). *Mao Tse-Tung on Guerrilla Warfare*. Frederick Praeger Publisher.

Jain, B. (2013, February 17). Andhra Greyhound model for other Maoist-hit states on anvil. *Times of India*. Anti-Maoist Special Forces: Andhra Greyhound model for other Maoist-hit states on anvil | India News - Times of India. https://timesofindia.indiatimes.com/india/Andhra-Greyhound-model-for-other-Maoist-hit-states-on-anvil/articleshow/18538474.cms

Lynch, T. F. (2016). *India's Naxalite Insurgency: History, Trajectory, and Implications for U.S.-India Security Cooperation on Domestic Counterinsurgency*. Institute for National Strategic Studies (Strategic Perspectives, No. 22).

Majumdar, C. (1965). What Possibility the Year 1965 is Indicating. In *The Collected Works of Charu Majumdar*, Deshabrati Prakashani (publishing house of the Undivided C.P.I. (M-L)): Calcutta. Available from the Charu Majumdar Internet Archive. https://www.marxists.org/reference/archive/mazumdar/index.htm

Mathews, R. D. (2011). The Telangana Movement: Peasant Protests in India, 1946–51. In *People's Struggles in India*. Ritimo. https://www.ritimo.org/The-Telengana-Movement-Peasant-Protests-in-India-1946-51

Miklian, J. (2009). The Purification Hunt: The *Salwa Judum* Counterinsurgency in Chhattisgarh, India. *Dialectical Anthropology, 33*, 441–459.

Mohanty, M. (2015). *Red and Green: Five Decades of the Indian Maoist Movement*. Setu Prakashani.

Myrdal, J. (2012). *Red Star Over India: As the Wretched Earth Are Rising*. Setu Prakashani.

Navlakha, G. (2012). *Days and Nights in the Heartland of Rebellion*. Penguin.

Prasad, R. (2016). *Heart of India's Development Conflict*. Hachette India: Gurgaon India.

Ramasubbu, K. (2008). How the *Salwa Judum* Experiment Went Wrong. https://www.livemint.com/Politics/aegTjKka79aqBcS2ZbFrQJ/How-the-Salwa-Judum-experiment-went-wrong.html

Roy, A. (2011). *Broken Republic*. Hamish Hamilton.

Shah, A., & Jain, D. (2017). Naxalbari At Its Golden Jubilee: Fifty Recent Books on the Maoist Movement in India. *Modern Asian Studies, 51*, 1165–1219.

Simon, M. S. (2022). India's Internal Security: Issues, Challenges and Options. In A. Behera & S. Mishra (Eds.), *Varying Dimensions of India's National Security: Emerging Perspectives* (pp. 107–120). Springer.

Singh, P. (2006). *The Naxalite Movement in India*. Rupa Publications.

Strategy and Tactics of the Indian Revolution. (2004). https://archive.org/details/strategy-tactics-of-the-indian-revolution2/mode/2up

Sundar, N. (2022). *The Burning Forest*. Juggernaut: New Delhi

Sundarayya, P. (1972). *Telangana People's Struggle and Its Lessons*. Communist Party of India (Marxist).

Weili, S., & Yingli, Z. (1992). On Mao Zedong's Geographic Strategic Concept of Encircling the Cities from the Countryside. *Human Geography, 7*, 1–6.

CHAPTER 4

'Sons of the Soil' Conflicts in India's Northeast

4.1 Background to Northeastern India

The Northeastern (NE) region of India comprises seven states: Arunachal Pradesh (pop: 1.38 million; area: 83,743 square kilometres), Assam (pop: 35 million; area: 78,348 square kilometres), Manipur (pop: 2.9 million; area: 22,300 square kilometres), Meghalaya (pop: 2.97 million; area: 22,400 square kilometres), Mizoram (pop: 1.1 million; 21,100 square kilometres), Nagaland (pop: 4.5 million; area: 16,600 square kilometres) and Tripura (pop: 3.7 million; area: 10,500 square kilometres).[1] A distinguishing feature of the region is that 98% of its borders are international boundaries with Bhutan and China to the North, Bangladesh to the West and Myanmar to the South (see Map 1.4 in Chapter 1). The only land connection between the NE and "mainland" India is a narrow strip of land, termed the "Siliguri corridor", about 200 km long and, at its narrowest point, 20 km wide and which is flanked by Nepal and Bhutan in the north and by Bangladesh in the south (Map 4.1; Upadhayay, 2006).[2]

[1] Though, sometimes, commentators add Sikkim to this list to make eight Northeastern states. This book, however, restricts itself to, as they are often termed, the "seven sisters".

[2] The town of Siliguri, in the state of West Bengal, is the major city in this area and the central point connecting Bhutan, Nepal, Bangladesh, Sikkim, Darjeeling, and Northeast India to one another.

V. K. Borooah, *The Political Economy of Terrorism*,
https://doi.org/10.1007/978-3-032-08553-5_4

Map 4.1 The Siliguri Corridor

Another distinguishing feature of the region is the multiethnicity of its population divided between Hindus and Muslims non-tribal persons living in the region's plains and a mosaic of tribes living in its plains and in its hills (Verghese, 1996). Taking the NE in its entirety: 54% of the population were Hindus (against 79.8% for India as a whole); 25.4% were Muslim (against the all-India figure of 14.2%); and 17.3% were Christian (against the all-India figure of 2.3%). Tripura had the largest proportion of Hindus (83.4%), followed by Assam (61.5%); Assam had the highest proportion of Muslims (34.2%), followed by Tripura and Manipur (respectively, 8.6% and 8.4%); Nagaland, Mizoram, and Meghalaya had the highest proportion of Christians (respectively, 87.9%, 87.2%, and 74.6%) followed by Manipur and Arunachal Pradesh (respectively, 41.3% and 30.3%).[3]

[3] All figures are from the 2011 Census for India and summarised in https://dhingcollegeonline.co.in/attendence/classnotes/files/1589983067.pdf.

The region is home to over 200 Hill and plains tribes and they constitute a substantial share of the states in the region: Mizoram, Nagaland, Meghalaya, and Arunachal Pradesh have the largest proportion of tribals in their populations (respectively, 95%, 89%, and 86%, and 64%) followed by Manipur (35%), Tripura (31%), and Assam (12%).[4] Prominent among the hill tribes are the *Dimasas* of Assam's North Cachar Hills, the *Khasis* and *Garos* of Meghalaya, the *Mizos, Brus and Hmars* of Mizoram, the *Nagas* of Nagaland (but also in Manipur and in Arunachal Pradesh), the *Kukis* of Manipur and the *Kokboroks* of Tripura. Prominent among the plains tribals are the *Bodos* of Assam and *Meiteis* of Manipur.[5]

The story of NE India is usually told in terms of *ethnic conflict*: combination of the region's porous international borders, and the multiplicity of ethnic identities within it, provides a rich source of conflicts and the protagonists often sought to resolve these conflicts through violence. The bedrock of the region's problems lies in a heightened sense of ethnic identity of those living in its constituent parts and conflicts arise as groups seek to defend, extend, or take advantage of their identities which, for a variety of reasons, they feel is under threat. In general, the NE of India feels neglected by the Government of India (GoI) in New Delhi which, in turn, this generates movements within different parts of the region for a separate "homeland".

The post-independence demand for separate tribal homelands derives from the (pre-independence) British practice of drawing a distinction in NE India between the "plains" and the "hills" of that region—the latter were regarded as the wild areas of the NE and an Inner Line Permit system, introduced in 1873, forbade entry into these hill areas without official authorisation. This system was an attempt to keep the residents of the fertile plains of Assam (as it then was) separate from the 'primitive' hill tribes and, thereby, protect the tribal homelands from encroachment by

[4] Figures from Sivakumar et al. (2013).

[5] Such a listing does not, however, take account of the detailed sub-division of tribes into clans and the further subdivision of clans into family lineage. For example, according to Haokip (2018, p. 61), the broad question "are you [from the tribe] a *Kuki*, *Naga*, or *Khasi*?" can be further refined as "are you [from the clan] an *Ao*, *Thadou*, or *Kom*?" and even further refined as "are you [from the family] Jamir, Haokip, or Sailo". As an illustration, the Nagas encompass various clans: for example, *Ao*, *Angam*, *Chakhesang*, *ChangLotha*, *Rengma*, *Sangtam*, *Sümi*. There are anywhere between 30–80 tribes that belong to the Naga ethnic group (Oppitz et al., 2008).

non-tribals. The colonial government allowed the tribes to govern themselves and such influence that the British did exercise was through the aegis of tribal chiefs. In contrast the plains of Assam were firmly under British rule and were actively administered by them (Vandekerckhove, 2009).

After independence, the Indian government continued the British policy of "protecting" hill tribes, with the Inner Line Permit system being reincarnated as the Sixth Schedule of the Indian Constitution. Under the Sixth Schedule, these tribes were now termed as "Scheduled Tribes": their language and culture were constitutionally protected, and they were given preferential access to government jobs, educational opportunities, and electoral representation. Under the Article 244 of the Constitution, they were also entitled to a claim a separate hill state subject to not jeopardising national interests. The important point of post-independent India was that, in respect of the hill tribes of Assam, it conflated ethnicity with territory. Consequently, after Indian independence, the different ethnic groups in the hill areas of Assam began to demand homelands for themselves, with clearly demarcated boundaries encompassing all the group's members. These demands were predicated on the notion of autochthony, that is the group "belonged" to that area by virtue of being 'rooted in its soil'.

The protection of tribes in Assam, initiated by the British in pre-independence times, was further extended by the post-independence Indian government when, in addition to the homeland demands of the *hill* tribes of Assam, it also acceded to the demands of the *plains* tribes for separate homelands. The most prominent of these concessions were to the Bodo, the Karbi, and the Dimasa and these are described in some detail in Vandekerckhove (2009) and in Kolås (2017).

In political terms, homeland demands took the form of independence from India or, failing that, full statehood within the Indian Union, or, failing that, an *Autonomous District Council* (ADC) within an existing state.86F[6] Independence from India has, of course, never been achieved

[6] Under the 6th Schedule of the Indian Constitution, an Autonomous District Council (ADC), for a particular tribe, grants that tribe considerable autonomy in the management of its affairs within its designated territory. The Sixth Schedule gives the ADC extensive powers of administration of justice as well as powers to establish primary schools, assess and collect land revenue and impose taxes, issue leases for prospecting or extracting minerals, and to regulate trading by non-tribals.

by any of the ethnic groups in NE India but Nagaland, Mizoram, and Meghalaya have succeeded in getting statehood, Manipur and Tripura were upgraded from Union Territories to full statehood and several ADC, catering to specific ethnic groups, have been established. There are three ADC in Assam (Bodoland Territorial Council, North Cachar Hills Autonomous Council, and Karbi Anglong Autonomous Council); three in Meghalaya (Autonomous Councils for the Garo, the Jaintia, and the Khasi Hills); three in Mizoram (Autonomous Councils for the Chakma, the Lai, and the Mara); and one in Tripura (Tripura Tribal Areas Autonomous District Council). These constitutionally mandated ADC are buttressed by several other *Statutory Autonomous District Councils* which are not constitutionally mandated but established under the aegis of the relevant state government and, therefore, with weaker powers than the ADC.

Going hand in hand with the notion of demanding a homeland to which one belonged, was the idea of exclusion or 'othering': persons not belonging to this group ('outsiders'), living in the 'homeland' were to be excluded from important rights and benefits, particularly in respect to acquiring land and the exercise of political rights, and in extreme cases, excluded *in toto* from the homeland's territories through ethnic cleansing. In these homelands, the struggle against the unwelcome "outsider" over property rights, economic benefits, and cultural symbols that might prevail in a more normal setting was simply resolved through the expedient of exclusion.[7] The establishment of Bodoland Territorial Council in 2003 was a bloody affair involving, as acts of ethnic cleansing, the killing of Bengali Muslims by Bodos both before and after Bodoland came into being. The establishment of Karbi Anglong also involved killing between the Karbi and the Dimasa tribes but this time the dispute was over who were the true 'sons of the soil' in the demarcated area (Vandekerckhove, 2009).

Under the broad umbrella of a sense of step-motherly treatment by 'mainland' India towards NE India, are specific identity-related grievances. In some parts of the NE, identity is seen as being threatened through illegal migration, which takes advantage of porous borders

[7] For example, in November 2024, the Khun Hynñiewtrep National Awakening Movement (KHNAM) asked the Khasi Hills Autonomous District Council deny non-Khasis the right to vote in Council elections https://highlandpost.com/khnam-calls-for-amendment-to-strip-non-khasis-of-khadc-voting-rights/.

with neighbouring countries, to enter an area and upset its ethnic balance: this is particularly true of Assam, Manipur, and Tripura. In other parts of the NE, minority ethnic groups were aggrieved by, what they perceived as, unfavourable treatment at the hands of the majority (Manipur and Tripura). Elsewhere, borders demarcating existing states have given rise to irredentist movements which seek to unite an ethnic group within a single boundary (Nagaland and Manipur) and competing irredentist claims (the Dimasas and the Nagas). Lastly, conflicts arise because some ethnic groups are resentful about being unfairly excluded from certain economic and social benefits which other, in their view, equivalent, groups receive (Assam and Manipur).

The next sections detail some of these identity-based conflicts that bedevil Northeastern India, and give rise to terrorist violence within it, for five of the states most affected by conflict: Nagaland, Mizoram, Manipur, Assam, and Tripura. When India became independent on 15 August 1947, the NE comprised just three states—Assam (encompassing contemporary Arunachal Pradesh—which was then the North East Frontier Agency or NEFA, Nagaland, Meghalaya, and Mizoram) and the princely states of Manipur and Tripura. The size of the area awarded to Assam, and the variety of the different ethnic groups that came under the purview of its government, was to become a cause of disagreement and, in less than a decade of Independence, the problem first emerged with the *Nagas*.

4.2 The Nagas: In Search of Nationhood

The Nagas were the first group in the NE of India to term themselves a "nation" rather than a "tribe" and their sense of nationhood was developed hand in hand with their conversion to Baptist Christianity (Baruah, 2020).[8] In fact, the Nagas adopted a distinctly Christian identity which was in stark opposition to the Hindu and Muslimidentities of most of India (Longkumer, 2009).

In the Naga imagination, a Naga nation (*Nagalim*) would encompass contiguous areas in the NE states of Arunachal Pradesh, Assam, Manipur and, in addition, include tracts of Burma (now Myanmar) as shown in

[8] The term Naga is not a linguistic label, and the people described as Naga speak a variety of languages (Post and Burling, 2003).

Map 4.2. Indeed, the Naga National Council (NNC), under the leadership of A.Z. Phizo, had declared independence from British rule on 14 August 1947, a day before Indian Independence. But Naga hopes were dashed when, with India becoming independent, the Naga territories in India were press-ganged into the state of Assam as one of its districts, with the Naga territories in Myanmar remaining part of that country.89F[9] Indeed, the first Indian Prime Minister, Jawaharlal Nehru wrote at that time, "Naga territory in Eastern Assam is much too small to stand by itself politically or economically... inevitability, therefore, this *Naga* territory must form part of India and Assam"[10] and Phizo quoted him as saying, during a stormy meeting between the two in New Delhi on 11 March 1952, that "it is inconceivable for the Nagas to have a sovereign state. They won't be allowed to become independent whatever happens, even if the heavens fall or India goes to pieces".[11]

So, much like the Kurds in Iraq and Turkey, territories in which *Nagas* were dominant straddled both sides of an international border. To add insult to injury, there were areas in which the Nagas were dominant in India, but which were in the neighbouring state of Manipur and Assam, with the result that persons of Naga ethnicity were divided by both international and national borders.

These perceived injustices then spawned the Naga insurrection, triggered by a boycott of the 1952 Indian General Election, of the 1950s which, in retaliation, was met by the GoI with brutal military force. A notorious feature of this military action (reprised, in the 1960s in Mizoram, and then again, between 2005 and 2011, in a different context, by the *Salwa Judum* against Left-Wing Extremists in the state of Chhattisgarh) was the village resettlement program which was underpinned by the assumption that all people in an insurgency area were potentially hostile and must, therefore, be quarantined in camps for the larger public good

[9] A district of an Indian state is an administrative geographical unit, headed by the District Commissioner (DC), who combines the offices of the District Magistrate, responsible for maintaining law and order in the unit, and District Collector, responsible for collection of revenue.

[10] Quoted in Upadhyay (2009, p. 38).

[11] New York Times, 12 March 1952 https://www.nytimes.com/1952/03/12/archives/nehru-rebuffs-nagas-indian-prime-minister-refuses-tribes-plea-for.html.

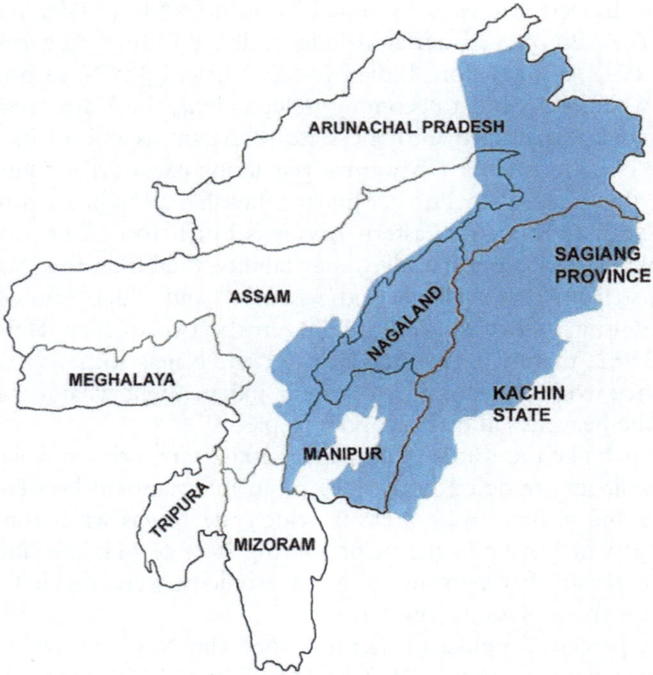

Map 4.2 Proposed Map of *Nagalim* (*Source* Wikimedia Commons)

(Sundar, 2011).[12] This counter-insurgency measure encapsulated a "cost–benefit approach" through which the *cost* to the public of supporting insurgents (in the form of having one's home destroyed, the denial of food, being tortured) was greater than the *benefit* (Jaffa, 2001; Kalvyas, 2006). The result was that in Nagaland support for insurgents increased greatly and the entire population went underground or, as the Nagas, preferred to term it, became "national workers" (Sundar, 2011, p. 49).

In a belated response to the Naga insurgents/Indian military violence, the Government of India (GoI) agreed to a separate state of Nagaland, comprising the (erstwhile) district of Nagaland in the state of Assam and the Tuensang Frontier Division, which was a part of NEFA, and this came

[12] During 1956–1959, it was under Nehru's orders that the Army burnt villages and grouped their inhabitants into camps (Sundar, 2011, p. 49).

into being in 1963. The subsequent "investment", in the form of grants and subsidies, by the GoI in Nagaland led to the creation of a Naga elite and bore fruit in the signing of the Shillong Accord of 1975 whereby a group of moderates in the Naga National Council accepted the compromise of statehood in lieu of nationhood and renounced violence (Baruah, 2020).

This Accord was, however, seen by other Nagas as a betrayal of the Naga demand for independence. Prominent among the dissenters were Isak Swu (who died in 2016) and Thuingaleng Muivah and this led to the formation of the *National Socialist Council of Nagaland (Isak-Muivah)*, hereafter NSCN (I-M) which continued hostilities and supported militant action by other Naga groups. Divisions among the Nagas led to a split in the NSCN(I-M) and a splinter entity, led by Khole Konyak Khaplang, the *National Socialist Council of Nagaland (Khaplang)*, hereafter NSCN(K) came into being.[13] This resulted in a period of internecine conflict between the NSCN(I-M) and the NSCN(K).[14]

On 25 July 1997, the GoI and the dominant faction of the National Socialist Council of Nagaland, the NSCN (I-M), entered into a ceasefire agreement the wording of which read: "For securing a peaceful political solution, discussion has been held between the Government of India and the NSCN leadership. It has been mutually decided to cease fire for a period of three (3) months with effect from the 1st of August 1997 and embark upon political level discussions". This was followed, in 2001, with a ceasefire agreement between the GoI and the NSCN(K). The thaw in India-Naga relations, embodied in these ceasefire agreements, culminated in a Peace Accord signed on 3 August 2015 between the GoI and the NSCN(I-M)—the other faction NSCN(K) having been declared a terrorist organisation after its part in an attack on an army convoy on 4 June 2015 which killed eighteen soldiers. This Peace Accord had a major flaw in that the NSCN(I-M) faction, which was the main signatory to this Accord, interpreted it to mean that sovereignty over Nagaland was now

[13] There exist myriad factions of the National Socialist Council of Nagaland, all breakaways from the parent NNC. The dominant faction is the Isak-Muivah group, NSCN(I-M), and derives its support is mostly from the Sema and the Tangkhul Nagas; the other large faction, the Khaplang group, NSCN(K) is supported by the Konyak Nagas. In addition, there are: NSCN(KK), NSCN(U), NSCN(R, NNC-A, NNC(N/A) and so on (Wouters, 2018).

[14] Uppsala Conflict Data Program https://ucdp.uu.se/additionalinfo/508/4.

to be *shared* between the GoI and the NSCN(I-M) and other factions and the GoI silently acquiesced to this (Baruah, 2020).

If one defines sovereignty as the rights to the legitimate use of force and to raise revenue through taxation, then it was the legitimately elected Nagaland government *and* the various factions of the NSCN which exercised these rights. Some of these details are in Baruah (2020): salaried persons paid 2% of their salaries to the "Government of the Peoples Republic of Nagaland" (GPRN),[15] government infrastructure projects paid 5% of their allocation, and the National Rural Employment Guarantee Scheme (NREGS) paid as much as 20%. Wouters (2018) writes about this state of affairs: "post the [1997] ceasefire, the mostly noble and selfless motivations of 'national workers', as cadres of Nagaland underground groups are called locally, quickly degenerated into greediness, intimidation and internal bickering ...it is widely held that the ceasefire has not made things better for ordinary Naga men and women" (p. 2).

4.3 The Mizos: In Search of Statehood

Mizoram, in the most southern part corner of NE India covers an area of approximately 21,000 square kilometres, with a population of 1.25 million, and is sandwiched between Myanmar to the east and south and Bangladesh to the west (see Map 4.3). Before Indian independence, it was known as the Mizo Hills district under British Rule and because the British excluded it from the Government of India Act of 1935—which introduced, for the first time, direct elections to provincial assemblies—hereditary chiefs ruled it right up to 1947. After Indian independence it became a part of the state of Assam and the GoI awarded it the status of District Council; the Mizo Union which won the District Council elections of 1952 was keen to be part of India and, thereby, end the rule of hereditary chiefs (Sundar, 2011).

A defining and catastrophic event occurred in Mizoram in 1959 with the cyclical 50-year flowering of the bamboo trees. Every 50 years or so, a bamboo species widespread in Mizoram suddenly blooms and die, a phenomenon referred to by Mizos as the *Mao Tham*. In its wake it leaves millions of seeds which are a prized food of rats, and this triggers a population explosion among the rodents with the average litter rising from

[15] This is the "parallel" government of the NSCN(I-M) to the official government.

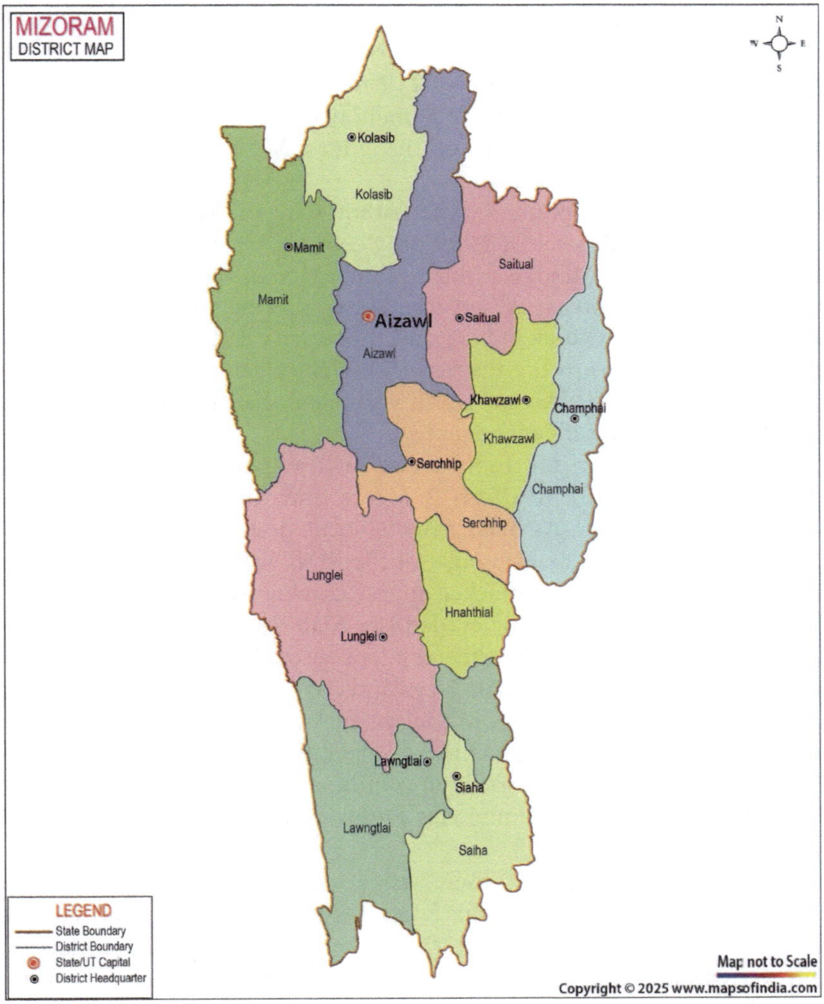

Map 4.3 Mizoram (*Source* Maps of India)

four to eighteen. Once the rats are through with the bamboo seeds, they devour crops and destroy fields leading—over a period of three years—to widespread famine and death by starvation, a phenomenon the Mizos refer to as the *Thing Tam*. (Nag, 2008; Rangasami, 1978).

The response of the Assam government, which bore responsibility for famine relief in Mizoram—a district of the state—was both scant and tardy. Of the total expenditure of ₹19 million, only ₹0.49 was spent of gratuitous relief and another ₹2.8 million on relief works (Rangasami, 1978). On one estimate, 5% of the entire Mizo population died of starvation (Dalrymple, 2025).

The indifferent response by the parent state of Assam to the Mizoram's Mao Tham disaster of 1959 provided the motive for Mizos, under the banner of the Mizo National Front (MNF), with Laldenga as its leader, to embark on an armed insurgency seeking independence from India. This began with an attack, on 28 February 1966, on Indian Army posts in three towns in the district—Lungleh, Champai, and Aizawl and on 1 March 1966, Laldenga and fifty-nine associates issued a statement unilaterally declaring independence.

The response from the Indians was swift and ruthless: Mizoram was declared a "disturbed area" on 2 March and, on 5–6 March, Aizawl was strafed by air and its main market burnt down. The Indian Army's counter-insurgency operations against the MNF were based on the observation that MNF fighters attacked supply convoys on the 20 mile stretch of the Vairengte-Aizawl-Lunglei road (see Map 4.4) and then escaped into the villages flanking it where their residents provided them with food and shelter. So, taking a leaf from its Nagaland copybook—which, in turn, was based on British Army tactics in Malaya against communist insurgents in 1948—the Indian Army launched an operation in 1967 to isolate the MNF from its village support by uprooting a total of 45,000 inhabitants living in 109 villages adjoining this highway, and moving them into 18 group centres (Jaffa, 2001).

Following this grouping, there was a second and third grouping so that, by 1972, 240,000 persons were herded into 109 group centres. Whatever the contribution that the grouping of the Mizo population into centres made to the success of counter-insurgency measures in the Mizo Hills there is little doubt that it scarred its socio-economic life. The displacement of villagers and their villages in Mizoram lasted fifteen years compared to just two or three in Nagaland. After grouping ended, most villagers in Nagaland returned to their original villages but in Mizoram they stayed on in the centres or else moved to Aizawl making Mizoram one of the most urbanised of Indian states—as Verghese (1996) noted, the proportion of the population that was urbanised increased from 5.4% in 1962 to 46.1% by 1991.

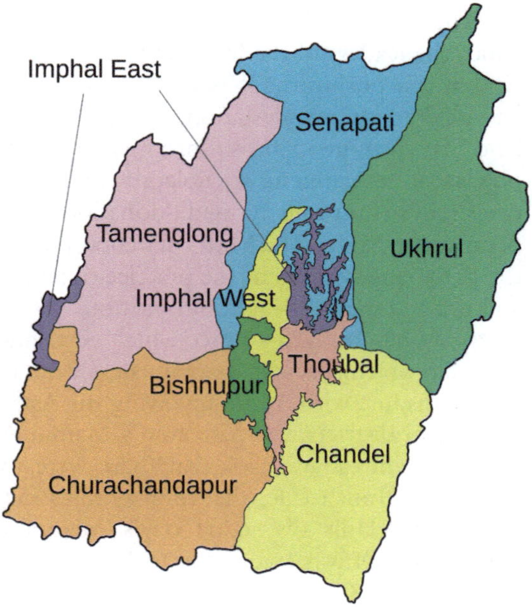

Map 4.4 District map of Manipur prior to 2016 reorganisation (*Source* Wikipedia, The Free Encyclopedia)

After two decades of warfare, peace was restored in Mizoram when a settlement in January 1972 resulted in Mizoram being elevated from a district of Assam to a Union Territory of India with two representatives (one each in the Lower and Upper Houses) in Parliament. A Peace Accord between the MNF and the GoI was signed in 1986 with Mizoram becoming a full state of the Indian Union under the Accord's terms. Furthermore, the incumbent Chief Minister Lal Thanhawla agreed to vacate his position in favour of Laldenga (the MNF's leader) and to serve as Deputy Chief Minister under a coalition government.

Three major differences emerge in comparing the insurgencies of Nagaland and Mizoram. First, the Nagas had set their sights on independence from India while the Mizos were content with statehood. So, even after Nagaland had become a fully fledged state on 1 December 1963, with Shilo Ao as the first Chief Minister, the Naga insurrection continued because the larger ambition of independence remained unfulfilled. On the other hand, Mizo aspirations were satisfied after Mizoram was awarded the status of statehood in 1986. Second, in Mizoram, the existing Chief Minister stepped down after Mizoram became a state and made way for

Laldenga, the leader of the MNF to assume this office. On the other hand, the leaders of the insurgents in Nagaland, Swu, and Muivah, never held official positions. Consequently, the concept of "shared sovereignty", and its practical manifestation, "parallel government" took hold in Nagaland. The insurgents broke into myriad factions all of which assumed the powers of government: to violently attack rivals and to collect ("extort") taxes (euphemistically termed "donations") from the public. In Mizoram because the MNF, which after statehood became a political party, was also the party of government the practice of parallel government did not exist and nor did the MNF split into factions. As a result, for the past 50 years, Mizoram has enjoyed a peace which Nagaland has not known.

The problems facing Mizoram stem from other sources. The first is the border dispute with Assam involving the Assam's Cachar, Hailakandi, and Karimganj districts and Mizoram's Mamit, Aizaw, and Kolasib districts. The problem essentially is that there were two notifications while India was under British rule: the 1875 notification set the boundary between the Lushai Hills district (today's Mizoram) and the Cachar district (Assam) which was favourable to Mizoram; however, a subsequent notification in 1933, revisited this and reset the boundaries this time now assigning some forest areas, previously awarded to Mizoram, to Assam. Obviously Mizoram would like the 1875, while Assam would want the 1933, notification to be the basis for drawing the border between the two states (Sarmah & Bhuyan, 2022).

The situation might seem trivial except for the fact that in an exchange of gunfire between Mizo and Assam security personnel in a disputed area called *Rengti Basti*, between Vairengte (Mizoram) and Lailapur (Assam), six policemen from Assam were killed on 26 July 2021.[16] In retaliation, on 2 August 2021, the Assam government blocked the national highway (NH306) from Silchar, in Assam, which is the main supply route into Mizoram. Although some essentials reached Mizoram through two other road routes from Tripura and Manipur, it was expensive to do so because of poor road conditions. Because of the blockade, there were food and medicine shortages in Mizoram.[17]

[16] https://theprint.in/india/there-were-bullets-stones-all-over-story-of-how-assam-mizoram-police-fought-each-other/705886/.

[17] https://theprint.in/india/veggies-are-expensive-medicines-in-short-supply-how-assam-blockade-is-hurting-mizoram/707113/.

The second issue in Mizoram is its treatment of minorities (that is, non-Mizo) in Mizoram. These comprise 27% of Mizoram's population and the largest of these are the *Chakmas* who form 8% of the state's population (Chakma, 2009). According to the Gogoi (2023), the Chakmas—who mostly live in the south of Mizoram, bordering the Chittagong Hill Tracts of Bangladesh and who are mostly Buddhist—are seen as a non-Indigenous people by the majority of Christian Mizos. The state government often treats them as non-citizens in Mizoram and they face cancellation of trade licenses, denial of their right to employment, deletion of names from electoral rolls, the withdrawal of healthcare and educational facilities and other forms of harassment. The Mizos in Mizoram also regard the Bru and Hmar tribals as aliens and subject them to similar neglect. Learning to live and respect minorities is, thus, an issue that Mizoram need to address in a humane and non-discriminatory manner.

4.4 Manipur: In Search of Inter-Tribal Harmony

The state of Manipur, sandwiched between Mizoram and Nagaland to the south and north, respectively, shares an international border with Myanmar to its east (see Map 1.4 in Chapter 1). It is from a combination of this geographical location and Manipur's ethnic composition that many of its problems emanate. Manipur has three rival ethnic groups between whom there is considerable friction, with a large part of this friction being based on geography. First, there are the (mostly Hindu) *Meiteis*, who like to think of themselves as Manipur's original inhabitants and who comprise about 54% of its population; second, there are the *Kukis* (mostly Christian), who belong to the same ethnic group as the *Mizos* in Mizoram and the *Chins* in Myanmar, and who comprise 14% of the state's population; and, third, there are the Nagas (also mostly Christian) who, in addition to having their own state of Nagaland, are present in large numbers in the districts of Manipur bordering Nagaland and constitute 26% of Manipur's population The remaining 6% of Manipur's population are *Meitei Muslim* and are locally referred to as *Pangals*.[18]

The *Meiteis* mostly live in the Imphal valley in the districts of Imphal East, Imphal West, Thoubal, and Bishnupur, with the *Pangals* mostly living in Bishnupur. These valley districts, collectively comprise 10% of

[18] These numbers are from Engineer and Dabhade (2024, p. 17).

Manipur's land. The. The hill districts, comprising the remaining land, are home to the *Kukis* and the *Nagas*: the *Kukis* are mostly to be found in the hill districts of Churachandpur and Chandel and the hill districts of Ukhrul, Senapati, Tamenglong, and Chandel are predominantly *Naga* (see Maps 4.4 and 4.5).[19]

Although the valley districts comprise only one-tenth of Manipur they are rich in terms of infrastructure: all the administrative offices, many of the educational institutions, hospitals, industries are located there. They are also rich in terms of political influence: of the 60 seats in the Manipur Assembly, 40 are based in the valley districts and only 20 are based in the hill districts. So, while the *Nagas* and *Kukis* constitute 40% of Manipur's population their districts have only one-third of the seats in Manipur's Assembly (Engineer & Dabhade, 2024, p. 17).

The first fault-line in this landscape of geographical and ethnic divisions is the *Meitei* demand that the GoI class them as a *Scheduled Tribe* (*ST*) and, thereby, put them on par with the *Nagas* and the *Kukis* who have always enjoyed this status. After India's Independence, some of the tribes in India were formally recognised as *ST* and Articles 341 and 342 of the Indian Constitution lists these tribes with the addendum that this list can be added to, or subtracted from, by the President of India. The criteria for being regarded as a *ST* have not been made explicit, but they include an indication of 'primitive' traits, 'distinctive' culture, geographical 'isolation', 'shyness' in connecting with the community at large, and economic and social 'backwardness' (Haokip, 2018).

Obtaining *ST* recognition then provides a passport to several tangible benefits: political representation through 'reserved' constituencies (that is, constituencies in which only members of a *ST* can be stand for election), reserved seats in government educational institutions, and reserved positions in public (that is, government, and government-supported, employment). Because of these benefits, tribes that the GoI does not currently recognise as "Scheduled" would like to obtain this status and social and political pressure from them has led to the number of *ST*s growing from 225 in 1960 to 700 in 2017 (Dragomir, 2017).

Of relevance to *Meiteis* in is the Manipur Land Revenue and Land Reforms Act of 1960 which restricts the non-*ST* Meiteis from buying land in the Hill Districts of Manipur which are the abode of the (ST)

[19] Roy (2016) and Engineer and Dabhade (2024).

Map 4.5 District map of Manipur after the 2016 reorganisation (*Source* Maps of India)

Kukis and *Nagas*.[20] The demand for ST status by the Meiteis stems from a desire to acquire land in the Hill Districts of Manipur and this demand is bitterly opposed by the *Kukis* and the *Nagas* who live there. The start of the current spate violence in Manipur, which continues into 2024, was the Manipur High Court's ruling on 14 April 2023 that the state government recommend to the GoI government that the *Meiteis* be granted ST status. In response to this ruling, on 3 May 2023, the All Tribals Students' Union Manipur (ATSUM) organised protest rallies all over the ten Hill Districts of Manipur and paralysed normal life there. Supporters of the *Meitei* demand for ST status—like the Scheduled Tribe Demand Committee Manipur (STDCM)—then organised counter-rallies in the Valley Districts.

With both sides to the dispute—the *Meiteis* on the one side, the *Nagas* and *Kukis* on the other—inflamed by these rallies the protests and counter-protests quickly spiralled into the most appalling violence. Ethnic cleansing was a facet of the violence, as *Nagas* and *Kukis* were forced out of their homes in the Valley Districts and Meiteis had to leave the Hill Districts. The consequence was that this population transfer resulted in over 3600 houses being burnt and 70,000 persons, from both sides of the ethnic divide, being made homeless and having to find shelter in relief camps. In the wake of this cleansing, more than 180 persons died, scores of women were raped and sexually assaulted, and many persons were reported missing. Armed personnel from both sides set up borders within Manipur preventing *Nagas* and *Kukis* from entering the Valley and *Meiteis* from entering the Hills (Engineer & Dabhade, 2024).

Even before the unceasing mayhem that engulfed Manipur from May 2023, anger and violence had always been part of life in Manipur. There was a large residue of anger in Manipur at, what it perceived as, high-handed treatment from India. Resentment emerged when Manipur was incorporated into the Indian Union in 1947 as a third-tier state, governed by a Chief Commissioner, rather than as a first or second-tier states which had Governors as their head of state. Manipuri resentment at India was exacerbated when, in 1953, Jawaharlal Nehru, India's first Prime Minister, as a gesture of goodwill, ceded the 7000 square mile Kubaw Valley, which historically had been a part of Manipur, to Burma. Then, in 1972, when

[20] Since the Act draws its powers from the Article 317 of the Indian Constitution, the state government cannot easily alter its proscriptions. Meiteis can only buy land in the Hill Districts with the consent of the District Councils which is difficult to get.

Manipur eventually did get full statehood it was nine years after Nagaland; and it was only in 1992 that the Manipuri language, notwithstanding its distinguished pedigree, was recognised by the GoI as one of India's official languages (Upadhyay, 2009).

Overlaying the tense Manipur-India relationship were the fraught relations between the main ethnic groups in Manipur. One issue was the Naga irredentist movement for a Naga nation (*Nagalim*) which would include not just the existing state of Nagaland but also the Hill districts in Manipur where the Nagas were predominant: Tamenglong; Senapati; Ukhru; and Chandel. Four Hill districts in Manipur. The Naga independence movement described earlier spilled over from Nagaland into these Manipur provinces under the aegis of the NSCN (I-M).

This irredentist movement had two tactical strands. The first was to assimilate *Kukis* into the Naga fold and this was successful with the "old *Kuki*" tribes. However, assimilation was unsuccessful, or not attempted, with the "New" *Kukis*.[21] The tactic here was to drive the *Kukis* that would not, or not asked to, become *Nagas*, out these four "Naga districts" to facilitate their incorporation into *Nagalim* (or "Greater Nagaland"). Consequently, *Kukis* in the northern district of Ukhrul fled to the Sadar Hills of Manipur or to the Kubaw valley in Burma (see Map 4.4) which was home to their ethnic counterparts (Haokip, 2023).

In 1980s the Kuki response to Naga intimidation changed from "flight" to "fight" through the formation of four armed groups: the Kuki National Front (KNA), the Kuki National Army (KNA), the Kuki Independent Army (KIA) and the Kuki Defence Force (KDF). This culminated in violent clashes between the *Kukis* and *Nagas* in 1992 which began in Manipur's border (with Myanmar) town of Moreh in the Tengnoupal district, and quickly spread to other parts of Manipur.[22] More than 1000 persons were killed in this conflict and 130,000 persons were made homeless with ethnically diverse villages, once common in Manipur, almost ceasing to exist (Butalia, 2008).

[21] The 1886 Gazetteer of Manipur, using census data, recorded approximately 8000 'old Kukis' in Manipur who traditionally lived in the state and about 17,000 'new Kukis' who had migrated from Lushai Hills in the south during the early nineteenth century (Engineer & Dabhade, 2024).

[22] Moreh is an important route through which drugs and small arms enter India. In addition, many of the NE India's insurgent groups have training camps across the border in Myanmar. Inhabited by Kuki-Chin groups and by Nagas (the Marin, Anals and Tangkhul tribes), the town has always been a source of ethnic tension (Butalia, 2008).

The *Kukis* also allied to their armed response to Naga hostility by demanding from the GoI a separate homeland like the demand by the *Bodo* tribe in Assam for a *Bodoland*. In 2012, a Kuki State Demand Committee (KSDC) announced a movement for *Kukiland* claiming 12,958 sq km—more than 60% of Manipur's area—for "*Kukis* and *Kukiland*". The territory of "*Kukiland*" was proposed to include the Sadar Hills (which surround the Imphal valley on three sides), the *Kuki*-dominated Churachandpur district, Chandel, which has a mix of Kuki and Naga populations, and even parts of Naga-dominated Tamenglong and Ukhrul (Roy, 2023).

The governmental response to The Naga-Kuki violence—and the twin demands by *Nagas* for *Nagalim* and *Kukis* for a *Kukiland*—has been two-fold. First, in 1980 the GoI extended the purview of the Armed Forces Special Powers Act (AFSPA), which was already in force in the Naga Hills, to include large parts of Manipur. This Act gives the Army, and the Central Armed Police Forces (CAPF), deployed in what were deemed "disturbed areas", the power to arrest or kill anyone breaking the law and to search premises without a warrant and, further, grants them immunity from prosecution and legal action against any of their actions. As Kakoti (2021) has argued, violence by the Armed Forces in Manipur is pervasive; it blurs the distinction between public and private spaces and specifically targets women.

Second, in 2016, the Manipur state government reorganised the districts in Manipur increasing their number from nine to 16 (Map 4.5 and compare it with Map 4.4). Before the reorganisation, the *Meiti*-majority valley had four districts—Imphal East, Imphal West, Thoubal and Bishnupur—while the remaining five districts of Ukhrul, Senapati, Chandel, Tamenglong and Churachandpur were tribal-majority hill districts: the *Kukis* dominated Churachandpur while *Nagas* dominated the other four. After the 2016 reorganisation, seven new districts were created with the most contentious being the creation of the Kuki-Zomi dominated Kangpokpi district, carved out from the Naga-dominated Senapati district in the Sadar Hills region of the state (Baruah, 2024).

The *Nagas* saw the move as an attempt by the Manipur's Congress government in 2016 to win over *Kuki* votes groups ahead of the elections at the expense of *Naga* interests. The United Naga Council, along with the largest insurgent group of the northeast, the NSCN (I-M), opposed the creation of the new districts, accusing the government of "appropriating" Naga villages and merging them with non-Naga areas. After the reorganisation, the United Naga Council imposed a blockade of highways into Manipur from November 2015 to March 2016, inflicting further violence on Manipur, demanding that the state government reverse its decision.

4.5 Assam: In Search of Ethnic Purity

Connected to the parent country by a narrow land corridor and largely separated from it by Bangladesh (see Map 4.1), the state of Assam—covering an area of 78,500 square kilometres with a population of just over 31 million[23]—is dominated by the mighty Brahmaputra River (Map 4.6). The Brahmaputra Valley has two main geographical features: the floodplain that is home to Hindus and Muslims and plains tribes (most prominent among these tribes being the *Bodo*, the *Miri*, and the *Rabha*) and the *Karbi* hills in the three districts of (Karbi Anglong, West Karbi Anglong, and Dima Hassao) populated by the *Karbi* and *Dimasa* tribes (Shrivastava & Heinen, 2005). In total, according to the 2011 Census of India, nearly 4 million persons in Assam (comprising 12.4% of its population) were classed as *ST* of whom 35% were *Bodo*, 18% were *Miri*, and 11% were *Karbi*.

Governance in Assam is complicated because the state has been divided based on ethnicity, quite often with overlapping jurisdictions. The state has: three Autonomous District Councils, under the Sixth Schedule of the Constitution, for the *Karbis*, the *Dimasas* and the Bodos, respectively; six Statutory Tribal Councils (Rabha, Mising, Tiwa, Deori, Thengal Kachari, and Sonowal Kachari); and a further eighteen Non-Statutory Ethnic Councils. In essence, therefore, Assam has become a state with several smaller states embedded within it (Kashyap, 2012).[24]

A consequence of this division of Assam by ethnic group is that the state is home to myriad ethnic groups, represented by a plethora of armed groups who offer to "liberate" them from the hegemony of their "oppressors"—sometimes perceived as the Indian government, sometimes the

[23] Respectively, 2.4% and 2.6% of India's area and population.

[24] See Samudra Gupta Kashyap, "The Assam Tangle", *The Indian Express*, August 26, 2012.

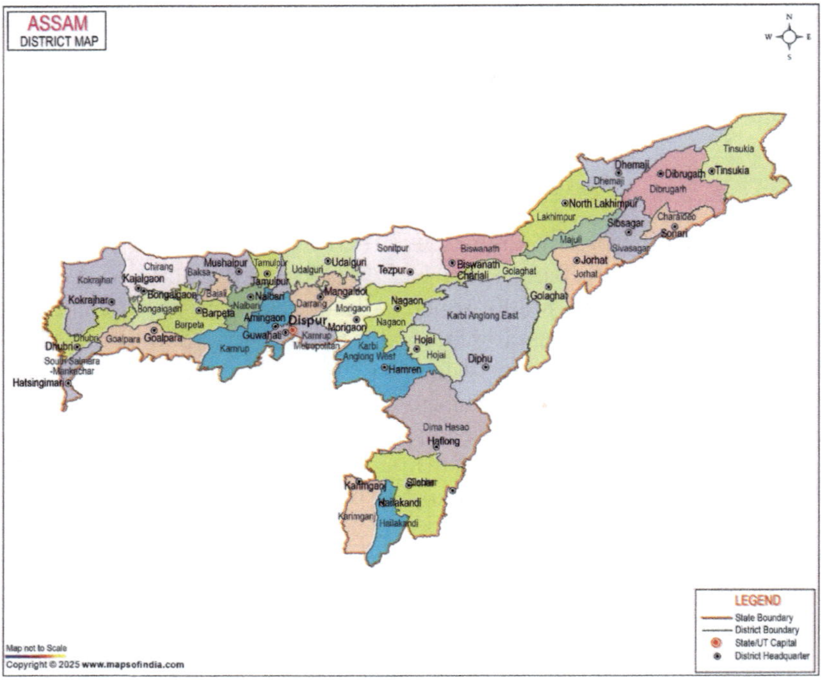

Map 4.6 Assam and its districts (*Source* Maps of India)

state government, and sometimes just other ethnic groups.[25] In consequence of the undercurrent of hostility between the various subgroups in Assam—engendered by a zero-sum competition for land and resources—life in the state is regularly punctuated by inter-tribal violence: *Karbis*

[25] Kashyap (2012) contains a comprehensive list of such groups: Dima Halam Daoga, Kuki Revolutionary Army, Hmar People's Convention, United Kukigam Defence Army, Adivasi People's Army, All Adivasi National Liberation Army, Santhal Tiger Force, Birsa Commando Force, Adivasi Cobra Military of Assam and Rabha Viper. In addition to these, are the Islamic terror groups: Muslim Security Council of Assam, United Liberation Militia of Assam, Islamic Liberation Army of Assam, Muslim Volunteer Force, Muslim Liberation Army, Muslim Security Force, Islamic Sevak Sangh, Islamic United Reformation Protest of India, Revolutionary Muslim Commandos, Muslim Tiger Force, Muslim Liberation Front, Muslim Liberation Tigers of Assam, Muslim United Liberation Front of Assamand Muslim United Liberation Tigers of Assam.

clash with *Kukis*, the *Dimasa* with the *Zeme*, *Rabhas* with *Garo*, *Bodos* with *Santhals*.

Despite their many arcane differences, the basic demand of all the militant groups in Assam—and, indeed, in NE India—has been demand for a homeland, whether in the form of an Autonomous District Council, a separate state, or even an independent country. These demands, taken collectively, are riddled with conflict-generating contradictions: the *Dima Halam Daogah* (DHD) want a separate state for the Dimasa called *Dimaraji* but the territory it demands overlaps with some of the area that the NSCN (I-M) wants for *Nagalim* which leads to violence between the two groups; then there is the *Hmar People's Convention-Democracy* (HPC-D) demanding an independent *Hmar* state covering Hmar-inhabited areas of Mizoram, Manipur, and Assam (including the North-Cachar Hills); the United People's Democratic Solidarity (UPDS) wants a separate territory for the *Karbi* tribe, covering Karbi Anglong, North-Cachar Hills, and contiguous 'Karbi dominated areas' of Meghalaya (Kolås, 2017). And so on!

Overshadowing these clashes, however, is the fact that, in the past 25 years or so, Assam has spawned some of the most egregious incidents of anti-immigrant violence in South Asia directed mainly, though not exclusively, against Bengali Muslims.106F[26] At the end of July 2012, *Bodo* tribesmen began a wave of killing of Bengali Muslims, and arson attacks on their homes in which, by August 2012, over 80 people had been killed (mostly Bengali Muslim, but some *Bodos*), with almost half a million persons, from nearly 400 villages, sheltering in refugee camps (*The Economist* August 24, 2012).

In earlier incidents, clashes between *Bodos* and Bengali Muslims in August–October 2008 resulted in 70 deaths with over 100,000 people made homeless; in July 1994, assaults on Bengali Muslims in Barpeta district resulted in 100 deaths (most of them Bengali Muslim); and in October 1993, 50 people were killed in Bongaigaon district in clashes

[26] Other immigrants have not escaped the fury of the native Assamese: in the 1960s there was violence against Bengali Hindus consequent upon Bengali being proposed, along with Assamese, as an official language of the state and, in November 2003, 30 persons were killed, in and around the town of Tinsukia in upper Assam, because of violence against immigrants from Bihar. http://www.rediff.com/news/2003/nov/20assam4.htm retrieved 9 September 2012.

between *Bodos* and Bengali Muslims.[27] The most egregious act of violence occurred on 14 February 1983 when a large group of armed men from the *Lalung* tribe in Assam raided fourteen villages, in close proximity to each other, in the district of Nagaon in Assam and killed over four thousand persons—men, women, and children—most of whom were Bengali Muslims. This was the infamous Nellie massacre, so named after one of the affected villages, in the aftermath of which nearly 250,000 persons were made homeless, and thousands fled the state (Weiner, 1983).[28]

The ostensible reason for attacks against Bengali Muslims is invariant: they are accused of being illegal immigrants who, taking advantage of the porous, 267 kilometres long border between Assam and Bangladesh, entered the state and occupied land belonging to the native population.[29] Moreover, through a rapid increase in their numbers, native Assamese see them as diluting and debasing traditional Assamese Hindu culture through the instruments of a foreign language (*Bengali*) and an alien religion (Islam). The political counterpart to these acts of violence is demands by political parties for the detection and expulsion of foreigners. The Assam Movement of 1979–1985 was a popular uprising which gave shape and voice to these demands and the resulting social unrest culminated in the signing of the Assam Accord of 1985.[30] By the terms of this Accord, immigrants who arrived before January 1, 1966 were to be regarded as Indian citizens; immigrants who arrived between 1 January 1966 and 25 March 1971 could remain in the country but would have their names removed from the electoral roll and would have to register themselves with the appropriate district offices but, after a period of

[27] http://www.firstpost.com/india/a-timeline-of-bodo-muslim-violence-in-assam-391475.html retrieved on 9 September 2012.

[28] The other villages were: Alisingha, Khulapathar, Basundhari, Bugduba Beel, Bugduba Habi, Borjola, Butuni, Indurmari, Mati Parbat, Muladhari, Mati Parbat no. 8, Silbheta, and Borburi.

[29] The Bangladesh border is the longest land border that India shares with any of its neighbours. It covers a length of 4095 kilometres, abutting the States of West Bengal, Assam, Meghalaya, Mizoram, and Tripura.

[30] These are comprehensively described by Weiner (1983), Baruah (1994), and Gosselink (1994).

10 years from registration, their right to vote would be restored; immigrants who arrived after 25 March 1971 were deemed to be "illegal" and would be deported.

Much of the violence that presaged the Accord was spearheaded by the United Liberation Front of Assam (ULFA), a group that was formed on 7 April 1979 with the intention of seeking a "sovereign socialist" Assam. It flowered during the first Assam Gana Parishad (AGP) government in Assam of 1986–1990 (Baruah, 2020) and could plausibly be viewed as the military arm of the Assam Movement, with the AGP party serving as the Movement's political wing. It established bases in Bangladesh and was allegedly under the patronage of Pakistan's Inter-Services Intelligence (ISI).[31]

Extortion was an important source of finance for ULFA and, towards the end of the AGP government's term of office, businessmen and traders in Assam complained to the GoI about how ULFA harassment had made doing business in Assam all but impossible. Responding to these complaints, the GoI dismissed the AGP government and imposed President's rule on 27 November 1990 with the Army simultaneously launching anti-ULFA operation (named "Operation Bajrang") followed by another offensive ("Operation Rhino"). After Operation Rhino, about 6000 ULFA activists surrendered and were renamed Surrendered United Liberation Front of Assam (SULFA). These "surrendered" members were then co-opted by the current government (ironically, the second AGP government 1996–2001 with P. K. Mahanta as Chief Minister) in Assam to identify—and then murder—with the collaboration of the security forces in Assam—members of ULFA who were still active. These killings by SULFA "death squads", which took place between 1998 and 2001, and described in detail in Talukdar et al. (2008). These methods—labelled by de Waal (2004) as "counterinsurgency on the cheap"—signalled the end of ULFA and, with its demise, also ended one of the bloodiest periods in the history of Assam (Baruah, 2020).[32]

A crucial point, however, about the Assamese agitation demanding the detection, and then expulsion, of illegal immigrants, is that, belying this *angst*, even in 1951, nearly one in four persons in Assam was Muslim. The

[31] See Talukdar et al. (2008).

[32] For a list of the killings by ULFA of Indian security personnel see https://uca.edu/politicalscience/home/research-projects/dadm-project/asiapacific-region/indiaassam-1967-present/.

Muslim migration to Assam occurred *circa* 1914 when "Bengali Muslims moved into the Brahmaputra valley from East Bengal…they reclaimed thousands of acres of land, cleared vast tracts of dense jungle along the south bank of the Brahmaputra, and occupied flooded lowlands all along the river" (Weiner, 1983, p. 283).

A further wave of Bengali Muslim migration into Assam occurred in the 1930s and 1940s when Bengali Muslims controlled Assam's government: Syed Muhammad Saadulla was Chief Minister from April 1937 to September 1938, then again from November 1939 to December 1941 and, finally, from August 1942 to February 1946. During this latter period, under the "Grow More Food Programme", immigrants from East Bengal were offered opportunities to settle in Assam by the Saadulla ministry, offering Muslim settlers, cultivation rights to wasteland and grazing reserves in the Nagaon, Darang, and Kamrup districts (Misra, 2012). Because of these two waves of migration from East Bengal, the proportion of Muslims in Assam's population increased from 16% in 1911 to 25% in 1951. The Muslim share in Assam's population remained steady at one-fourth in the 20-year period between 1951 and 1971 but, thereafter, it rose to 28% in 1991, to 31% in 2001, and, according to the 2011 Indian Census, to 34% in 2011.[33] It is this post-1971 nine percentage point increase (from 25 to 34%) in the percentage of Muslims in Assam's population that people ascribe to illegal migration and which is the font of apocalyptic warnings about the future of Assam.[34]

On Borooah's (2013) estimates, between 502,000 (maximum)—1 in 20 Muslims in Assam—and 125,000 (minimum)—1 in 100 Muslims in Assam—are illegal immigrants. To put the matter in perspective, in the 27 years between 15 August 1985, and 30 April 2012, 54,500 persons have been declared as "foreigners" from Bangladesh by the various Tribunals in Assam that adjudicate on these matters. Of these 54,500 persons, 12,782 entered Assam between 1966 and 1971 and, so, under the terms of the Assam Accord are eligible to stay in India: after a period of electoral disenfranchisement for 10 years from the date of registration the GoI would treat them as Indian citizens. So, in this 27-year period, 41,718 persons were identified as illegal immigrants who could,

[33] Because of the 2020–2022 Covid epidemic, the 2021 Census was not conducted.

[34] Illegal because, under the terms of the Assam Accord of 1985, discussed earlier, all post-1971 migrants from Bangladesh to Assam were deemed illegal.

in principle, be deported.[35] Although many Assamese Hindus and Hindu nationalists in the rest of India interpret the smallness of this number as a failure of administrative will to detect and deport, it may be small precisely because there are not that many illegal Bengali Muslim immigrants living in Assam.

Since 2014, the focus in Assam has been on the detection of illegal immigrants and this followed a Supreme order on 17 December 2014 that the National Register of Citizens (NRC) for Assam be updated to 25 March 1971 from the 1951 list of voters for the state. The heart of this updating process lay in "legacy data": an applicant had to demonstrate, with appropriate documents, a direct family lineage with a person who, on documented evidence, was indubitably an Indian citizen. On 31 August 2019, the head of the NRC exercise for Assam announced that out of 33 million applicants, 31.1 had been found to be "eligible" to vote and 1.9 million (or 5.8% of total applicants) were ineligible to vote and, in the parlance of the NRC, termed "doubtful" voters. To the President of the ruling BJP's Assam unit, Ranjeet Dass, this figure was unacceptably low and should have in the region of 3–5 million.[36] To their further chagrin, the list of 1.9 million non-citizens included some Bengali-speaking *Hindus* but excluded some Bengali-speaking *Muslims*. But, perhaps, the truth is that the number of illegal immigrants in Assam had, through repeated career-enhancing fulminations by politicians, grown and grown in the mind of the Assamese public until what people believed (or wanted to believe) to be true was totally at variance with reality.

Those who were regarded as doubtful voters could obviously not the deported to Bangladesh who refused to accept them. Instead, many of them were herded into detention camps where they languished indefinitely. On 3 December 2020, India's Minister of State for Home Affairs, G Kishan Reddy, in a written response, informed the Parliament that a detention centre in Goalpara had 201 inmates, another in Kokrajhar had 140 inmates, with other camps in Silchar (71 inmates), Dibrugarh

[35] Figures placed before the Assam Assembly by the Border Areas Development Minister in July 2012.

[36] Hiteswar Saikia, the late Chief Minister of Assam, had claimed that there were 3 million illegal immigrants in Assam; The Minister of State of Home Affairs, Sriprakash Jaiswal had put this figure at 5 million (as cited in Saha, 2021).

(40 inmates), Jorhat (196 inmates), and Tezpur (322 inmates).117F[37] These Centres—complete with high walls and watch towers and, typically, located in remote areas of Assam—house nursing mothers and children. In May 2023 the Supreme Court ordered the government to release detainees who had spent more than three years in such centres. Media estimates place this number at over 300 but the government has permitted the release of only 56 detainees.[38]

In the heat of the debate about illegal immigration into Assam it is worth making a counter point. The value of Bengali Muslims (pejoratively termed *miyas*) in Assam is posed entirely in terms of the supposed costs they imposed: by importing a foreign language and religion, they dilute (and have done so for decades) the purity of Assamese culture. By ignoring the benefits they brought, the discussion of Bengali Muslims immigrants proceeds as though they made no useful contribution to the host society and that the native population learnt nothing useful from them. This is patently not true of Bengali Muslims in Assam.

In general, migrants from East Bengal introduced better techniques of cultivation in Assam, greater crop variety (including several vegetables hitherto unknown in Assam), and multiple cropping, the last of which was not practised in Assam till the arrival of the immigrants (Weiner, 1978; Madhab, 2006). Moreover, immigrants settled on all available land, even on land previously thought uncultivable like the *chars* (sandbars) of the Brahmaputra (Goswami, 2007). During the colonial days, *Bodos* and other tribal communities—practising, as they did, *jhoom* ("slash and burn") methods of cultivation—had an aversion to acquiring permanent tenure over land. Bengali Muslims iintroduced settled cultivation with permanent tenure over land (Misra, 2012). In consequence of all these innovative practices, Assam had a surplus of rice production by 1947 (Bhaumik, 2003).

Most ominously, the position of native Assamese Hindus (the *Ahomiyas*) is itself threatened by the alienation of Muslims and Assam's fragmentation along tribal lines. The percentage of persons in Assam claiming Assamese as their mother tongue fell from 57.8% in 1991

[37] https://www.aljazeera.com/news/2020/1/2/how-is-it-human-indias-largest-detention-centre-almost-ready.

[38] https://abdulkazad.wordpress.com/2023/06/01/the-stories-of-people-in-assams-detention-camps-are-harrowing-mothers-separated-from-children-wives-from-husbands/.

to 48.4% in 2011.[39] So where did all the Assamese speakers go? The answer is that throughout the Censuses from 1951 to 1991 several non-*Ahomiya* persons—in particular Bengali-speaking Muslims—often declared their mother tongue as Assamese. For example, Weiner (1978, 1983) makes the point that Bengali Muslims, as supporters of the *Ahomiya*-dominated government in Assam, often claimed Assamese as their mother tongue and, also, accepted the use of Assamese, rather than Bengali, as the medium of instruction in schools. For similar reasons, *Bodo*-speakers might have claimed Assamese, rather than *Bodo*, as their mother tongue. On Borooah's (2013) estimate, of the 12,958 thousand Assamese speakers in Assam in 1991, 1593 thousand (or 12%) were non-*Ahomiyas*.

In the decade since 1991, however, the alienation of Bengali Muslims and tribal fragmentation have meant that non-*Ahomiyas* have begun to declare their native language, rather than Assamese, as their mother tongue. This tendency is mirrored in a rise in the proportion of Bengali speakers (that is, those claiming Bengali as their mother tongue) in Assam from 21.7% in 1991 (4857 thousand) to 27.5% (7343 thousand) in 2001—an unprecedented rise of 5.8 percentage points in just 10 years. After abstracting from the natural increase in Bengali speakers, Borooah (2013) estimates is that 58% (or 1440 thousand persons) of the total increase of 2486 thousand Bengali speakers, over the 1991–2001 period, was due to Bengali speakers switching their declared mother tongue from Assamese to Bengali. On the same estimate, 118,000 *Bodo* speakers switched their declared mother tongue from Assamese to *Bodo* and 155,000 persons switched their declared mother tongue from Assamese to other languages indigenous to Assam (for example, *Santali*, *Dimasa*, *Karbi*, *Deori*, *Rabha*, *Mishing*, and *Lalung*). So, all in all, it would appear that, since 1991, non-*Ahomiyas* have lost their desire to identify with the Assamese language. This leaves *Ahomiyas*—along with a few, stray non-*Ahomiyas*—as the only persons in Assam claiming Assamese as their mother tongue. This, in consequence, as the 2011 Census for Assam shows, has reduced "Assamese speakers" to a minority within the state.

[39] Language Atlas of India (2011).

4.6 Tripura: In Search of Ethnic Balance

The state of Tripura, covering 10,491 square kilometres is the third smallest state in India,[40] with a population of 3.7 million people, and is bordered on the west, south, and north by Bangladesh—with whom it shares an 832 km long international border—and on the east by Mizoram and Assam (see Map 4.1). Like Manipur, Tripura was a princely state which joined the Indian Union in 1949 as a Class C state, subsequently becoming a union territory from 1st Nov. 1956, and attaining full statehood on 21 January 1972. Like Assam, Tripura received waves of migration from Bangladesh with two distinct episodes. In the first episode, an estimated 200,000 Bengali *Hindus* fled the communal riots in the districts of Chittagong, Sylhet, and Noakhali, in erstwhile East Pakistan, which broke out in 1950, three years after partition in 1947, and sought sanctuary in Tripura. In the second episode, there was another wave of migration into Tripura in 1971 following the war between the two wings of Pakistan (Choudhuri, 2019).

A notable difference between Tripura and Assam is that Bengalis (the immigrant group) constitute the largest ethnic group in Tripura, comprising nearly 70% of the total population with the tribals who, in 1951, constituted 52% of population having been reduced to minority; in Assam, however, native Assamese remain the single largest group though, with 48.8% of the Assamese population claiming Assamese as their first language, they do not constitute a majority. The second difference between Tripura and Assam is that, in the former, the Bengali immigrants were Hindus while, in the latter, they were Muslim. Thus, the Hindu/Muslim divide which exists in Assam was not replicated in Tripura being replaced, instead, by a tribal/non-tribal division (Kolås, 2023).

After a series of demands by Tripura's tribal groups, the Tripura Tribal Areas Autonomous District Council (TTAADC) Act, 1979 was passed by the Indian parliament and the first elected members to the TTAADC were sworn in on 18 January 1982. Nonetheless, violent conflict involving a bewildering array of groups, with no clear aims or ideological perspectives, remained a serious problem in Tripura. Prominent among these groups were the National Liberation Front of Tripura (NLFT)—with two main factions, the Biswa Mohan Debbarma and the Nayanbasi Jamatiya factions—and the All-Tripura Tiger Force (ATTF). Both organisations

[40] Ahead of Sikkim (7096 sq. km.) and Goa (3702 sq. km.).

operated from several bases in Bangladesh, and both were proscribed by the GoI in 1997 under the Unlawful Activities Prevention Act.[41]

The emergence of the Tipra Motha Party (TMP) in February 2021 by Pradyot Kishore Manikya Debbarma, a member of Tripura's royal family of the Manikya dynasty, has, however, dampened violence in Tripura. The party combines its demands for a separate state within Tripura to protect the rights and culture of the tribals with the assurance that they are not against any community and, unlike the demands in Assam, certainly do not seek the deportation of Bengalis to Bangladesh (Kolås, 2023).

4.7 Concluding Remarks

In Plato's allegory of the cave (Jowett, 2017), a group of men chained to a wall ("have their legs and necks chained so they cannot move and only see before them") in a cave can only see, on the opposite wall, the shadows of people moving outside the cave. Since the chained men have no experience of life outside the cave, they regard these shadows as representing reality ("the truth is literally nothing but the shadows of these images"). And what would happen if one of them were released and disabused of their error? According to Plato, "the glare would distress him, and he would be unable to see the realities of which in his former state he had seen as shadows".

And so, it is with the hill tribes of NE India. Chained by the Inner Line Permit system, introduced in 1873 by the British, to their domiciles in the hills, with entry by outsiders forbidden except without official authorisation, they were kept isolated from life in mainstream India, the shadows of which they perceived only through the occasional visits of selected outsiders. The British policy of quarantining the hill tribes of the NE was continued, after independence, by the Indian government. Under the Sixth Schedule of the Indian Constitution in conjunction with Article 244, the tribes, now designated as "Scheduled Tribes", were entitled to claim their own "ethnic homeland" from which "outsiders" (even Indian citizens) could be excluded.

In dealing with its neglected NE region, the GoI faced two competing objectives: the first was to protect the culture and interests of the hill tribes against social and economic exploitation by those foreign to the

[41] See https://www.satp.org/terrorism-assessment/india-insurgencynortheast-tripura.

region; the second was to integrate people from these tribes, as fully functioning citizens of the country, into the mainstream of Indian life. Faced with these objectives, the GoI plumped for the first. It decided to continue the British policy of 'exceptionality' towards the hill tribes of Assam by conceding their demand for ethnic homelands and, indeed, to extend this privilege to *plains* tribes.

By conflating ethnicity with territory, the Government of India (GoI) sowed the seeds of various 'sons-of-the soil' movements in the NE India which, in the fullness of time, became the bedrock of the region's politics and the principal source of concern of its inhabitants. This, in turn, spawned an endless cycle of violence predicated on ethnic cleansing: tribes clashed over territory in the belief that were the "true autochthons", and "outsiders" were forced, at great personal cost, to leave various ethnic homelands because they did not "belong".

The demand for ethnic homelands was spearheaded by a plethora of armed groups to which the government response was two-fold. Initially, it was to engage militarily with the insurgent groups, beginning with Nagaland. Later on, since the mid-1990s, there was a policy change and the GoI, seeking to avoid armed confrontation between its security forces and the insurgents, began negotiating agreements—negotiations in which the armed groups played a prominent role—for ethnic homelands, sometimes in the form of separate states (Meghalaya, Mizoram, Nagaland), sometimes by establishing new districts, and lately, through setting up separate Autonomous Territorial Councils.

Since 1997, the GoI has signed several ceasefires (or, as they are termed, 'Suspension of Operations') agreements with various militant groups in the NE: both factions of the National Socialist Council of Nagaland—the Isak-Muivah and the Khaplang groups; the National Democratic Front of Bodoland; the United Peoples' Democratic Solidarity in Karbi Anglong; the *Dima Halam Daogah* in the North-Cachar Hills. In all these negotiations, the militant groups were treated generously. The ground rules for the ceasefires were that the militants would live in designated camps, mutually agreed by the state and the relevant group, *while retaining their weapons* and not engage in violence or illegal activity like extortion, kidnapping, etc.

Notwithstanding, these ceasefire agreements, many of which treated the militant groups generously, the violence continues. The difference being that post-ceasefire, violence was largely inter- and intra-tribal and only minimally directed towards the government forces. For example, of the 15,000 insurgent related fatalities, recorded between 1992 and 2010, in the three most violent states of NE India—Assam, Manipur, and Nagaland—less than 2000 were of security force members (Kolås, 2012).

So, what explains this continued violence? Firstly, some of these ethnic homeland demands involved overlapping jurisdictions and this provided a source of conflict to be resolved by violent means. As Kolås (2012) pointed out, overlapping territories were claimed by the National Socialist Council of Nagaland for a unified *Nagalim*; by the *Dima Halam Daogah* for a unified *Dimaraji* (a state comprising all *Dimasa* inhabited areas); by the United Peoples' Democratic Solidarity for a Karbi state; and by the Kuki Revolutionary Army for a Kuki Regional Council.

Second, there was little done to stop militants who had signed ceasefire agreements to continue with their demands for routine payments of 'taxes'. Indeed, according to Kolås (2015), the ceasefire regime made it easier for armed groups to run their extortion businesses because law enforcement agencies adopted a "mission accomplished" attitude and withdrew from their duty to protect the civilian population from the depredations of militants.

Third, a significant part of the government funds provided to the various Autonomous, Territorial, and District Councils was siphoned off by the militant groups, that had "surrendered" under the terms of the various ceasefires and provided them with a rich source of revenue. The enrichment of the "surrendered" members of the United Liberation Front of Assam (SULFA) is documented by Sahni and Routray (2024) while Wouters (2018) describes the myriad ways in which government provided development funds is sliced between various interested parties.

The fact that militant groups receive their "cut" of government funds is also likely to have led to factionalism among the various militant groups that plague the NE of India. As Table 1.12 in Chapter 1 of the book shows, the *Kukis* are split into eight factions, the *Nagas* into ten factions and so on. Insurgency groups in NE India have shown themselves to be predatory organisations which value economic over social gain and greed over grievances (Beardsley & McQuinn, 2009; Collier & Hoeffler, 2004). Increasing the amount of swill poured into a trough resulting in increasing the number of snouts at it.

All this raises the question of why the GoI has been willing to enter ceasefire agreements with militants in NE India. It is true, that post these agreements, armed clashes between militants and security forces have fallen but, on the other hand: internecine killings have increased;

corruption has been entrenched; members of militant groups have been enriched; and extortion and kidnappings have caused the welfare of ordinary citizens in the region to deteriorate. To explain the indifference of the GoI to the welfare of citizens in its Northeastern regions, one must hark back to the British Prime Minister's, Neville Chamberlain, appeasement of Hitler in the 1930s. In response to Hitler's annexation of Czechoslovakia, Chamberlain justified British inaction by declaring, on 27 September 1938, that it was "a quarrel in a faraway country, between people of whom we know nothing". And so, it is with mainland India and its Northeastern states.

References

Baruah, S. (1994). The State and Separatist Militancy in Assam: Winning a Battle and Losing the War? *Asian Survey, 34*, 863–877.

Baruah, S. (2020). *In the Name of the Nation: India and its Northeast*. Stanford University Press.

Baruah, S. (2024). Decode Politics: Why New Districts Created in 2016 Talking Point Now in Strife-Torn Manipur. *Indian Express*. https://indianexpress.com/article/political-pulse/new-districts-created-in-2016-strife-torn-manipur-9517327/

Beardsley, K., & McQuinn, B. (2009). Rebel Groups as Predatory Organisations. *The Journal of Conflict Resolution, 53*, 624–645.

Bhaumik, S. (2003). Flower Garden or Fluid Corridor: A Conceptual Framework for Refugee Inflows, Migration, and Internal Displacement in Northeast India. In O. Mishra & A. J. Majumdar (eds.), *The Elsewhere People: Cross Border Migration, Refugee Protection and State Response*. Lancer Books.

Borooah, V. K. (2013). The Killing Fields of Assam. *Economic and Political Weekly, 48*, 43–52.

Butalia, U. (2008). *Interrogating Peace: The Naga-Kuki Conflict in Manipur*. Evangelischer Entwicklungsdienst e.V (EED).

Chakma, P. (2009). Mizoram: Minority Report. *Economic and Political Weekly, 44*, 20–21.

Choudhuri, G. (2019). Partition, Migration and the Ethnic Movement in Tripura. *IOSR Journal of Humanities and Social Science (IOSR-JHSS), 24*, 1–8.

Collier, P., & Hoeffler, A. (2004). Greed and Grievance in Civil War. *Oxford Economic Papers, 56*, 123–146.

Dalrymple, S. (2025). *Shattered Lands: Five Partitions and the Making of Modern Asia*. Harper Collins.

de Waal, A. (2004). Counterinsurgency on the cheap. *London Review of Books*, No. 15 (5 August).

Dragomir, C.-I. (2017). *Scheduled Tribe Classification: The Need for Clarification*, Centre for the Advanced Study of India, Philadelphia: University of Pennsylvania. https://casi.sas.upenn.edu/iit/cristinaioanadragomir (accessed 15 November 2024).

Engineer, I., & Dabhade, N. (2024). *Peace Eludes Manipur: State Apathy Towards the Ongoing Conflict*. Centre for Study of Society and Secularism.

Gogoi, S. (2023). *In Mizoram, A Refugee Crisis Highlights Mizo Tribal Affinities and Hostility*. Centre for Governance Studies.

Gosselink, R. G. (1994). Minority Rights and Ethnic Conflict in Assam. *Boston College Third World Journal, 14*, 83–116.

Goswami, U. (2007), *Internal Displacement, Migration, and Policy in Northeastern India*, Working Paper. East West Centre.

Haokip, P. (2018). Clans, Tribes and Unions of Tribes: Nomenclature of Northeast India. *Economic and Political Weekly, 53*, 61–66.

Haokip, T. (2023). Home and Belonging in Northeast India: Ethnic-Territoriality, Conflict and Citizenship in the India-Myanmar Borderlands. In A. Ranjan & D Chattoraj (Eds.), *Migration and the Search for a Home in Eastern South Asia*. Palgrave Macmillan.

Jaffa, V. S. (2001). Counterinsurgency Warfare: The Use and Abuse of Military Force. In K. P. S. Gill (Ed.), *Terror and Containment: Perspectives of India's Internal Security.* Gyan Publishing House. Also available on https://www.satp.org/satporgtp/publication/faultlines/volume3/fault3-jafaf.htm

Jowett, B. [Translated] (2017). *The Allegory of the Cave*, from Book VII of *The Republic* by Plato. Enhanced Media.

Kakoti, C. (2021). *Militarised Violence and Women's Resistance in Manipur, India*. London School of Economics. https://blogs.lse.ac.uk/wps/2021/09/02/militarised-violence-and-womens-resistance-in-manipur-india/

Kalvyas, S. (2006). *The Logic of Violence in Civil War*. Cambridge University Press.

Kashyap, S. G. (2012, August 26). The Assam Tangle. *The Indian Express*. https://indianexpress.com/article/news-archive/web/the-assam-tangle/

Kolås, A. (2012). What's Up with the Territorial Council? *Seminar* 640.

Kolås, A. (2015), Framing the tribal: ethnic violence in Northeast India, *Asian Ethnicity*, 18: 22–37,

Kolås, A. (2017). Framing the Tribal: Ethnic Violence in Northeast India. *Asian Ethnicity, 18*, 22–37.

Kolås, A. (2023). This World and the "Other": Muslim Identity and Politics on the Indo-Bangladesh Border. *Alternatives: Global, Local, Political, 48*, 223–241.

Language Atlas of India (2011).

Longkumer, A. (2009). Exploring the Diversity of Religion: The Geo-Political Dimensions of Fieldwork and Identity in the Northeast of India. *Fieldwork in Religion, 4*, 46–66.

Madhab, J. (2006). Illegal Migration and the Economy of the Northeast. In B. B. Kumar (Ed.), *Illegal Migration from Bangladesh*. Concept Publishing Company.

Misra, U. (2012). Bodoland: The Burden of History. *Economic and Political Weekly, 47*, 36–42.

Nag, S. (2008). *Pied Pipers in Northeast India: Bamboo Flowers*. Manohar Publications.

Oppitz, M., Kaiser, T., von Stockhausen, A., & Wettstein, M. (2008). *Naga Identities: Changing Local Cultures in the Northeast of India*. Snoeck.

Post, M. W., & Burling, R. (2003). The Tibeto-Burman Languages of Northeastern India. In G. Thurgood & R. J. LaPolla (Eds.), *The Sino-Tibetan Languages*. Routledge.

Rangasami, A. (1978). Mizoram: Tragedy of Our Own Making. *Economic & Political Weekly, 13*, 653–662.

Roy, E. (2016). Simply Put: Seven New Districts that Set Manipur Ablaze. *Indian Express*. https://indianexpress.com/article/explained/manipur-violence-new-districts-okram-ibobi-united-naga-council-4436039/. Accessed 15 November 2024.

Roy, E. (2023). The Demand for a Kuki Homeland, Its History and Rationale. *Indian Express*, 27 August.

Saha, A. (2021). *No Land's People: The Untold Story of Assam's NRC Crisis*. Harper Collins.

Sahni, A., & Routray, B. P. (2024). SULFA: Terror by Another Name. *South Asian Terror Portal*. Available at https://www.satp.org/satporgtp/publication/faultlines/volume9/article1.htm

Sarmah, J. K., & Bhuyan, P. (2022). "Interstate Border Disputes in Northeast India, The Case of Assam and Mizoram. *Economic & Political Weekly, 57*, 26–28.

Shrivastava, R. J., & Heinen, J. T. (2005). Migration and Home Gardens in the Brahmaputra Valley. *Journal of Ecological Anthropology, 9*, 20–34.

Sivakumar, P. S., Anantharaman, M., Thirunanavel, A., Ramanathan, S., & Punitha, P. (2013). *Traditional Tuber Crop Foods of Northeastern India*. Central Tuber Crops Research Institute.

Sundar, N. (2011). Interning Insurgent Populations: The Buried Histories of Indian Democracy. *Economic and Political Weekly, 46*, 47–57.

Talukdar, M., Borpujari, U., & Deka, K. (2008). *The Secret Killings of Assam*. Nanda Talukdar Foundation.

Upadhayay, A. (2006). Terrorism in the Northeast. *Economic and Political Weekly, 41*, 4993–4999.

Upadhyay, A. (2009), Terrorism in the North-East: Linkages and Implications. *Economic and Political Weekly, 41*, 4993–4999.

Vandekerckhove, N. (2009). We Are Sons of the Soil: The Endless Battles Over Indigenous Homelands in Assam, India. *Critical Asian Studies, 41*, 523–548.

Verghese, B. G. (1996). *India's Northeast Resurgent: Ethnicity, Insurgency, Governance, Development*. Konark Publishers.

Weiner, M. (1978). *When Migrants Succeed and Natives Fail: Assam and its Migrants*, Chapter 3 in Myron Weiner (author), Sons of the Soil: Migration and Ethnic Conflict in India, Princeton, NJ: Princeton University Press.

Weiner, M. (1983). The Political Demography of Assam's Anti-Immigrant Movement. *Population and Development Review, 9*(2), 279–292.

Weiner, M. (2015). *Sons of the soil: Migration and ethnic conflict in India*. Princeton University Press.

Wouters, J. J. P. (2018). *In the Shadows of Naga Insurgency: Tribes, State, and Violence in Northeast India*. Oxford University Press.

CHAPTER 5

Fatalities from Terrorist Incidents

5.1 Introduction

The previous chapters set out the issues underlying militant activity in India's three theatres of war—Jammu and Kashmir (J&K) in Chapter 2, the "Red Corridor" in Chapter 3, and the Northeast in Chapter 4. Against this background, this chapter and the next go beyond a *qualitative* discussion of underlying issues to undertake a *quantitative* analysis of militancy in each of these theatres using data from the University of Maryland's Global Terrorism Database (GTD).[1] Since this was described in Chapter 1, a summary here will suffice. The GTD contains an event-by-event record of all known terrorist incidents in the world from 1970 till June 2021, with ancillary information about the nature of these incidents: *inter alia* the country, and the country sub-region, in which the incident occurred; the terrorist group involved; the intended target; the weapons used in the incident; and the casualties (if any) that resulted from the incident in terms of deaths of the perpetrators, security personnel, and

[1] See Lafree and Dugan (2007) and Lafree *et. al.* (2015).

V. K. Borooah, *The Political Economy of Terrorism*,
https://doi.org/10.1007/978-3-032-08553-5_5

civilians.[2] The quantitative analysis in this chapter focuses on the *fatalities* resulting from terrorist activities.

It is commonly believed that deaths from terrorism are rare relative to other deaths from other forms of violence like armed conflict and homicide. Indeed, the Global Terrorism Index (2024) claims that between 20,018 and 2019, globally there were just under 120,000 deaths from terrorism in contrast to 1.1 million deaths from armed conflict, 5.5 million deaths through homicide, and 8.7 million deaths through suicide. It further suggests that nearly half of terrorist incidents did not result in any deaths. Notwithstanding these aspects of terrorist-related fatalities, terrorist attacks assume importance because, unlike other forms of violence, they instil in the public at large a sense of fear and anxiety which is disproportionate to the number of resulting fatalities (Vorsina et al., 2017).

The issue of terrorist related deaths has been addressed by Hultman (2007): employing monthly data on 60 rebel groups, involved in armed conflict in the period January 2002 to December 2004, she showed that rebels killed more civilians the more fighters they lost in battle. Piazza (2009) examined the hypothesis that Islamist terrorist groups are more dangerous than non-Islamist groups because they cause more casualties. The rise in the casualty rate from terrorism (the average number of dead and wounded from terrorist incidents), from 2.08 between 1968 and 1979 to 10.89 for the period 2000 to 2005, is conventionally explained by the parallel rise in religious (i.e. Islamic) terrorism. Using data from the Terrorism Knowledge Base for 135 groups and 383 incidents he showed that such a sweeping conclusion needed to be tempered by the "ideological orientation" of the Islamist groups with groups associated with *al-Qaida* being much more lethal than other, more secular, Islamist groups.

[2] To be considered a "terrorist incident"by the GTD, the event had to have been committed by non-state actors, had to have been violent, and intentional. In addition, the act must have met two of the following three criteria: (i) it must have been aimed at attaining a political, economic, religious, or social goal. In terms of economic goals, the exclusive pursuit of profit did not satisfy this criterion; (ii) there must have been evidence of an intention to coerce, intimidate, or convey some other message to a larger audience (or audiences) than the immediate victims; (iii) the action must have been outside the context of legitimate warfare activities, i.e. the act must have been outside the parameters permitted by international humanitarian law and, particularly, the admonition against deliberately targeting civilians or non-combatants (Global Terrorism Index, 2019).

The analysis of fatalities in this chapter distinguishes between non-terrorist and terrorist deaths resulting from terrorist incidents. Tables 1.1 and 1.2 of Chapter 1 showed that, between 2004 and 2021, there were 8749 terrorist-related deaths in India compared to say, Pakistan's 21,725 terrorist-related deaths and a total of 330,445 terrorist related deaths world-wide. The issue of terrorist-related deaths raises the question of the lethality of the different terrorist groups which, in turn was conditioned by *inter alia* the geographical areas in which they operated, the weapons they used, and their choice of targets. This chapter discusses these issues with respect to India's terrorist wars.

5.1.1 The Kill-Ratio

In analysing fatalities, the chapter suggests a measure for the effectiveness of government against terrorists and that is the *kill-ratio* which is the number of terrorists killed as a ratio of non-terrorists. The higher this ratio, the greater the effectiveness of government in combatting terrorism. Since there are sub-regions within a particular region of terrorist activity, an interesting question is the contribution that these sub-regions made to the overall kill-ratio.

This chapter uses a novel decomposition method, pioneered by Borooah and Lee (1988) in an application to the labour market, to show how the overall kill-ratio can be decomposed in terms of the sub-regional kill-ratios. This decomposition, which is implemented in respect of the districts of Kashmir and the states of the Red Corridor and the Northeast shows that the *relative* attraction of the sub-regions in terms of terrorist incidents, and the *relative* lethality of these incidents, were important determinants of the contribution they made to the overall kill-ratio.

5.1.2 Political Economy

The quantitative analysis of fatalities is cast in the framework of political economy. As Chapter 1 argued, circumstances in India about elections and government since the new millennium have offered a natural experiment for judging the government's effectiveness against terrorism. Firstly, between the period 2004 and 2021 (which is the last year for which GTD data are available) India had, in succession, two governments of different ideological make-ups. The United Progressive Alliance (UPA), headed by the Congress Party, and led by Prime Minister, Manmohan

Singh from the Congress, governed India in the decade between 2004 and 2013. Hereafter, this government is referred to as simply a "Congress government". The subsequent general elections of 2014 and 2019 saw the Bhartiya Janata Party (BJP) swept into power and, since 2014, the BJP, led by Prime Minister Narendra Modi, has been India's party of government.[3]

The GTD allows quantitative answers to question of how effective India's two main political parties—the Congress and the Bhartiya Janata Party (BJP) were in dealing with terrorism. These answers are based on a general methodology, articulated in this paper, for evaluating the effectiveness of a government's anti-terrorist policies: Are governments more effective in dealing with certain types of terrorists? In certain regions of the country? Against certain types of weapons? The answers to these questions then result in a more nuanced comparison of inter-government differences—specifically here between the BJP (in government since 2014) and the Congress (in government, as the largest member of a coalition, between 2004 and 2014) in India.

5.2 Fatalities from Terrorist Activity in India: J&K, the Red Corridor, and the Northeast

The number of terrorist incidents by district in J&K are shown in Table 5.1 for each year from 2004 to (June) 2021. During this period there were a total of 2073 terrorist incidents divided between 535 and 1538 incidents, respectively, for the periods of Congress (2004–2013) and BJP (2014 onwards) governments in New Delhi. The GTD reported incidents according to village/town location; these were converted by the author into districts.

The number of fatalities associated with these incidents are shown in Table 5.2, by districts in J&K, for three items: the number of non-terrorist fatalities; the number of total fatalities; and the number of terrorist fatalities, where the latter is the difference between total fatalities and total non-terrorist fatalities. There were a total 1372 non-terrorist deaths

[3] Though the BJP lost its parliamentary majority in the 2024 General Election, it continued in government as part of a coalition.

Table 5.1 Terrorist incidents by year and district in Jammu & Kashmir

	AN	*BN*	*BA*	*BU*	*DO*	*GA*	*JM*	*KA*	*KI*	*KL*	*KP*	*PN*	*PU*	*RJ*	*RA*	*RE*	*SA*	*SH*	*SR*	*UD*	*Total*
2004	12	1	6	4	3	3	5	0	0	1	1	6	7	5	1	1	0	3	13	0	72
	16.7	*1.4*	*8.3*	*5.6*	*4.2*	*4.2*	*6.9*	*0.0*	*0.0*	*1.4*	*1.4*	*8.3*	*9.7*	*6.9*	*1.4*	*1.4*	*0.0*	*4.2*	*18.1*	*0.0*	*100*
2005	7	2	9	2	4	0	1	1	1	3	5	3	7	3	2	2	0	2	28	3	85
	8.2	*2.4*	*10.6*	*2.4*	*4.7*	*0.0*	*1.2*	*1.2*	*1.2*	*3.5*	*5.9*	*3.5*	*8.2*	*3.5*	*2.4*	*2.4*	*0.0*	*2.4*	*32.9*	*3.5*	*100*
2006	2	1	13	2	7	1	1	0	0	3	1	2	3	0	1	0	0	0	34	3	74
	2.7	*1.4*	*17.6*	*2.7*	*9.5*	*1.4*	*1.4*	*0.0*	*0.0*	*4.1*	*1.4*	*2.7*	*4.1*	*0.0*	*1.4*	*0.0*	*0.0*	*0.0*	*46.0*	*4.1*	*100*
2007	2	2	5	1	0	2	0	0	1	1	3	0	5	2	0	0	0	1	10	0	35
	5.7	*5.7*	*14.3*	*2.9*	*0.0*	*5.7*	*0.0*	*0.0*	*2.9*	*2.9*	*8.6*	*0.0*	*14.3*	*5.7*	*0.0*	*0.0*	*0.0*	*2.9*	*28.6*	*0.0*	*100*
2008	2	0	8	2	11	1	1	1	5	0	5	0	1	1	3	2	2	2	3	1	51
	3.9	*0.0*	*15.7*	*3.9*	*21.6*	*2.0*	*2.0*	*2.0*	*9.8*	*0.0*	*9.8*	*0.0*	*2.0*	*2.0*	*5.9*	*3.9*	*3.9*	*3.9*	*5.9*	*2.0*	*100*
2009	0	0	0	0	5	1	1	0	0	1	2	0	3	2	0	0	0	1	5	2	23
	0.0	*0.0*	*0.0*	*0.0*	*21.7*	*4.4*	*4.4*	*0.0*	*0.0*	*4.4*	*8.7*	*0.0*	*13.0*	*8.7*	*0.0*	*0.0*	*0.0*	*4.4*	*21.7*	*8.7*	*100*
2010	1	0	2	0	1	0	0	0	2	1	1	0	2	1	0	0	1	1	0	0	13
	7.7	*0.0*	*15.4*	*0.0*	*7.7*	*0.0*	*0.0*	*0.0*	*15.4*	*7.7*	*7.7*	*0.0*	*15.4*	*7.7*	*0.0*	*0.0*	*7.7*	*7.7*	*0.0*	*0.0*	*100*
2011	2	3	12	3	0	1	1	0	2	0	2	0	4	1	0	0	0	0	7	0	38
	5.3	*7.9*	*31.6*	*7.9*	*0.0*	*2.6*	*2.6*	*0.0*	*5.3*	*0.0*	*5.3*	*0.0*	*10.5*	*2.6*	*0.0*	*0.0*	*0.0*	*0.0*	*18.4*	*0.0*	*100*
2012	6	1	18	3	1	2	1	0	2	2	2	0	7	0	1	0	2	1	18	0	67
	9.0	*1.5*	*26.9*	*4.5*	*1.5*	*3.0*	*1.5*	*0.0*	*3.0*	*3.0*	*3.0*	*0.0*	*10.5*	*0.0*	*1.5*	*0.0*	*3.0*	*1.5*	*26.9*	*0.0*	*100*
2013	5	0	16	3	3	1	0	1	0	2	9	5	12	1	0	0	2	4	13	0	77
	6.49	*0*	*20.78*	*3.9*	*3.9*	*1.3*	*0*	*1.3*	*0*	*2.6*	*11.69*	*6.49*	*15.6*	*1.3*	*0.0*	*0.0*	*2.6*	*5.2*	*16.9*	*0.0*	*100*
Total Congress 2004–2013	39	10	89	20	35	12	11	3	13	14	31	16	51	16	8	5	7	15	131	9	535
	7.3	*1.9*	*16.6*	*3.7*	*6.5*	*2.2*	*2.1*	*0.6*	*2.4*	*2.6*	*5.8*	*3.0*	*9.5*	*3.0*	*1.5*	*0.9*	*1.3*	*2.8*	*24.5*	*1.7*	*100*
2014	8	1	28	3	0	1	5	2	0	4	8	8	29	2	0	0	0	10	15	0	124
	6.5	*0.8*	*22.6*	*2.4*	*0.0*	*0.8*	*4.0*	*1.6*	*0.0*	*3.2*	*6.5*	*6.5*	*23.4*	*1.6*	*0.0*	*0.0*	*0.0*	*8.1*	*12.1*	*0.0*	*100*

(continued)

Table 5.1 (continued)

	AN	*BN*	*BA*	*BU*	*DO*	*GA*	*JM*	*KA*	*KI*	*KL*	*KP*	*PN*	*PU*	*RJ*	*RA*	*RE*	*SA*	*SH*	*SR*	*UD*	*Total*
2015	13	0	26	4	0	4	3	1	1	6	9	2	9	2	0	0	3	11	11	4	109
	11.9	*0.0*	*23.9*	*3.7*	*0.0*	*3.7*	*2.8*	*0.9*	*0.9*	*5.5*	*8.3*	*1.8*	*8.3*	*1.8*	*0.0*	*0.0*	*2.8*	*10.1*	*10.1*	*3.7*	*100*
2016	33	4	21	14	1	4	5	1	0	9	21	6	38	2	2	0	2	17	22	1	203
	16.3	*2.0*	*10.3*	*6.9*	*0.5*	*2.0*	*2.5*	*0.5*	*0.0*	*4.4*	*10.3*	*3.0*	*18.7*	*1.0*	*1.0*	*0.0*	*1.0*	*8.4*	*10.8*	*0.5*	*100*
2017	39	11	15	15	1	0	3	0	1	22	12	8	55	1	0	1	1	42	29	1	257
	15.2	*4.3*	*5.8*	*5.8*	*0.4*	*0.0*	*1.2*	*0.0*	*0.4*	*8.6*	*4.7*	*3.1*	*21.4*	*0.4*	*0.0*	*0.4*	*0.4*	*16.3*	*11.3*	*0.4*	*100*
2018	44	16	40	22	2	10	7	0	3	24	19	11	112	8	0	1	1	46	41	0	407
	10.8	*3.9*	*9.8*	*5.4*	*0.5*	*2.5*	*1.7*	*0.0*	*0.7*	*5.9*	*4.7*	*2.7*	*27.5*	*2.0*	*0.0*	*0.3*	*0.3*	*11.3*	*10.1*	*0.0*	*100*
2019	19	2	20	8	2	1	5	0	4	16	9	10	46	4	2	0	0	23	27	1	199
	9.6	1.0	10.1	4.0	1.0	0.5	2.5	0.0	2.0	8.0	4.5	5.0	23.1	2.0	1.0	0.0	0.0	11.6	13.6	0.5	100
2020	21	5	24	10	2	2	0	1	1	17	7	7	30	3	2	0	0	10	23	2	167
	12.6	*3.0*	*14.4*	*6.0*	*1.2*	*1.2*	*0.0*	*0.6*	*0.6*	*10.2*	*4.2*	*4.2*	*18.0*	*1.8*	*1.2*	*0.0*	*0.0*	*6.0*	*13.8*	*1.2*	*100*
2021	11	0	6	4	1	1	6	0	1	2	2	2	10	3	0	0	1	4	18	0	72
	15.3	*0.0*	*8.3*	*5.6*	*1.4*	*1.4*	*8.3*	*0.0*	*1.4*	*2.8*	*2.8*	*2.8*	*13.9*	*4.2*	*0.0*	*0.0*	*1.4*	*5.6*	*25.0*	*0.0*	*100*
Total BJP 2014-(June) 2021	188	39	180	80	9	23	34	5	11	100	87	54	329	25	6	2	8	163	186	9	1538
	12.2	*2.5*	*11.7*	*5.2*	*0.6*	*1.5*	*2.2*	*0.3*	*0.7*	*6.5*	*5.7*	*3.5*	*21.4*	*1.6*	*0.4*	*0.1*	*0.5*	*10.6*	*12.1*	*0.6*	*100*

AN = Anantnag; BN = Bandipore; BA = Baramulla; BU = Budgam; DO = Doda; GA = Ganderbal; JM = Jammu; KA = Kathua; KI = Kishtwar; KL = Kulgam; KP = Kupwara; PN = Poonch; PU = Pulwama
RJ = Rajouri; RA = Ramban; RE = Reasi; SA = Samba; SH = Shopian; Sr = Srinagar; UD = Udhampur
Numbers in Italics are Percentages of Row Totals
Source Own Calculations from GTD

between 2004-(June) 2021 divided between 720 and 652 deaths, respectively, for the periods of Congress (2004–2013) and BJP (2014 onwards) governments in New Delhi.

Table 5.2 shows that the largest number of non-terrorist deaths during a Congress government in New Delhi occurred in the districts of Srinagar (167 deaths); Baramulla (82); Pulwama (74); Doda (58); and Anantnag (53). Together, these five districts accounted for 60% of the total of 720 deaths in this period. During the period of the BJP government, the largest number of deaths were in Pulwama (154); Baramulla (106); Anantnag (85); and Shopian (52); and Srinagar (51). These five districts collectively accounted for 69% of the total of 652 non-terrorist deaths in this period.

It is often commented that across the two regions of J&K—*Jammu* (comprising the districts of: Doda; Jammu; Kathua; Kishtwar; Poonch; Rajouri; Ramban; Reasi; Samba; and Udhampur) and *Kashmir* (comprising the districts of: Anantnag; Bandipore; Baramulla; Budgam; Ganderbal; Kulgam; Kupwara; Pulwama; Shopian; and Srinagar), it was the Kashmir region that was mostly affected by terrorism and that the Jammu region escaped relatively lightly. This is quantified in Table 5.3.

Table 5.3 shows that of the 2073 terrorist incidents that occurred in J&K in the period 2004–(June) 2021, 1787 (or 86%) occurred in the Kashmir region and of the total of 1372 non-terrorist fatalities in the period 2004–(June) 2021, 1064 (or 78%) occurred in the Kashmir region.

Table 5.4 shows information on fatalities for the Red Corridor, following the same format in as for J&K, except that now the information is conveyed in the context of states rather than, as with J&K, in terms of districts. Table 5.4 shows that between 2004 and (June) 2021 there were 3899 instances of Left-Wing Extremist (LWE) violence in the seven affected states—Andhra Pradesh, Bihar, Chhattisgarh, Jharkhand, Orissa, Telangana, and West Bengal—which was considerably more than the 2073 reported for J&K during the same period. These 3899 incidents were almost equally divided between the Congress (1885) and BJP (2014) regimes and, of these 3899 terrorist incidents, 2203 (57%) occurred in just two states, Chhattisgarh and Jharkhand.

Table 5.5 shows the fatalities in the Red Corridor resulting from these 3899 incidents of LWE militancy. In total, there were 3784 deaths from such activity during the period 2004–(June) 2021 (of which 433 were terrorist deaths) and these were divided between the Congress (2528

Table 5.2 Fatalities from terrorist incidents by year and district in Jammu & Kashmir

	AN	*BN*	*BA*	*BU*	*DO*	*GA*	*JM*	*KA*	*KI*	*KL*	*KP*	*PN*	*PU*	*RJ*	*RA*	*RE*	*SA*	*SH*	*SR*	*UD*	*Total*
2004	38	0	24	8	7	8	14	NA	NA	11	2	20	24	5	1	4	NA	4	17	NA	187
2005	4	1	15	4	9	NA	5	2	2	4	11	2	19	2	5	11	NA	2	63	14	175
2006	0	0	7	1	33	1	1	NA	NA	21	1	7	6	NA	0	NA	NA	NA	46	16	140
2007	3	4	9	4	NA	3	NA	NA	1	1	0	NA	6	6	NA	NA	NA	1	3	NA	41
2008	0	NA	2	0	7	0	0	0	5	NA	3	NA	0	0	5	3	6	2	7	0	40
2009	NA	NA	NA	NA	1	0	5	NA	NA	1	2	NA	3	3	NA	NA	NA	0	1	2	18
2010	0	NA	1	NA	0	NA	NA	NA	1	0	0	NA	1	1	NA	NA	0	1	NA	NA	5
2011	2	1	5	1	NA	1	0	NA	2	NA	0	NA	1	0	NA	NA	NA	NA	4	NA	17
2012	4	1	6	0	0	0	0	NA	2	1	0	NA	1	NA	0	NA	0	0	6	NA	21
2013	2	NA	13	2	1	3	NA	6	NA	1	4	5	13	0	NA	NA	4	2	20	NA	76
Total Non-Terrorist Deaths Congress: 2004–2013	53	7	82	20	58	16	25	8	13	40	23	34	74	17	11	18	10	12	167	32	720
Total Deaths Congress 2004–2013	55	7	92	21	61	17	31	8	13	40	27	35	81	21	11	18	13	15	195	32	793
Total Terrorist Deaths Congress: 2004–2013	*2*	*0*	*10*	*1*	*3*	*1*	*6*	*0*	*0*	*0*	*4*	*1*	*7*	*4*	*0*	*0*	*3*	*3*	*28*	*0*	*73*

	AN	*BN*	*BA*	*BU*	*DO*	*GA*	*JM*	*KA*	*KI*	*KL*	*KP*	*PN*	*PU*	*RJ*	*RA*	*RE*	*SA*	*SH*	*SR*	*UD*	*Total*
Non-Terrorist Deaths per Incident Congress: 2004–2013	1.36	0.70	0.92	1.00	1.66	1.33	2.27	2.67	1.00	2.86	0.74	2.13	1.45	1.06	1.38	3.60	1.43	0.80	1.27	3.56	1.35
2014	3	0	17	0	NA	0	8	3	NA	2	3	4	20	0	NA	NA	NA	4	3	NA	67
2015	6	NA	11	0	NA	3	0	5	0	3	11	0	2	1	NA	NA	3	3	0	2	50
2016	7	0	31	2	0	0	8	0	NA	3	13	1	16	0	3	NA	0	2	4	1	91
2017	28	3	1	3	1	NA	1	NA	0	4	5	3	30	2	NA	0	0	21	8	3	113
2018	9	6	25	7	0	0	7	NA	4	9	8	1	24	3	NA	0	0	12	14	NA	129
2019	14	1	3	3	1	0	3	NA	2	8	3	0	50	3	1	NA	NA	8	4	0	104
2020	12	3	8	2	1	2	NA	0	3	6	6	0	8	0	1	NA	NA	2	12	3	69
	AN	BN	BA	BU	DO	GA	JM	KA	KI	KL	KP	PN	PU	RJ	RA	RE	SA	SH	SR	UD	Total
2021	6	NA	10	2	0	0	0	NA	0	1	0	0	4	0	NA	NA	0	0	6	NA	29
Total Non-Terrorist Deaths BJP: 2014–(June) 2021	85	13	106	19	3	5	27	8	6	36	49	9	154	9	5	0	3	52	51	9	652

(continued)

Table 5.2 (continued)

	AN	*BN*	*BA*	*BU*	*DO*	*GA*	*JM*	*KA*	*KI*	*KL*	*KP*	*PN*	*PU*	*RJ*	*RA*	*RE*	*SA*	*SH*	*SR*	*UD*	*Total*
Total Deaths BJP:2014–(June) 2021	88	20	130	25	3	9	40	13	9	44	80	13	177	11	11	5	5	60	67	11	821
Total Terrorist Deaths BJP:2014–(June) 2021	3	7	24	6	0	4	13	5	3	8	31	4	23	2	6	5	2	8	16	2	169
Non-Terrorist Deaths per Incident BJP: 2014–(June) 2021	0.45	0.33	0.59	0.24	0.33	0.22	0.79	1.60	0.55	0.36	0.56	0.17	0.47	0.36	0.83	0.00	0.38	0.32	0.27	1.00	0.42

AN = Anantnag; BN = Bandipore; BA = Baramulla; BU = Budgam; DO = Doda; GA = Ganderbal; JM = Jammu; KA = Kathua; KI = Kishtwar; KL = Kulgam; KP = Kupwara; PN = Poonch; PU = Pulwama
RJ = Rajouri; RA = Ramban; RE = Reasi; SA = Samba; SH = Shopian; Sr = Srinagar; UD = Udhampur
Numbers in Italics are Percentages of Row Totals
Source Own Calculations from GTD

Table 5.3 Terrorist incidents and fatalities by Jammu and Kashmir regions, by year

	Jammu Region						*Kashmir Region*					
	Congress			*BJP*			*Congress*			*BJP*		
	Incidents	*Non-Terrorist Fatalities*	*Terrorist Fatalities*	*Incidents*	*Non-Terrorist Fatalities*	*Terrorist Fatalities*	*Incidents*	*Non-Terrorist Fatalities*	*Terrorist Fatalities*	*Incidents*	*Non-Terrorist Fatalities*	*Terrorist Fatalities*
2004	21	51	4				51	136	9			
2005	20	52	3				65	123	17			
2006	14	57	2				60	83	5			
2007	3	7	0				32	34	10			
2008	27	26	4				24	14	2			
2009	10	11	0				13	7	1			
2010	5	2	0				8	3	1			
2011	4	2	0				34	15	0			
2012	7	2	0				60	19	3			
2013	12	16	4				65	60	8			
2014				17	15	7				107	52	18
2015				16	11	5				93	39	12
2016				20	13	11				183	78	24
2017				17	10	2				240	103	29
2018				33	15	8				374	114	21
2019				28	10	3				171	94	13
2020				18	8	3				149	61	11

(continued)

Table 5.3 (continued)

	Jammu Region						*Kashmir Region*					
	Congress			*BJP*			*Congress*			*BJP*		
	Incidents	*Non-Terrorist Fatalities*	*Terrorist Fatalities*	*Incidents*	*Non-Terrorist Fatalities*	*Terrorist Fatalities*	*Incidents*	*Non-Terrorist Fatalities*	*Terrorist Fatalities*	*Incidents*	*Non-Terrorist Fatalities*	*Terrorist Fatalities*
(June) 2021				14	0	0				58	29	2
Total	123	226	17	163	82	39	412	494	56	1375	570	130

The Jammu Region comprised the following districts: Doda; Jammu; Kathua; Kishtwar; Poonch; Rajouri; Ramban; Reasi; Samba; and Udhampur
The Kashmir Region comprised the following districts: Anantnag; Bandipore; Baramulla; Budgam; Ganderbal; Kulgam; Kupwara; Pulwama; Shopian; and Srinagar
Source Own calculations from the GTD

Table 5.4 Terrorist incidents by year and state in the Red Corridor

	Andhra Pradesh	*Bihar*	*Chhattisgarh*	*Jharkhand*	*Orissa*	*Telangana*	*West Bengal*	*Total*
2004	0	2	1	3	0	NI	1	7
	0.0	*28.6*	*14.3*	*42.9*	*0.0*		*14.3*	*100*
2005	4	0	3	2	2	NI	0	11
	36.36	0.00	27.27	18.18	18.18		0.00	100
2006	2	3	14	8	0	NI	2	29
	6.9	*10.3*	*48.3*	*27.6*	*0.0*		*6.9*	*100*
2007	1	4	4	4	1	NI	3	17
	5.9	*23.5*	*23.5*	*23.5*	*5.9*		*17.7*	*100*
2008	9	32	31	46	24	NI	9	151
	6.0	*21.2*	*20.5*	*30.5*	*15.9*		*6.0*	*100*
2009	8	63	55	88	71	NI	100	385
	2.1	*16.4*	*14.3*	*22.9*	*18.4*		*26.0*	*100*
2010	25	86	68	84	84	NI	150	497
	5.0	*17.3*	*13.7*	*16.9*	*16.9*		*30.2*	*100*
2011	19	83	69	112	63	NI	42	388
	4.9	*21.4*	*17.8*	*28.9*	*16.2*		*10.8*	*100*
2012	2	17	45	44	81	NI	3	192
	1.0	*8.9*	*23.4*	*22.9*	*42.2*		*1.6*	*100*
2013	5	39	66	54	40	NI	4	208
	2.4	*18.8*	*31.7*	*26.0*	*19.2*		*1.9*	*100*
Total Congress: 2004–2013	75	329	356	445	366	NI	314	1885
	4.0	*17.5*	*18.9*	*23.6*	*19.4*		*16.7*	*100*
2014	21	45	78	110	55	0	3	312
	6.7	14.4	25.0	35.3	17.6	0.0	1.0	100
2015	18	27	166	70	45	7	0	333
	5.4	8.1	49.9	21.0	13.5	2.1	0.0	100
2016	9	39	162	81	48	8	6	353
	2.6	11.1	45.9	23.0	13.6	2.3	1.7	100
2017	16	36	136	68	46	8	0	310
	5.2	11.6	43.9	21.9	14.8	2.6	0.0	100
2018	6	27	145	45	21	16	0	260
	2.3	10.4	55.8	17.3	8.1	6.2	0.0	100
2019	5	15	82	63	25	6	2	198
	2.5	7.6	41.4	31.8	12.6	3.0	1.0	100
2020	1	14	76	47	15	6	1	160
	0.6	8.8	47.5	29.4	9.4	3.8	0.6	100

(continued)

Table 5.4 (continued)

	Andhra Pradesh	*Bihar*	*Chhattisgarh*	*Jharkhand*	*Orissa*	*Telangana*	*West Bengal*	*Total*
2021	2	2	51	22	6	4	1	88
	2.3	2.3	58.0	25.0	6.8	4.6	1.1	100
Total BJP: 2014–(June) 2021	78	205	896	506	261	55	13	2014

Telangana was formed on 2 June 2014
Numbers in Italics are Percentages of Row Totals
Source Own Calculations from GTD

deaths of which 220 were of terrorists) and BJP (1256 deaths of which 213 were of terrorists).

Tables 5.6 and 5.7 show the incidence of terrorism, and resultant fatalities, in India's seven Northeastern states. Between 2004 and (June) 2021, there were 2536 incidents in the Northeastern states (fewer than in the Red Corridor but more than in J&K) and these were divided between the Congress (1353 incidents) and BJP (1183 incidents) regimes. Of the 2536 incidents, 893 occurred in Assam and 1121 occurred in Manipur—thus these two states contributed 2014 (79%) to the total of 2536 incidents in the Northeast, (79%) that occurred between 2004 and (June) 2021.

The terrorist incidents in the Northeast resulted in 1504 fatalities of which 134 were terrorist deaths. Of these fatalities, 1068 deaths (98 terrorists killed) occurred under the Congress regime and 436 deaths (36 terrorists killed) occurred under the BJP regime.

5.3 Measuring the Government's Effectiveness Against Terrorists

It is a truism to say that the business of terrorists is to create—and, by creating, to spread—terror amongst the general population. This they do through a variety of means—to name a few, killings, kidnappings, extortion, arson, bombings. For the purposes of the analysis in this chapter, it is assumed that, from this plethora of terror-inducing measures, the *number*

Table 5.5 Fatalities from terrorist incidents in the Red Corridor

	Non-terrorist deaths							
	Andhra Pradesh	*Bihar*	*Chhattisgarh*	*Jharkhand*	*Orissa*	*Telangana*	*West Bengal*	*Total*
2004	NI	7	0	33	NI	NI	4	44
2005	16	NI	40	18	6	NI	NI	80
2006	3	0	129	52	NI	NI	4	188
2007	3	9	85	26	3	NI	11	137
2008	5	28	37	54	48	NI	12	184
2009	9	44	140	99	47	NI	71	410
2010	14	75	191	70	59	NI	268	677
2011	6	26	93	78	34	NI	27	264
2012	1	19	40	32	34	NI	3	129
2013	7	44	49	66	28	NI	1	195
Total Non-Terrorist Deaths: Congress 2004–2013	64	252	804	528	259	NI	401	2308
Total Deaths Congress: 2004–2013	73	280	889	561	284	NI	441	2528
Total Terrorist Deaths Congress: 2004–2013	9	28	85	33	25	NI	40	220
Non-Terrorist Deaths per Incident Congress: 2004–2013	0.97	0.85	2.50	1.26	0.78	NI	1.40	1.34
2014	8	15	72	46	33	NI	0	174
2015	9	4	75	12	22	1	NI	123
2016	3	21	71	41	22	1	0	159
2017	39	16	78	24	27	2	NI	186
2018	3	14	107	16	11	3	NI	154
2019	3	9	42	27	10	2	0	93
2020	2	8	61	14	3	1	0	89
(June) 2021	1	0	56	6	2	0	0	65

(continued)

Table 5.5 (continued)

	Non-terrorist deaths							
	Andhra Pradesh	*Bihar*	*Chhattisgarh*	*Jharkhand*	*Orissa*	*Telangana*	*West Bengal*	*Total*
Total Non-Terrorist Deaths BJP: 2014–(June) 2021	68	87	562	186	130	10	0	1043
Total Deaths BJP: 2014–(June) 2021	69	95	759	189	134	10	0	1256
Total Terrorist Deaths BJP: 2014–(June) 2021	1	8	197	3	4	0	0	213
Non-Terrorist Deaths per Incident BJP: 2014–(June)2021	0.87	0.42	0.63	0.37	0.50	0.18	0.00	0.52

Telangana was formed on 2 June 2014
NI = No incidents
Source Own calculations from GTD

of (non-terrorist) fatalities resulting from terrorist incidents is a summary measure of the amount of terror created.

Following from this, a measure of the *productivity* of terrorists is $\frac{\text{number of non - terrorist fatalities}}{\text{number of terrorist incidents}}$. The productivity of terrorists will be high when many fatalities can be produced from a small number of incidents while this productivity will be low when it takes many incidents to generate a small number of fatalities. On the other hand, the *cost* to terrorists from their activities can be summarised in terms of the number of terrorists killed per incident expressed as $\frac{\text{number of terrorist fatalities}}{\text{number of terrorist incidents}}$ and this will be high when many terrorists are killed from a small number of incidents while it will be low when it takes many incidents to generate a small number of terrorist fatalities.

The government's effectiveness against terrorism can now be defined by the "kill-ratio" (KR) defined as:

Table 5.6 Terrorist incidents by year and state in northeast India

	Arunachal Pradesh	*Assam*	*Manipur*	*Meghalaya*	*Mizoram*	*Nagaland*	*Tripura*	*Total*
2004	0	19	1	0	0	1	1	22
	0.0	*86.4*	*4.6*	*0.0*	*0.0*	*4.6*	*4.6*	*100*
2005	0	28	1	0	0	1	1	31
	0.0	*90.3*	*3.2*	*0.0*	*0.0*	*3.2*	*3.2*	*100*
2006	0	38	4	0	0	0	2	44
	0.0	*86.4*	*9.1*	*0.0*	*0.0*	*0.0*	*4.6*	*100*
2007	0	57	10	0	0	1	0	68
	0.0	*83.8*	*14.7*	*0.0*	*0.0*	*1.5*	*0.0*	*100*
2008	0	93	89	1	0	26	7	216
	0.0	*43.1*	*41.2*	*0.5*	*0.0*	*12.0*	*3.2*	*100*
2009	1	108	73	2	0	6	6	196
	0.5	*55.1*	*37.2*	*1.0*	*0.0*	*3.1*	*3.1*	*100*
2010	1	32	56	6	0	1	2	98
	1	*33*	*57*	*6*	*0*	*1*	*2*	*100*
2011	1	50	75	21	1	5	7	160
	0.63	*31.25*	*46.88*	*13.13*	*0.63*	*3.13*	*4.38*	*100*
2012	0	59	131	42	2	1	4	239
	0.0	*24.7*	*54.8*	*17.6*	*0.8*	*0.4*	*1.7*	*100*
2013	0	102	116	48	2	8	3	279
	0.0	*36.6*	*41.6*	*17.2*	*0.7*	*2.9*	*1.1*	*100*
Total Congress: 2004–2013	3	586	556	120	5	50	33	1353
	0.2	*43.3*	*41.1*	*8.9*	*0.4*	*3.7*	*2.4*	*100*
2014	0	102	120	50	6	4	8	290
	0.0	*35.2*	*41.4*	*17.2*	*2.1*	*1.4*	*2.8*	*100*
2015	*4.0*	*51.0*	*115.0*	*53.0*	*3.0*	*24.0*	*1.0*	*251*
	1.59	20.32	45.82	21.12	1.2	9.56	0.4	100
2016	4	59	127	31	0	6	0	227
	1.8	*26.0*	*56.0*	*13.7*	*0.0*	*2.6*	*0.0*	*100*
2017	*5.0*	*31.0*	*89.0*	*35.0*	*1.0*	*9.0*	*3.0*	*173*
	2.89	17.92	51.45	20.23	0.58	5.2	1.73	100
2018	6	24	46	7	3	11	1	98
	6	*24*	*47*	*7*	*3*	*11*	*1*	*100*
2019	*3*	*17*	*40*	*2*	*0*	*6*	*1*	*69*
	4.35	24.64	57.97	2.9	0	8.7	1.45	100
2020	3	15	18	11	1	3	2	53
	5.7	*28.3*	*34.0*	*20.8*	*1.9*	*5.7*	*3.8*	*100*
2021	*1.0*	*8.0*	*10.0*	*0.0*	*0.0*	*2.0*	*1.0*	*22*
	4.55	36.36	45.45	0	0	9.09	4.55	100

(continued)

Table 5.6 (continued)

	Arunachal Pradesh	*Assam*	*Manipur*	*Meghalaya*	*Mizoram*	*Nagaland*	*Tripura*	*Total*
Total BJP: 2014–(June) 2021	26	307	565	189	14	65	17	1183
	2.2	25.95	47.76	15.98	1.18	5.49	1.44	100

Numbers in Italics are Percentages of Row Totals
Source Own calculations from GTD

$$\mathrm{KR} = \frac{\text{cost to terrorists}}{\text{productivity of terrorists}} \times 100 = \frac{\text{number of terrorist deaths}}{\text{number of non - terrorist deaths}} \times 100$$

The kill-ratio, KR, represents the number of terrorists killed per hundred non-terrorist deaths. The greater the value of KR, the greater the relative cost to terrorists. Indeed, the *KR* may be interpreted as ***the price that society pays*** for terrorist activities: $KR = 10$ implies that ten terrorists are killed per hundred non-terrorists (or in other words, it takes 100 non-terrorist deaths to "buy" ten dead terrorists) while, if $KR = 0.25$, forty terrorists are killed per hundred non-terrorists (or in other words, the price falls because now it takes "only" forty non-terrorist deaths to "buy" a hundred dead terrorists). The kill-ratio is, therefore, an indicator of the government's effectiveness against terrorism: the higher the kill-ratio, the higher will government effectiveness.

The use of the kill-ratio as a measure of a government's effectiveness against terrorism, however, has two possible problems. First, there could be incidents in which terrorists are killed but without any concomitant loss of non-terrorist lives. In such cases, the kill-ratio will not be defined. This occurred in the district of Reasi in J&K when five terrorists were killed between 2014–(June) 2021 without any non-terrorist fatalities (see Table 5.2). Secondly, terrorists could be killed *outside* the ambit of incidents as recorded in the GTD. This is the phenomenon of extra-judicial killings (or, euphemistically, "encounter" killings) of terrorists. For example, Burhan Wani, the leader of *Hizbul Mujahideen*, was in a village in Anantnag district when he was killed in a gun battle with Indian security forces on 8 July 2016. His death would not be recorded in the

Table 5.7 Fatalities from terrorist incidents in Northeastern States

	Arunachal Pradesh	*Assam*	*Manipur*	*Meghalaya*	*Mizoram*	*Nagaland*	*Tripura*	*Total*
2004	NI	60	4	NI	NI	12	5	81
2005	NI	34	2	NI	NI	0	8	44
2006	NI	66	6	NI	NI	NI	6	78
2007	NI	138	27	NI	NI	0	NI	165
2008	NI	153	33	0	NI	12	5	203
2009	0	141	11	0	NI	2	11	165
2010	0	29	6	2	NI	0	2	39
2011	0	20	22	14	0	3	1	60
2012	NI	11	21	15	0	0	0	47
2013	NI	26	26	31	0	2	3	88
Total Non-Terrorist Deaths Congress: 2004–2013	0	678	158	62	0	31	41	970
Total Deaths Congress: 2004–2013	2	716	190	63	0	56	41	1068
Total Terrorist Deaths Congress: 2004–2013	2	38	32	1	0	25	0	98
Non-Terrorist Deaths per Incident Congress: 2004–2013	0.00	1.16	0.28	0.52	0.00	0.62	1.24	0.72
2014	NI	103	24	16	0	0	5	148
2015	6	11	41	16	3	11	0	88
2016	2	26	22	5	NI	0	NI	55
2017	0	8	24	2	0	3	1	38
2018	2	9	12	4	1	6	0	34
2019	13	3	3	1	NI	3	0	23
2020	2	0	3	0	0	2	0	7
(June) 2021	0	6	0	NI	NI	0	1	7
Total Non-Terrorist Deaths BJP 2014–(June) 2021	25	166	129	44	4	25	7	400

(continued)

Table 5.7 (continued)

	Arunachal Pradesh	*Assam*	*Manipur*	*Meghalaya*	*Mizoram*	*Nagaland*	*Tripura*	*Total*
Total Deaths BJP: 2014–(June) 2021	30	181	139	46	4	29	7	436
Total Terrorist Deaths BJP: 2014–(June) 2021	5	15	10	2	0	4	0	36
Non-Terrorist Deaths per Incident BJP: 2014–(June)2021	0.96	0.54	0.23	0.23	0.29	0.38	0.41	0.34

NI = No incidents
Source Own Calculations from GTD

GTD because it was not the consequence of a terrorist incident initiated by *Hizbul Mujahideen*.

Tables 5.2, 5.5, and 5.7 show the number of non-terrorist deaths *per incident* (that is, the "productivity" of terrorists), for J&K (by district) and for the Red Corridor and the Northeast (by state). Table 5.2 shows that in the 2004–2013 period there were 1.35 non-terrorist deaths per incident in J&K (720 deaths from 535 incidents) while in the 2014–2021 period, the number of non-terrorist deaths per incident in J&K fell to 0.42 (652 deaths from 1538 incidents).

Table 5.5 shows that, in the Red Corridor, the number of non-terrorist fatalities-per-incident was 1.34 under the Congress (very similar to the comparable figure for J&K) and 0.52 under the BJP (slightly higher than the comparable figure for J&K). Similarly, Table 5.7 shows that, for the Northeast, the number non-terrorist fatalities-per-incident was 0.72 under the Congress and 0.34 under the BJP, both values being considerably lower than comparable values for J&K and the Red Corridor.

Figure 5.1 shows that during the 2004–2013 period, the 720 non-terrorist deaths in J&K were accompanied by 73 terrorists being killed resulting in a "kill-ratio" of 10.1. This meant that, on average, 10.1 terrorists were killed for every hundred non-terrorists fatalities or, put it differently, the "price" of one dead terrorist was 9.9 non-terrorist deaths in J&K during the 2004–2013 (Congress) period; during the 2014–2021 (BJP) period, the 652 non-terrorist deaths, accompanied by 169 terrorists being killed, resulting in a "kill-ratio" of 25.9 which meant that now 25.9 terrorists were killed for every hundred non-terrorists fatalities. This meant that the "price" that civil society had to pay for a dead terrorist *fell* from 9.9 non-terrorist deaths during 2004–2013 to 3.9 non-terrorist deaths during 2014–21 (Figs. 5.2, 5.3, 5.4).

Figure 5.1 shows, for the Red Corridor, that during the 2004–2013 period, the 2308 non-terrorist deaths were accompanied by 220 terrorists being killed resulting in a "kill-ratio" of 9.5, while during the 2014–2021 (BJP) period, the 1043 non-terrorist deaths, accompanied by 213 terrorists being killed, resulted in a "kill-ratio" of 20.4. This meant that the "price" that civil society had to pay for a dead terrorist in the Red Corridor *fell* from 10.5 non-terrorist deaths during 2004–2013 to 4.9 non-terrorist deaths during 2014–21.

The price of a dead terrorist—the number of terrorist deaths per non-terrorist death—in the Red Corridor was 0.1 for the Congress regime (meaning one terrorist was killed for every *ten* non-terrorist fatalities) and

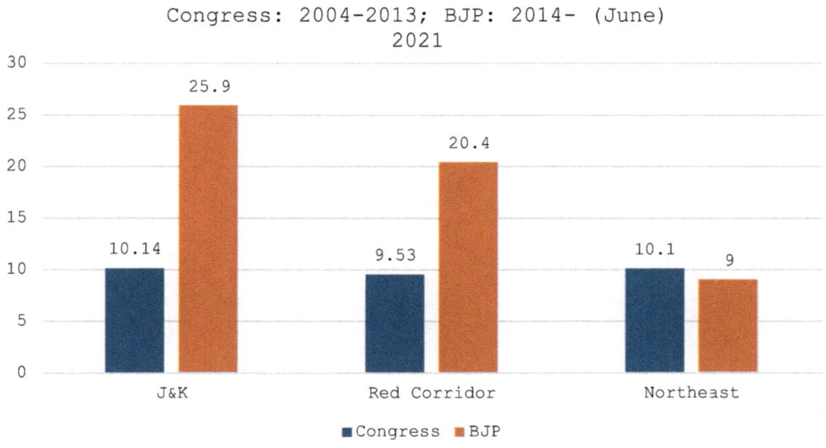

Fig. 5.1 The "Kill-Ratio" under Congress and BJP governments: J&K, the Red Corridor, and the Northeast. The Kill-Ratio is the number of terrorists killed per 100 non-terrorist deaths (*Source* Own calculations from GTD)

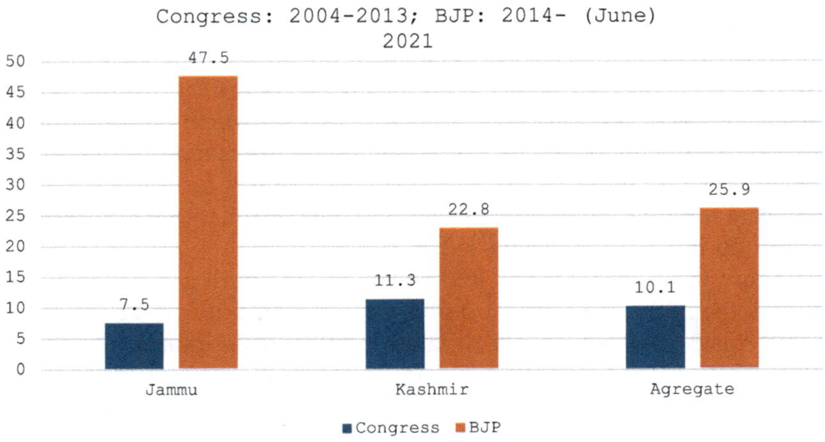

Fig. 5.2 The "Kill-Ratio" under Congress and BJP governments: Jammu and Kashmir Regions. The Kill-Ratio is the number of terrorists killed per 100 non-terrorist deaths (*Source* Own calculations from GTD)

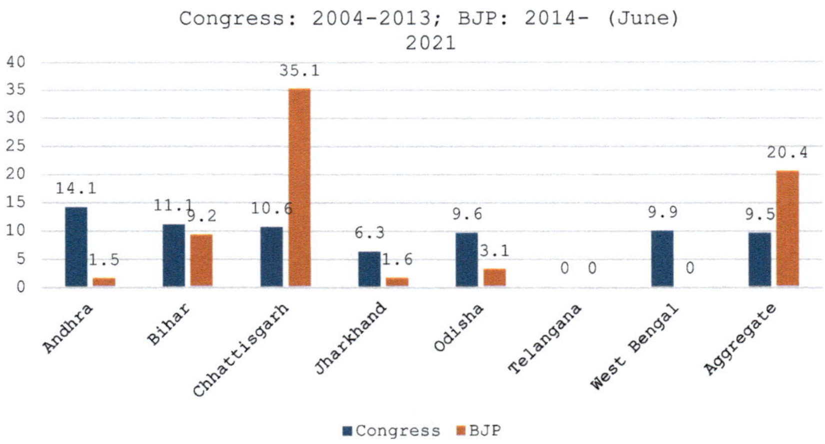

Fig. 5.3 The "Kill-Ratio" under Congress and BJP governments in the States of the Red Corridor. The Kill-Ratio is the number of terrorists killed per 100 non-terrorist deaths (*Source* Own Calculations from GTD)

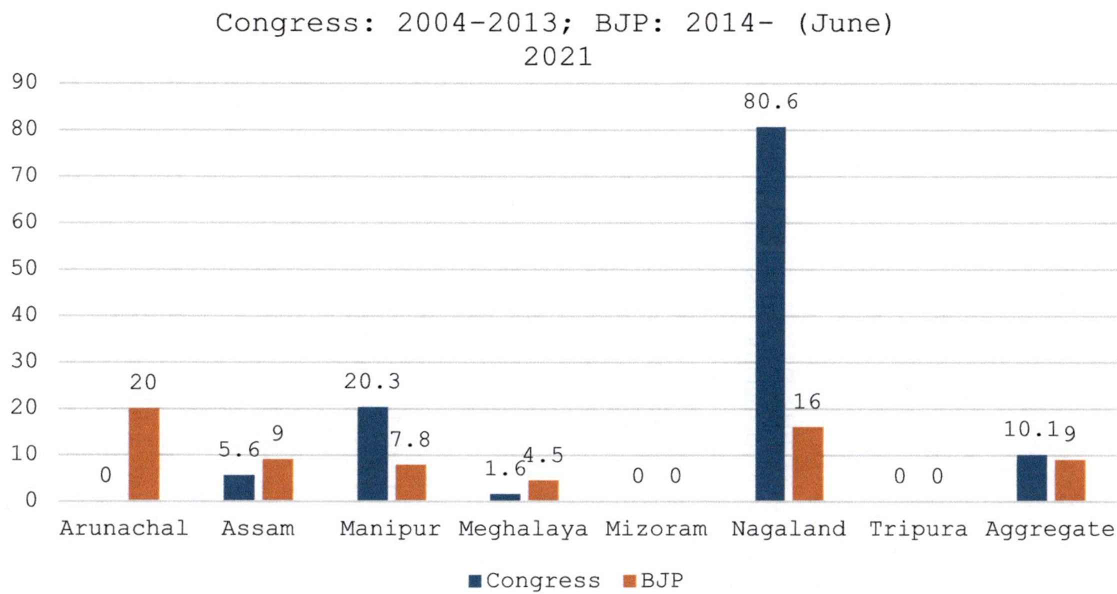

Fig. 5.4 The "Kill-Ratio" under Congress and BJP governments in the States of the Northeast. The Kill-Ratio is the number of terrorists killed per 100 non-terrorist deaths (*Source* Own Calculations from GTD)

0.2 for the BJP regime (meaning one terrorist was killed for every *five* non-terrorist fatalities). These figures were very similar to those obtained for J&K reported earlier in the context of Table 5.2: the "kill-ratio" was almost *twice* as high—the price of a dead terrorist was half—under the BJP than under the Congress regimes in both J&K and the Red Corridor.

Lastly, Fig. 5.1 shows, for the Northeast, that during the 2004–2013 period, the 970 non-terrorist deaths were accompanied by 98 terrorists being killed resulting in a "kill-ratio"" of 10.1, while during the 2014–2021 (BJP) period, the 400 non-terrorist deaths, accompanied by 36 terrorists being killed, resulted in a "kill-ratio" of 9.0. This meant that the "price" that civil society had to pay for a dead terrorist in the Northeast *rose* from 9.9 non-terrorist deaths during 2004–2013 to 11.1 non-terrorist deaths during 2014–21.

In a manner analogous to that for J&K and the Red Corridor, one can calculate the price of a terrorist death as the number of non-terrorist deaths it took to kill a single terrorist—for the Congress regime, this was 0.10 (meaning that one terrorist was killed for every *ten* non-terrorist fatalities) while for the BJP regime this was 0.09 (meaning that one terrorist was killed for every *eleven* non-terrorist fatalities).

5.4 The Decomposition of the Kill-Ratio by Sub-Regions

Each of the three regions of terrorist activity—J&K, the Red Corridor, and the Northeast—contained subregions. In the case of J&K it was districts, enumerated in Tables 5.1 and 5.2, as well as the two broad subregions of Jammu and of Kashmir. In respect of the Red Corridor and the Northeast the subregions were states, enumerated in Tables 5.4 and 5.5 for the Red Corridor and in Tables 5.6 and 5.7 for the Northeast. This section analyses the contribution that sub-regional kill-ratios made to the overall kill-ratio in a particular theatre of terrorist warfare. This is achieved by employing a novel decomposition method—first applied to labour markets by Borooah and Lee (1988)—which identifies the factors which influence the aggregate kill-ratio (hereafter, KR ratio). There are essentially two factors—the structure of *post-incident* outcomes in respect of the deaths of terrorists and of non-terrorists in the sub-regions, and the *relative* nature of terrorist incidents in the sub-regions.

Suppose that a region of terrorist activity in a country has K sub-regions, indexed ($k = 1, 2,\ldots,K$) such that F_k and M_k are, respectively, terrorist and non-terrorist deaths in sub-region *k*, ($k = 1, 2,\ldots,K$). Then $F = \sum_{k=1}^{K} F_k$ and $M = \sum_{k=1}^{K} M_k$ are, respectively, the total number of terrorists and non-terrorists killed in that region.

The aggregate kill-ratio, F/M, can be written as:

$$\frac{F}{M} = \sum_{k=1}^{K} \frac{F_k}{M_k} \times \frac{M_k}{M} \tag{5.1}$$

where F_k and M_k are, respectively, terrorist and non-terrorist fatalities in sub-region *k*, ($k = 1, 2,\ldots,K$).

Equation (5.1) expresses the aggregate kill-ratio ratio, F/M, as a weighted average of the sub-regional kill-ratios, F_k/M_k, the weights being the shares of non-terrorist deaths in the various sub-regions, M_k/M.

If N_k represents the number of terrorist incidents in sub-region *k*, and $N = \sum_{k=1}^{K} N_k$ is the total number of terrorist incidents in the region, the weights may be expanded to yield:

$$\begin{aligned} KR = \frac{F}{M} &= \sum_{k=1}^{K}\left(\frac{F_k}{M_k} \times \frac{M_k}{M}\right) = \sum_{k=1}^{K}\left(\frac{F_k}{M_k} \times \frac{N_k}{N} \times \frac{N}{M} \times \frac{M_k}{N_k}\right) \\ &= \sum_{k=1}^{K}\left(\frac{F_k}{M_k} \times \frac{N_k}{N} \times \left[\frac{M_k}{N_k} \Big/ \frac{M}{N}\right]\right) = \sum_{k=1}^{K} C_k \end{aligned} \tag{5.2}$$

The C_k in Eq. (5.2) shows the contributions that sub-region *k*, ($k = 1,2,\ldots,K$), makes to the overall KR while the terms *within* the summation sign show the various components of this contribution. Thus, C_k and, therefore, the aggregate KR may change because of:

1. Changes in the sub-regional KR, represented by the terms F_k/M_k.
2. "Relative Incident Effects" which show the proportion of the total number of terrorist incidents that occur in a sub-region, represented by the terms N_k/N.
3. "Relative Fatality effects" as represented by the terms $\frac{M_k}{N_k}/\frac{M}{N}$ which show the non-terrorist deaths-per-incident in a sub-region, $\frac{M_k}{N_k}$, *relative* to non-terrorist deaths-per-incident for the entire region $\frac{M}{N}$.

5.5 Empirical Results Based on the Decomposition Methodology

5.5.1 *J&K by Districts and Regions*

Table 5.8 shows the results of using Eq. (5.2) to decompose the aggregate KR, *F/M*, ratio for two time periods: 2004–2013, the period of a Congress government in New Delhi and 2014- (June) 2021, the period of a BJP government. As the numbers in the last row and the penultimate columns of Table 5.9 show, the aggregate kill-ratios (*FM*) ratios were, respectively, 10.1 and 25.2. Each of these numbers is arrived at by summing the individual district contributions.

So, for example, in Table 5.8, the KR (F/M) in the district of Anantnag was, respectively, 3.8 and 3.5 during Congress and BJP rule (in New Delhi). This was then multiplied by Anantnag's share in the totality of terrorist incidents,$N_k/N = 0.073$ (meaning, 7.3% of total incidents in J&K occurred in Anantnag) and by the "relative lethality" effect, $\frac{M_k}{E_k}/\frac{M}{E}$ = 1. This last effect was obtained by the fact that the number of non-terrorist deaths per incident, $\frac{M_k}{N_k}$, was 1.35 in Anantnag which was the same as number of non-terrorist deaths per incident, $\frac{M}{N}$ in J&K in its entirety: hence the "relative fatality factor" in Anantnag was one. Multiplying these three terms yielded the *absolute* contribution of Anantnag of 0.28 to the overall kill-ratio (FM) for J&K of 10.1. Column 6 of Table 5.8 then shows the *percentage* contribution of Anantnag as (0.28/10.1) × 100 implying that, during the period 2004–2013, Anantnag contributed 2.8% to the overall kill-ratio of 10.1 in J&K.

By contrast, during this period, Srinagar district (with a district kill-ratio of 16.8, a relative incident effect of 0.25, and a relative fatality effect of 0.94) contributed 38.4% to the overall kill-ratio; Baramulla district (with a district kill-ratio of 12.2, a relative incident effect of 0.17, and a relative fatality effect of 0.68) contributed 13.7% to the overall kill-ratio; and Pulwama district (with a district kill-ratio of 9.5, a relative incident effect of 0.095, and a relative fatality effect of 1.1) contributed 9.6% to the overall kill-ratio.

Compared to the 2004–2013 period, the single biggest change that occurred in the 2014–(June) 2021 period was the fall in the contribution of Srinagar district to the overall kill-ratio from 38.4% in the earlier period to 9.8% in the later period. Although the kill-ratio in Srinagar rose from 16.8 in 2004–2013 to 31.4 in 2014–(June) 2021, Srinagar's share in

Table 5.8 The decomposition of the kill-ratio for Jammu and Kashmir by districts and regions using the methodology of Eq. (5.2)

Districts	*Congress: 2004–2013*					*BJP: 2014-(June) 2021*				
	$\frac{F_k}{M_k}$ *District Kill-Ratios (1)*	$\frac{N_k}{N}$ *Relative Incident Effects (2)*	$\frac{M_k}{N_k}/\frac{M}{N}$ *Relative Fatality Effect (3)*	*Product of Columns 1–3*	*Percentage contribution of district to overall FM ratio*	$\frac{F_k}{M_k}$ *District anti-terrorism effects (1)*	$\frac{N_k}{N}$ *District Incidence Occurrence Effects (2)*	$\frac{M_k}{N_k}/\frac{M}{N}$ *Relative Fatality Effect by District (3)*	*Product of Columns 1–3*	*Percentage contribution of district to overall FM ratio*
Shows Anantnag	3.77	0.073	1.35/1.35	0.278	2.74	3.53	0.12	0.45/0.42	0.46	1.83
Bandipore	0	0.019	0.7/1.35	0	0.00	53.85	0.03	0.33/0.42	1.07	4.27
Baramulla	12.20	0.167	0.92/1.35	1.39	13.71	22.64	0.12	0.59/0.42	3.68	14.64
Budgam	5	0.037	1/1.35	0.139	1.37	31.58	0.05	0.24/0.42	0.92	3.66
Doda	5.17	0.065	1.66/1.35	0.417	4.11	0.00	0.01	0.33/0.42	0.00	0.00
Ganderbal	6.25	0.022	1.33/1.35	0.139	1.37	80.00	0.01	0.22/0.42	0.61	2.44
Jammu	24	0.021	1.33/1.35	0.833	8.21	48.15	0.02	0.79/0.42	1.99	7.93
Kathua	0	0.005	2.67/1.35	0	0.00	62.50	0.00	1.60/0.42	0.77	3.05

(continued)

Table 5.8 (continued)

Districts	*Congress: 2004–2013*					*BJP: 2014-(June) 2021*				
	$\frac{F_k}{M_k}$ *District Kill-Ratios (1)*	$\frac{N_k}{N}$ *Relative Incident Effects (2)*	$\frac{M_k}{N_k}/\frac{M}{N}$ *Relative Fatality Effect (3)*	*Product of Columns 1–3*	*Percentage contribution of district to overall FM ratio*	$\frac{F_k}{M_k}$ *District anti-terrorism effects (1)*	$\frac{N_k}{N}$ *District Incidence Occurrence Effects (2)*	$\frac{M_k}{N_k}/\frac{M}{N}$ *Relative Fatality Effect by District (3)*	*Product of Columns 1–3*	*Percentage contribution of district to overall FM ratio*
Kishtwar	0	0.024	1/1.35	0	0.00	0.00	0.01	0.82/ 0.42	0.00	0.00
Kulgam	0	0.026	2.86/ 1.35	0	0.00	22.22	0.07	0.36/ 0.42	1.23	4.88
Kupwara	17.39	0.058	0.74/ 1.35	0.556	5.48	63.27	0.06	0.56/ 0.42	4.75	18.90
Poonch	2.94	0.030	2.13/ 1.35	0.139	1.37	44.44	0.04	0.17/ 0.42	0.61	2.44
Pulwama	9.46	0.095	1.45/ 1.35	0.972	9.59	14.94	0.21	0.47/ 0.42	3.53	14.03
Rajouri	23.53	0.030	1.06/ 1.35	0.556	5.48	22.22	0.02	0.36/ 0.42	0.31	1.22
Ramban	0	0.015	1.38/ 1.35	0	0.00	120.00	0.00	0.83/ 0.42	0.92	3.66

Districts	Congress: 2004–2013					BJP: 2014-(June) 2021				
	$\frac{F_k}{M_k}$ District Kill-Ratios (1)	$\frac{N_k}{N}$ Relative Incident Effects (2)	$\frac{M_k}{N_k} / \frac{M}{N}$ Relative Fatality Effect (3)	Product of Columns 1–3	Percentage contribution of district to overall FM ratio	$\frac{F_k}{M_k}$ District anti-terrorism effects (1)	$\frac{N_k}{N}$ District Incidence Occurrence Effects (2)	$\frac{M_k}{N_k} / \frac{M}{N}$ Relative Fatality Effect by District (3)	Product of Columns 1–3	Percentage contribution of district to overall FM ratio
Reasi	0	0.009	3.6/ 1.35	0	0.00	0.000	0.00	0.00/ 0.42	0.00	0.00
Samba	30	0.013	1.43/ 1.35	0.417	4.11	66.67	0.01	0.38/ 0.42	0.31	1.22
Shopian	25	0.028	0.8/ 1.35	0.417	4.11	15.38	0.11	0.32/ 0.42	1.23	4.88
Srinagar	16.77	0.245	1.27/ 1.35	3.89	38.36	31.37	0.12	0.27/ 0.42	2.45	9.76
Udhampur	0	0.017	3.56/ 1.35	0	0.00	22.22	0.01	1.00/ 0.42	0.31	1.22
Total FM Ratio				10.14	100				25.15	100
Regions										
Jammu	7.52	0.230	1.84/ 1.35	2.36	23.27	47.56	10.6	0.50/ 0.42	5.98	23.1

(continued)

Table 5.8 (continued)

Districts	*Congress: 2004–2013*					*BJP: 2014-(June) 2021*				
	$\frac{F_k}{M_k}$ *District Kill-Ratios (1)*	$\frac{N_k}{N}$ *Relative Incident Effects (2)*	$\frac{M_k}{N_k} / \frac{M}{N}$ *Relative Fatality Effect (3)*	*Product of Columns 1–3*	*Percentage contribution of district to overall FM ratio*	$\frac{F_k}{M_k}$ *District anti-terrorism effects (1)*	$\frac{N_k}{N}$ *District Incidence Occurrence Effects (2)*	$\frac{M_k}{N_k} / \frac{M}{N}$ *Relative Fatality Effect by District (3)*	*Product of Columns 1–3*	*Percentage contribution of district to overall FM ratio*
Kashmir	11.34	0.770	1.20/ 1.35	7.78	76.73	22.81	89.4	0.41/ 0.42	19.94	76.9
Total FM Ratio				10.14	100				25.92	100

The Jammu Region comprised the following districts: Doda; Jammu; Kathua; Kishtwar; Poonch; Rajouri; Ramban; Reasi; Samba; and Udhampur
The Kashmir Region comprised the following districts: Anantnag; Bandipore; Baramulla; Budgam; Ganderbal; Kulgam; Kupwara; Pulwama; Shopian; and Srinagar
The Kill-Ratio is the Number of Terrorists Killed per 100 Non-Terrorist Deaths
Source Own calculations from GTD

Table 5.9 The decomposition of the Kill-Ratio for the Red Corridor and the northeast by states using the methodology of Eq. (5.2)

	Red Corridor									
	Congress: 2004–2013					*BJP: 2014–(June) 2021*				
States	$\frac{F_k}{M_k}$ *District kill-ratios (1)*	$\frac{N_k}{N}$ *Relative Incident Effects (2)*	$\frac{M_k}{N_k} / \frac{M}{N}$ *Relative Fatality Effect (3)*	*Product of Columns 1–3*	*Percentage contribution of district to overall FM ratio*	$\frac{F_k}{M_k}$ *District anti-terrorism effects (1)*	$\frac{N_k}{N}$ *District Incidence Occurrence Effects (2)*	$\frac{M_k}{N_k} / \frac{M}{N}$ *Relative Fatality Effect by District (3)*	*Product of Columns 1–3*	*Percentage contribution of district to overall FM ratio*
Andhra Pradesh	14.06	0.04	0.85/1.22	0.39	4.09	1.47	0.04	0.87/0.52	0.10	0.47
Bihar	11.11	0.17	0.77/1.22	1.21	12.72	9.20	0.10	0.42/0.52	0.77	3.76
Chhattisgarh	10.57	0.19	2.26/1.22	3.68	38.62	35.05	0.44	0.63/0.52	18.89	92.49
Jharkhand	6.25	0.24	1.19/1.22	1.43	15.05	1.61	0.25	0.37/0.52	0.29	1.41
Orissa	9.65	0.19	0.71/1.22	1.08	11.36	3.08	0.13	0.50/0.52	0.38	1.88
Telangana	0.00	0.00	0.00/1.22	0.00	0.00	0.00	0.03	0.18/0.52	0.00	0.00
West Bengal	9.98	0.17	1.28/1.22	1.73	18.17	0.00	0.01	0.00/0.52	0.00	0.00
Total FM Ratio				9.54	100				20.42	100

(continued)

Table 5.9 (continued)

States	*Red Corridor*									
	Congress: 2004–2013					*BJP: 2014–(June) 2021*				
	$\frac{F_k}{M_k}$ *District kill-ratios (1)*	$\frac{N_k}{N}$ *Relative Incident Effects (2)*	$\frac{M_k}{N_k} / \frac{M}{N}$ *Relative Fatality Effect (3)*	*Product of Columns 1–3*	*Percentage contribution of district to overall FM ratio*	$\frac{F_k}{M_k}$ *District anti-terrorism effects (1)*	$\frac{N_k}{N}$ *District Incidence Occurrence Effects (2)*	$\frac{M_k}{N_k} / \frac{M}{N}$ *Relative Fatality Effect by District (3)*	*Product of Columns 1–3*	*Percentage contribution of district to overall FM ratio*
	The Northeast Congress: 2004–2013					**BJP: 2014–(June) 2021**				
Arunachal Pradesh	0.00	0.00	0.00/ 0.72	0.00	0.00	20.00	0.02	0.96/ 0.34	1.25	13.89
Assam	5.60	0.43	1.16/ 0.72	3.92	39.58	9.04	0.26	0.54/ 0.34	3.75	41.67
Manipur	20.25	0.41	0.28/ 0.72	3.30	33.33	7.75	0.48	0.23/ 0.34	2.50	27.78
Meghalaya	1.61	0.09	0.52/ 0.72	0.10	1.04	4.55	0.16	0.23/ 0.34	0.50	5.56
Mizoram	0.00	0.00	0.00/ 0.72	0.00	0.00	0.00	0.01	0.29/ 0.34	0.00	0.00

States	*Red Corridor*									
	Congress: 2004–2013					*BJP: 2014–(June) 2021*				
	$\frac{F_k}{M_k}$ *District kill-ratios (1)*	$\frac{N_k}{N}$ *Relative Incident Effects (2)*	$\frac{M_k}{N_k} / \frac{M}{N}$ *Relative Fatality Effect (3)*	*Product of Columns 1–3*	*Percentage contribution of district to overall FM ratio*	$\frac{F_k}{M_k}$ *District anti-terrorism effects (1)*	$\frac{N_k}{N}$ *District Incidence Occurrence Effects (2)*	$\frac{M_k}{N_k} / \frac{M}{N}$ *Relative Fatality Effect by District (3)*	*Product of Columns 1–3*	*Percentage contribution of district to overall FM ratio*
Nagaland	80.65	0.04	0.62/ 0.72	2.58	26.04	16.00	0.05	0.38/ 0.34	1.00	11.11
Tripura	0.00	0.02	1.24/ 0.72	0.00	0.00	0.00	0.01	0.41/ 0.34	0.00	0.00
Total FM Ratio				9.90	100				9.00	100

The Kill-Ratio is the Number of Terrorists Killed per 100 Non-Terrorist Deaths
Source Own calculations from GTD

the totality of terrorist incidents in J&K fell from 24.5% in the period of Congress rule to 12% in the period of BJP rule with an accompanying fall in the relative fatality effect from 0.94 to 0.64—the number of deaths per incident in Srinagar district was now 0.27 compared to the overall J&K figure of 0.42.

The other big change was the rise in the contributions of Kupwara and Pulwama districts from, respectively, 5.5% and 9.6% in 2004–2013 to 18.9% and 14% in 2014–(June) 2021. The kill-ratio in Kupwara rose from 17.4 (four terrorists and 23 non-terrorists killed) during the period of Congress rule in New Delhi to 63.3 (31 terrorist and 49 non-terrorist deaths) during the period of the BJP government; Kupwara's share of total incidents did not change (from around 6%) but the relative fatality rose from 0.54 in the first period to 1.33 in the latter period.

The kill-ratio in Pulwama rose from 9.5 (seven terrorists and 74 non-terrorists killed) during the period of Congress rule in New Delhi to 14.9 (23 terrorist and 154 non-terrorist deaths) during the period of the BJP government; Pulwama's share of total incidents increased from 9.5% in the first period to 21% in the second period but the relative fatality was more or less unchanged between the periods.

Table 5.8 also shows, in its lower panel, the results of the decomposition of Eq. (5.2) with respect to the two regions of J&K: *Jammu* (comprising the districts: Doda; Jammu; Kathua; Kishtwar; Poonch; Rajouri; Ramban; Reasi; Samba; and Udhampur) and *Kashmir* (comprising the districts of Anantnag; Bandipore; Baramulla; Budgam; Ganderbal; Kulgam; Kupwara; Pulwama; Shopian; and Srinagar).

As Table 5.8 shows, in the 2004–2013 period, the overall kill-ratio in J&K was 10.1 and, to this, the Jammu region contributed 23.3% and Kashmir contributed 76.7%. This was partly because Jammu had a lower kill-ratio than Kashmir (7.5 versus 11.3) but largely because only 23% of terrorist incidents occurred in Jammu with the remainder occurring in Kashmir. In the 2014–(June) 2021 period, the kill-ratio in Jammu rose to 47.6 (from 7.5 in 2004–2013) which was a much steeper rise than the kill-ratio for Kashmir (11.3 to 22.8). Simultaneously, however, the proportion of terrorist incidents occurring in Jammu fell from 23% in 2004–2013 to 10.6% in 2014–(June) 2021 with the result that the contributions of the Jammu and Kashmir regions to the overall kill-ratio remained virtually unchanged at, respectively, 23% and 77%.

Table 5.9 shows in its upper and lower panels the results of the decomposition of Eq. (5.2) with respect to the states of the Red Corridor and the Northeast, respectively. In the Red Corridor, the state of Chhattisgarh made the largest contribution to its overall kill-ratio: 38.6% to its overall kill-ratio of 9.5 during the Congress period 2004–2013 and 92.5% to its overall kill-ratio of 20.4 during the BJP period 20,014-(June) 2021. In the Northeast, the states of Assam and Manipur made the largest contributions to its overall kill-ratio: 39.6% and 41.7%, respectively, to the overall kill-ratios of 9.9 during the Congress period 2004–2013 and 41.7% and 27.8% to its overall kill-ratio of 9.0 during the BJP period 20,014–(June) 2021.

5.6 Inequality Analysis of Deaths from Terrorist Incidents in India

The previous discussion was based on an analysis of the average number of fatalities from incidents for which terrorist groups in India were responsible. However, focusing exclusively on the average ignores the distribution of the total number of deaths across incidents: the total number of fatalities may be the result of a few spectacular incidents which result in many deaths, with most incidents being relatively light on fatalities, or it may also be the result of a relatively equal distribution of fatalities across incidents.

To address the distributional issue, we computed the Gini coefficient for the distribution of fatalities, in terrorist incidents in the three theatres of conflict—J&K, the Red Corridor, and the Northeast—for two major types of attack: armed assault and bombing. The program used to compute inequality (*ineqdeco* in Stata) would not accept zero values and hence all those incidents which had resulted in zero non-terrorist fatalities were dropped from the calculations.[4]

If N is the number of incidents, with which there was associated at least one non-terrorist fatality, and M_i is the number of (non-terrorist) deaths from incident i $(i = 1 \ldots N)$, and $\mu = \sum_{i=1}^{N} M_i / N$ represents the

[4] These were: 1,401 incidents for J&K; 2,379 for the Red Corridor; and 1,900 for the Northeast.

average number of deaths, the Gini coefficient is defined as:

$$G = \frac{1}{2N^2\mu}\sum_{i=1}^{N}\sum_{j=1}^{N}|M_i - M_j| \tag{5.3}$$

In other words, the Gini coefficient is computed as half the mean of the difference in the number of deaths between pairs of incidents, divided by the average (μ). So, $G = 0.45$ implies that the ***difference in the number of deaths between two incidents chosen at random*** will be 90 percent of the average number of deaths: if $\mu = 1$, this difference will be 0.9 fatalities.

The Gini coefficient measures the extent to which the distribution of fatalities between incidents deviates from a perfectly equal distribution. The value of the coefficient varies from 0 (no deviation) or 1 (complete deviation) or, in percentage terms, from 0 to 100. A value of zero indicates perfect equality with higher values indicating higher inequality.

Table 5.10 shows that, judging by the values of the Gini coefficient, inequality in the distributions of deaths, resulting from the armed assault incidents, was lowest in J&K and highest in the Red Corridor for both the periods, 2004–2013 and 2014–(June) 2021 (0.440 and 0.617, respectively, for the earlier period and 0.248 and 0.570, respectively, for the later period). This was also the case for inequality in the distributions of deaths, resulting from bombing incidents: inequality was lowest in J&K and highest in the Red Corridor. In terms of fatalities, however, terrorist incidents involving armed assault were most deadly in the Northeast and least deadly in the Red Corridor with average deaths per incident of 2.9 and 1.5, respectively, for 2004–2013 and 2.1 and 0.74 for 2014–(June) 2021.

5.6.1 *The Equally Distributed Equivalent Fatality Rate*

What is the social loss from terrorist incidents? If the number of fatalities is used as an indicator of loss, then both the average number of deaths and the inter-incident distribution of deaths should serve to determine the size of social loss. For example, Anand and Sen (1997) compared the Honduras (with an average literacy rate of 75%, distributed between men and women as 78%,:73%) with China (with an average literacy rate of 80%, distributed between men and women as 92%: 68%) and asked which country should be regarded as having the "better" achievement with regard to literacy: China with a higher overall rate or the Honduras

Table 5.10 Gini coefficients by terrorist group and type attack

	Congress: 2004–2013				*BJP: 2014-(June) 2021*			
	Armed attack incidents	*Bombing incidents*	*Mean deaths from armed assault incidents*	*Mean deaths from bombing incidents*	*Armed attack incidents*	*Bombing incidents*	*Mean deaths from armed assault incidents*	*Mean deaths from bombing incidents*
Jammu & Kashmir	0.440	0.472	2.2	3.3	0.248	0.548	1.4	3.1
The Red Corridor	0.617	0.898	1.5	1.1	0.570	0.913	0.74	0.37
The North-east	0.523	0.529	2.9	3.1	0.424	0.414	2.1	2.4

Source Own calculations from GTD

with greater gender equality? To answer this question both the average (China does better) and the distribution (the Honduras does better) need to be factored in to arrive at an assessment.

But how to arrive at an assessment? The answer to this begins with the concept of a social loss function. If there are N incidents with M_1, M_2, ...M_N associated non-terrorist deaths, social loss, L, is determined by these N values:

$$L = L(M_1, M_2, ..., M_N) = \sum_{i=1}^{N} h(M_i) \tag{5.4}$$

The function L of Eq. (5.4) says that social loss is the *sum* of losses resulting from deaths caused by the ***individual*** terrorist incidents or, in other words, it is written in an ***additively separable form***. The functions *h(.)* in Eq. (5.4) is society's valuation of the loss to it from incident i resulting in M_i deaths. A given average number of deaths, computed over all incidents, $\overline{M}$, will generate different values of social loss, depending on how it is distributed across the incidents (M_1, M_2, ...M_N). Social loss, L, increases as the number of deaths from an incident increases (so an incident which involves 20 deaths inflicts more social loss than one with which only four deaths are associated). Moreover, the rate of increase of social loss increases with number of deaths meaning that, if the number of deaths from a particular incident increased by one (from M_i to $M_i + 1$), the *rise* in social loss would be *greater* when, say, $M_i = 20$ than when $M_i = 4$. It follows from this that social loss from terrorist incidents, L, will be *minimised* when all the incidents result in the *same* number of deaths $(M_1 = M_2 = \ldots M_N)$.[5]

In his seminal paper on income inequality, Atkinson (1970) argued that "society" would be prepared to accept a reduction in average income, ***provided the lower income was equally distributed***, from a higher average income which was unequally distributed.[6] The size of this reduction depended upon our degree of "inequality aversion" which Atkinson (1970) measured by the value of an "inequality aversion" parameter $\varepsilon \geq 0$.[7]

This idea can, equally well, be applied to the measurement of the social loss from terrorism.[8] If one is to averse to spectacular, high-profile incidents—9/11 in New York, 26/11 in Mumbai, 7/7 in London—in which a large number of innocent lives are lost, with the consequence that the prevailing socio-political mood becomes one of fear, insecurity, and paranoia, then one might "prefer" low-grade terrorism with several low-fatality incidents, without any high-fatality ones, to a few iconic incidents which inflict death on a large scale.

[5] To see this, suppose there are two incidents, 1 and 2, such that $M1 > M_2$. Now suppose a death is "transferred" from incident 1 to 2. Then a reduction by one death from the first incident will reduce social loss, while an increase of one death from the second incident will increase social loss. But, by the argument in the main text, the reduction in social loss will exceed the increase. So long as $M1 > M_2$, transfers of fatalities from incident 1 to 2 will reduce social loss with the result that it will be minimised when $M1 = M_2$.

[6] In the language of economics, the two situations would yield the same level of social welfare, i.e. be 'welfare equivalent'.

[7] When $\varepsilon = 0$, we are not at all averse to inequality implying that we would not be prepared to accept even the smallest reduction in average income to secure an equitable distribution. The degree of inequality aversion increases with the value of ε: the higher the value of ε, the more averse we would be to inequality and, in order to secure an equitable distribution of income, the greater the reduction in average income we would find acceptable.

[8] See Borooah (2002) for a derivation of the loss function and its application to measuring unemployment.

One would then be willing increase the average number of deaths from terrorist incidents in a country,$\overline{M}$, by the amount of inter-incident inequality in fatalities, to arrive at M^e, an "equity sensitive" fatality rate, ***which was equally distributed across the incidents***, for the country, $M^e \geq \overline{M}$.. We refer to M^e as the *equally distributed equivalent fatality rate (ede)*: when *every* terrorist incident results in exactly M^e deaths, M^e imposes the same social loss as (or is *welfare equivalent* to)$\overline{M}$.

Following from this, Atkinson's (1970) index, defined with respect to the parameter, ε, as applied to differences between terrorist incidents in their number of deaths, yields:

$$A_\varepsilon = (M^e/\overline{M}) - 1 = \left[\sum_{i=1}^{N} N^{-1}\left(\frac{M_i}{\overline{M}}\right)^{1+\varepsilon}\right]^{1/(1+\varepsilon)} - 1 \qquad (5.5)$$

When $\varepsilon = 0$, society is indifferent about the inter-incident distribution of a given total of deaths from terrorist incidents and $M^e = \overline{M}$; for $\varepsilon > 0$, $M^e > \overline{M}$ and $A_\varepsilon > 0$. The higher the value of the inequality aversion parameter, ε, the greater will the value of M^e and hence of A_e.

The above points can be illustrated diagrammatically in Fig. 5.5. If there are two incidents (that is, $N = 2$), each point on *QQ* represents a (M_1, M_2) combination that yields the same (given) total of deaths, $M = M_1 + M_2$ and, therefore the same (given) value of $\overline{M} = M/2 = F/2$: *QQ* is the "iso-fatality" locus corresponding to M and its slope is -1. Call this the "iso-fatality" line.

For $N = 2$, the curves represent the combinations of incident-specific deaths (M_1 and M_2) which represent a *constant* level of social loss. Call these the "iso-loss" curves. They are obtained by fixing the value of L at different levels in Eq. (5.2) and then solving for the different M_1 and M_2 combinations which would result in that (constant) level of L. The curve further away from the origin represents a higher level of social loss because it is associated with a higher level of fatalities, M.

These iso-loss curves are superimposed upon the iso-fatality line, *QQ* in Fig. 5.5. Social loss is minimised at a point where an iso-loss curve is tangential to the iso-fatality line QQ: this will occur at the point A when $M_1 = M_2$. In other words, tangency between the iso-loss curve and *QQ* occurs at a point (A) on the 45^0 line: equilibrium results when both incidents result in an identical number of deaths so that social loss from a given number of deaths, M, is minimised.

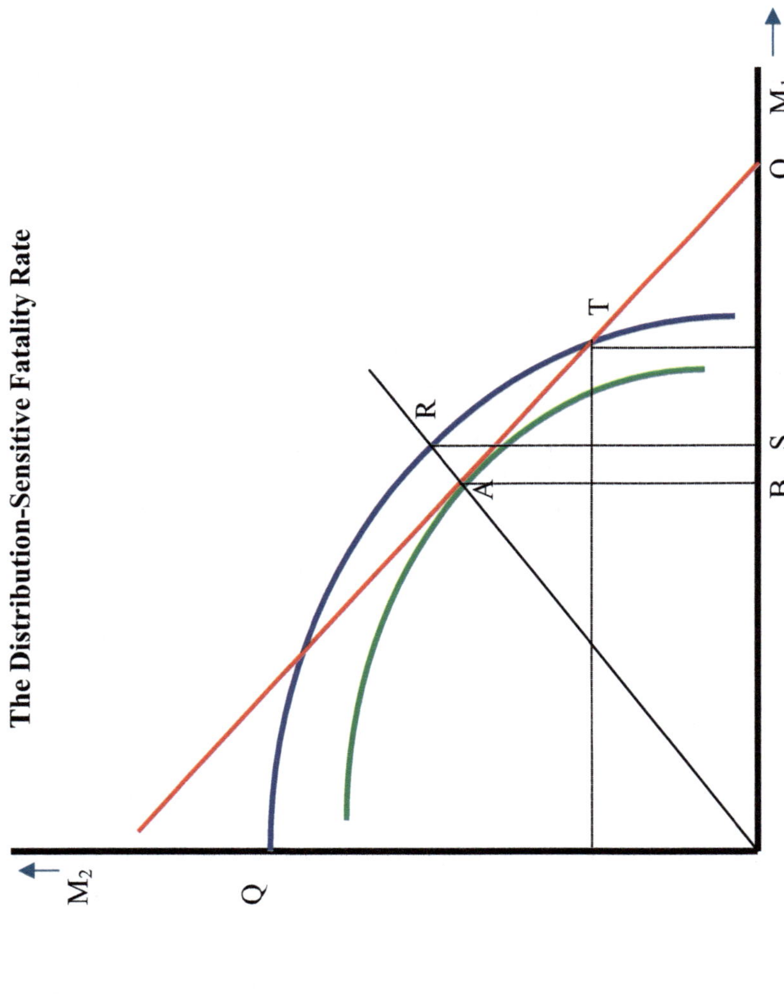

Fig. 5.5 The distribution-sensitive fatality rate

If, however, the outcomes with respect to the two incidents are at T so that fatalities from the first incident exceed those from the second, so that $M1 > M_2$), then the total number of deaths, $2 \times AB$, if distributed according to the point T of QQ, results in the same social loss (is "welfare-equivalent) to a larger total of fatalities, $2 \times RS$, when $2 \times RS$ is equally distributed between the two incidents. The percentage amount by which the social loss from locating at T exceeds its minimum value at A is $(RS/AB)-1$. The greater the ***aversion to inequality***, the more bowed will be the iso-loss curves and the higher will R be along the 45° line, and the greater will be the social loss associated with the point T.

The total number of deaths, $2 \times RS$ is referred to as the equally distributed equivalent (***ede***) fatalities to the total number of deaths, $2 \times AB$ distributed according to point T. In other words, a ***larger*** number of deaths $2 \times RS$, if ***distributed equally*** between the two incidents—so that each incident results in RS deaths—will yield the same amount of social loss as a smaller number of deaths, $2 \times AB$, distributed unequally between the incidents, so that the first and second incidents results in M_1 and M_2 deaths, respectively, $M_1 + M_2 = 2 \times AB$ but $M1 > M_2$.

To compute RS, note that if A_ε is the value of the inequality index (as defined in Eq. (5.5) at point T in Fig. 5.5, for an inequality aversion parameter, ε, then:

$$RS = AB(A_\varepsilon + 1) \text{ or, equivalently, } M^e = \overline{M}(A_\varepsilon + 1) \qquad (5.6)$$

Applying Eq. (5.6), allows one to compute the values of M^e for the ***given*** value of $\overline{M}$ and ***different*** values of A_ε, the values of which vary according to the value assigned to ε, the inequality aversion parameter. When $\varepsilon = 0$ (so that there is no aversion to inequality and society is indifferent as to how fatalities are distributed over incidents), $M^e = \overline{M}$; when $\varepsilon > 0$, $M^e > \overline{M}$ and the greater the value of ε, the greater the difference between the two quantities. Four special cases, contingent upon the value assumed by ε, may be distinguished:

1. When $\varepsilon = 0$, M^e is the ***arithmetic mean*** of the fatalities
2. When $\varepsilon = 0.5$ there is mild inequality aversion
3. When $\varepsilon = 1$, M^e is the ***geometric mean*** of the fatalities
4. When $\varepsilon = 2$, M^e is the ***harmonic mean*** of the fatalities

These calculations for the equally distributed equivalent fatality rate, M^e, with respect to different values of ε are shown in Table 5.11 for the three main areas of terrorist activity in India (J&K, the Red Corridor, The Northeast), for the two main attack types (armed assault and bombing).

When $\varepsilon = 0.5$ (mild inequality aversion), "society", under the Congress regime of 2004–2013, would have been prepared to tolerate a fatality rate of 2.59 deaths from armed assault (as compared to the actual fatality rate of 2.21) and a fatality rate of 3.90 deaths from bombing (as compared to the actual fatality rate of 3.30) from terrorist incidents in J&K *provided these higher numbers were equally distributed between the incidents.* Under the BJP regime of 2014-(June) 2021, under mild inequality aversion, the corresponding numbers were a fatality rate of 1.51 deaths from armed assault (as compared to the actual fatality rate of 1.41) and a fatality rate of 3.95 from bombing (as compared to the actual fatality rate of 3.14) from terrorist incidents in J&K *provided these higher numbers were equally distributed between the incidents.*

In the Red Corridor and the Northeast, the *equally distributed equivalent* fatality rates, under $\varepsilon = 0.5$, were 2.62 and 3.53, respectively, for armed assault under the Congress regime (as compared to the actual fatality rates of 2.16 and 2.85) and, respectively, 1.44 and 2.41 for armed assault under BJP rule (as compared to the actual fatality rates of 1.35 and 2.06) on the assumption that the *ede* rates *were equally distributed between the incidents.* For bombings, the *ede* fatality rates, under $\varepsilon = 0.5$, were 7.00 and 3.78 for the Red Corridor and the Northeast, respectively, under the Congress regime (as compared to the actual fatality rates of 5.73 and 3.06) and 3.47 and 2.75 for the Red Corridor and the Northeast, respectively, under the BJP government (as compared to the actual fatality rates of 2.83 and 2.38) on the assumption that the *ede* rates *were equally distributed between the incidents.*

As aversion to inequality increased, from $\varepsilon = 0.5$, to $\varepsilon = 1.0$, to $\varepsilon = 2.0$, the *ede* fatality rate rose; to compensate for the unequal distribution of deaths between the different terrorist incidents, "society" would be prepared to tolerate increasingly higher fatality rate, *provided this was equally distributed between the incidents.*

Table 5.11 Equally distributed equivalent number of deaths and fatality rates for terrorist groups in India: armed assault and bombing

	Congress 2004–2013 *Armed assaults* *J&K*	*Red Corridor*	*The Northeast*	*Bombings* *J&K*	*Red Corridor*	*The Northeast*
Number of Incidents for which there was at least one non-terrorist death	174	482	183	84	115	105
Mean fatality rate	2.21	2.16	2.85	3.30	5.73	3.06
Equally distributed equivalent fatality rate with $\varepsilon = 0.5$	2.59	2.62	3.53	3.90	7.00	3.78
Equally distributed equivalent fatality rate with $\varepsilon = 1.0$	2.84	2.85	3.92	4.34	7.97	4.22
Equally distributed equivalent fatality rate with $\varepsilon = 2.0$	3.10	3.05	4.29	4.97	9.16	4.64
	BJP 2014–(June) 2021 *Armed Assaults* *J&K*	*Red Corridor*	*The Northeast*	*Bombings* *J&K*	*Red Corridor*	*The Northeast*
Number of Incidents for which there was at least one non-terrorist death	288	296	109	71	109	61
Mean fatality rate	1.41	1.35	2.06	3.14	2.83	2.38

(continued)

Table 5.11 (continued)

	Congress 2004–2013 *Armed assaults* *J&K*	*Red Corridor*	*The Northeast*	*Bombings* *J&K*	*Red Corridor*	*The Northeast*
Equally distributed equivalent fatality rate with $\varepsilon = 0.5$	1.51	1.44	2.41	3.95	3.47	2.75
Equally distributed equivalent fatality ratewith $\varepsilon = 1.0$	1.58	1.50	2.62	4.41	3.88	2.99
Equally distributed equivalent fatality rate with $\varepsilon = 2.0$	1.67	1.57	2.83	4.83	4.26	3.26

The equally distributed equivalent fatality rate = mean fatality rate × (1 + value of Atkinson Index)
Source Own calculations from GTD

5.7 Conclusions

This chapter provided a quantitative analysis of fatalities resulting from terrorist activities in India's three main conflict zones: Jammu & Kashmir, the Red Corridor, and the Northeast. Using data from the Global Terrorism Database (GTD), it examined trends in terrorist and non-terrorist deaths, the effectiveness of government responses as measured by the "kill-ratio", and the inequality in the distribution of fatalities across incidents.

The chapter's first contribution was to use the "kill-ratio", defined as the number of terrorists killed per hundred non-terrorist deaths, as an indicator of government's effectiveness against terrorism. A higher kill-ratio is interpreted as greater government effectiveness because it signifies a higher relative cost to terrorists for their activities. It suggests that the government is more effective in neutralising terrorists while minimising civilian casualties. Indeed, as was explained earlier in this chapter, the kill-ratio may be interpreted as the price that society pays for terrorist activities in terms of non-terrorist deaths: the lower the kill-ratio, the higher the price.

In this context, the kill-ratio was almost twice as high under the BJP regime compared to the Congress regime in both J&K and the Red Corridor: this suggested that counterterrorism was more effective during the BJP's, compared to the Congress', tenure. However, in the Northeast, the kill-ratio was slightly lower under the BJP regime.

The use of metrics like the kill-ratio in war or conflict has historical precedents, although the interpretation and value placed on such metrics have varied significantly. In the Vietnam War, the "body count" was a widely used for measuring effectiveness. In the First World War, the concept of attrition warfare was central to the strategies employed on the Western Front. The goal was to gradually wear down the enemy's forces through sustained casualties with the battles of Verdun and the Somme being prime examples of this approach. In the Second World War, the US military often focused on inflicting maximum casualties on Japanese forces, even at the cost of prolonging battles. This was partly due to the perceived fanaticism of Japanese soldiers and the belief that they would not surrender easily. It is arguable that the same fanaticism is evidenced in the jihadist terrorists in J&K and the Maoist guerrillas in the Red Corridor.

The chapter's second contribution was to employ a novel decomposition method to analyse the contribution of sub-regional kill-ratios to the *overall* kill-ratio. This analysis suggested that, apart from the kill-ratios in the sub-regions, this contribution depended on the position of a sub-region *relative* to other sub-regions in terms of the number of incidents and the lethality of incidents. This analysis could then quantify, for each sub-region, the contribution of each of these factors to the overall kill-ratio. For instance, it showed that the contribution of Srinagar district to the overall kill-ratio in J&K decreased significantly under the BJP regime, while the contributions of Kupwara and Pulwama districts increased.

The third contribution of this chapter was to use the Gini coefficient to highlight differences in the distribution of deaths resulting from armed assaults and bombings across the three regions. The Red Corridor consistently exhibited the highest inequality in the distribution of deaths, while J&K showed the lowest.

Lastly, the chapter developed the concept of the *Equally Distributed Equivalent Fatality Rate*. This incorporated society's aversion to inequality in the distribution of fatalities across incidents and led it to shun terrorist incidents which caused a large number of fatalities. This measure allowed one to quantify the social loss from terrorism, considering both the average number of deaths and the inter-incident distribution of deaths.

Taken together, the analysis in this chapter offers insights into the dynamics of terrorist-related fatalities in India which can lead to the development of more effective and targeted counter-terrorism strategies. By understanding the factors that influence the kill-ratio, the contributions of different sub-regions, and the social loss associated with different patterns of fatalities, policymakers can better allocate resources and tailor interventions to mitigate the human cost of terrorism. Future research could explore the underlying causes of the observed trends and assess the long-term impact of counter-terrorism measures on reducing fatalities and promoting stability in the affected regions.

References

Anand, S., & Sen, A. (1997). *Concepts of Human Development and Poverty: A Multidimensional Perspective*. Human Development Report 1997 Papers, New York, UNDP

Atkinson, A. B. (1970). On the Measurement of Inequality. *Journal of Economic Theory, 2*, 244–263.

Borooah, V. K., & Lee, K. C. (1988). The Effect of Changes in Britain's Industrial Structure on Female Relative Pay and Employment. *Economic Journal, 98*, 818–832.

Borooah, V. K. (2002). A Duration Sensitive Measure of the Unemployment Rate: Theory and Application. *Labour, 16*: 453–468.

Hultman, L. (2007). 'Battle Losses and Rebel Violence: Raising the Costs for Fighting.' *Terrorism and Political Violence, 19*, 205–222.

Global Terrorism Database. (2019). *Codebook: Inclusion Criteria and Variables*. University of Maryland.

Global Terrorism Index. (2024). *Measuring the Impact of Terrorism*. Institute for Economics and Peace.

Lafree, G., & Dugan, L. (2007). Introducing the Global Terrorism Database. *Terrorism and Political Violence, 19*, 181–204.

Lafree, G., Dugan, L., & Miller, E. (2015). *Putting Terrorism in Context: Lessons from the global terrorism database*. Routledge.

Piazza, J. A. (2009). 'Is Islamist Terrorism More Dangerous? An Empirical Study of Group Ideology Organization, and Goal Structure.' *Terrorism and Political Violence, 21*, 62–88.

Vorsina, M., Manning, M., Flemming, C. M., Ambrey, C. L., & Smith, C. (2017). The Welfare Cost of Terrorism. *Terrorism and Political Violence, 29*, 1066–1086.

CHAPTER 6

The Likelihood of Terrorist Attacks Being Successful

6.1 Introduction

Using data from the University of Maryland's Global Terrorism Database (GTD),[1] the previous chapter examined terrorist incidents in the three main regions of terrorist activity in India—J&K, the Red Corridor, and the Northeast—from the perspective of fatalities arising from such incidents. In this context it proposed a measure for judging the effectiveness of government action against terrorists. This was the "kill-ratio"—the number of terrorists killed as a ratio of the number of non-terrorist deaths caused by terrorists and the higher this ratio the greater the effectiveness of government in fighting terrorism.

Within the context of the GTD, this chapter turns to a different aspect of terrorism, namely the likelihood that terrorist attacks would be "successful".[2] Since the GTD was described in Chapter 1, a summary here will suffice. The GTD contains an event-by-event record of all known terrorist incidents in the world from 1970 till June 2021, with ancillary information about the nature of these incidents: *inter alia* the country, and the country sub-region, in which the incident occurred; the terrorist group involved; the intended target; the weapons used in the incident; and the

[1] See Lafree and Dugan (2007) and Lafree et al. (2015).

[2] The terms "probability" and "likelihood" are used interchangeably in this paper.

V. K. Borooah, *The Political Economy of Terrorism*,
https://doi.org/10.1007/978-3-032-08553-5_6

casualties (if any) that resulted from the incident in terms of deaths of the perpetrators, security personnel, and civilians.[3]

A particular feature of the GTD is defining whether a particular terrorist incident was, from the point of view of the terrorists a "success". As the Global Terrorism Database (2019) explains[4]:

> The definition of a successful attack depends on the type of attack. Essentially, the key question is whether the attack type took place. If a case has multiple attack types, it is successful if *any* [emphasis added] of the attack types are successful, except for assassinations, which are only successful if the intended target is killed. The success of a terrorist strike is defined according to the tangible effects of the attack. Success is *not* judged in terms of the larger goals of the perpetrators. For example, a bomb that exploded in a building would be counted as a success even if it failed in bringing the building down or inducing government repression. (pp. 26–27)

This variable, termed *success*, indicated whether, *from the perspective of the terrorists*, the incident had been successful *(success=1)* or unsuccessful *(success=0)*. As the GTD makes clear, "the success of a terrorist attack is defined according to the tangible effects of the attack and not in terms of the larger goal of the perpetrators". An incident involving multiple attack types (firearms, explosives, etc.) would be regarded as a "success" if any of

[3] To be considered a "terrorist incident" by the GTD, the event had to have been committed by non-state actors, had to have been violent, and intentional. In addition, the act must have met two of the following three criteria: (i) it must have been aimed at attaining a political, economic, religious, or social goal. In terms of economic goals, the exclusive pursuit of profit did not satisfy this criterion; (ii) there must have been evidence of an intention to coerce, intimidate, or convey some other message to a larger audience (or audiences) than the immediate victims; and (iii) the action must have been outside the context of legitimate warfare activities, i.e. the act must have been outside the parameters permitted by international humanitarian law and, particularly, the admonition against deliberately targeting civilians or non-combatants (Global Terrorism Database, 2019).

[4] See also Lafree and Dugan (2007) and Lafree et al.(2015).

the attack types were successful".[5] A quantitative analysis of the "success" of terrorist incidents in India is the subject of this chapter.

In pursuit of this, the chapter uses the following statistical methods:

1. Logit Model: This is a statistical model that predicts the probability of a binary outcome (in this case, whether a terrorist incident was successful or not). The logit model is used to analyse the relationship between the success of terrorist incidents and various political and non-political factors. This method is used in conjunction with statistical testing using z-values which are used to determine if the difference in synthetic probabilities between different scenarios (e.g. Congress vs. BJP) was statistically significant.
2. Method of Recycled Proportions and Synthetic Probabilities: This method is used to isolate the effect of specific variables (like the party in power) on the probability of terrorist incidents being successful. It involves creating hypothetical scenarios where all incidents occurred under one condition (e.g. all incidents occurred under a Congress government) and then comparing the predicted probabilities with scenarios where all incidents occurred under a different condition (e.g. all incidents occurred under a BJP government).

6.2 The Success Rate of Terrorists by Area of Activity, Type of Attack, and Nature of Target

Table 6.1 shows, for J&K, the success and failure of terrorist activities in terms of district and Table 6.2 does the same in terms of its two broad regions, Jammu and Kashmir. Over the period of a Congress government in New Delhi (2004–2013), there were a total of 535 terrorist incidents in J&K in its entirety of which 59 were "unsuccessful" and 476 were "successful", yielding a success rate of 89%. Similarly, over the period of BJP government in New Delhi for which data was available (2014—(June)

[5] Global Terrorism Database, *Codebook: Inclusion Criteria and Variables* 26–27. For example, a bomb that explodes would be counted as a success even if it did not hit the intended target. An armed assault is successful if the attack occurs and a target is hit (people and/or property). A hijacking is successful if the hijackers obtain control of the vehicle. Hostage taking is successful if, at any point, the terrorists take control of individuals. An attack on infrastructure is successful if the facility is damaged. An unarmed assault is successful if there is a victim who has been injured.

2021), there were a total of 1538 terrorist incidents in J&K of which 379 were "unsuccessful" and 1159 were "successful", yielding a *lower* success rate of 75.4%.

The sample sizes for the districts were small but, in the 2004–2013 period, Anantnag (39 incidents, 32 successes) had a success rate of 82.1% while Srinagar (131 incidents, 120 successes) and Baramulla (89 incidents, 84 successes) had success rates of, respectively, 91.6% and 94.4%. During the 2014–(June) 2021 period, the success rate in Srinagar fell to 75.3% (186 incidents, 140 successes) and the success rate in Baramulla fell to 78.3% (180 incidents, 141 successes). In terms of J&K's broad regions, the success rate in the Jammu and Kashmir regions was both lower in the 2014–(June) 2021 than in the 2004–2013 period (Jammu: 69.9% versus 86.2%; Kashmir: 89.8% versus 75.4%).

Tables 6.3 and 6.4 show the success and failure rates of terrorist activities in terms of states for, respectively, the Red Corridor and the Northeast. The overall success rate for the Red Corridor (Table 6.3) was 93.6% during the 2004–2013 period (1885 incidents, 121 failures, 1764 successes) and this fell to 79.9% during the 2014–(June) 2021 period (2014 incidents, 405 failures, 1609 successes). The success rate, between the two periods, fell in all the Red Corridor states but the falls were largest in Bihar (from 96% to 78.5%) and in Jharkhand (from 90.3% to 77.3%).

The largest number of incidents in the states of the Northeast occurred in Assam and in Manipur. The success rates rates in Assam and Manipur during 2004–2013 were, respectively, 84.6% and 73.6%. During the 2014–(June) 2021 period, the success rate in Assam fell to 73% while that in Manipur remained virtually unchanged at 74%.

The fact that the success rate of terrorist activities was lower in the "BJP" period than in the earlier "Congress" period cannot be taken as evidence of the BJP's greater effectiveness in combatting terrorism. This is because the success of terrorist incidents, quite apart from the political climate under which they occurred, would also depend upon the type of target chosen and the mode of attack. It could be that the "mix" of targets and weaponry differed between the political regimes and this in part, or in whole, was responsible for the BJP appearing to do better than the Congress. To arrive at a considered view about inter-party differences in effectiveness against terrorist attacks, one must "control" for these non-political factors.

The GTD distinguished between four separate targets: private sector targets (persons, private property, businesses); government personnel and

Table 6.1 Success and failure of terrorist incidents by district in Jammu & Kashmir

	Congress Government in New Delhi: 2004–2013																				
	AN	*BN*	*BA*	*BU*	*DO*	*GA*	*JM*	*KA*	*KI*	*KL*	*KP*	*PN*	*PU*	*RJ*	*RA*	*RE*	*SA*	*SH*	*SR*	*UD*	*Total*
Total number of incidents	39	10	89	20	35	12	11	3	13	14	31	16	51	16	8	5	7	15	131	9	535
Total number of failed incidents	7	1	5	2	5	1	2	1	0	2	3	3	7	2	1	0	2	3	11	1	59
Total number of successful incidents	32	9	84	18	30	11	9	2	13	12	28	13	44	14	7	5	5	12	120	8	476
Success rate	82.1	90.0	94.4	90.0	85.7	91.7	81.8	66.7	100.0	85.7	90.3	81.3	86.3	87.5	87.5	100.0	71.4	80.0	91.6	88.9	89.0
	BJP Government in New Delhi: 2014-(June) 2021																				
	AN	*BN*	*BA*	*BU*	*DO*	*GA*	*JM*	*KA*	*KI*	*KL*	*KP*	*PN*	*PU*	*RJ*	*RA*	*RE*	*SA*	*SH*	*SR*	*UD*	*Total*
Total number of incidents	188	39	180	80	9	23	34	5	11	100	87	54	329	25	6	2	8	163	186	9	1538
Total number of failed incidents	29	13	39	23	3	8	15	0	2	21	24	13	74	10	0	1	4	53	46	1	379

(continued)

Table 6.1 (continued)

	BJP Government in New Delhi: 2014-(June) 2021																				
	AN	*BN*	*BA*	*BU*	*DO*	*GA*	*JM*	*KA*	*KI*	*KL*	*KP*	*PN*	*PU*	*RJ*	*RA*	*RE*	*SA*	*SH*	*SR*	*UD*	*Total*
Total number of successful incidents	159	26	141	57	6	15	19	5	9	79	63	41	255	15	6	1	4	110	140	8	1159
Success rate (%)	84.6	66.7	78.3	71.3	66.7	65.2	55.9	100.0	81.8	79.0	72.4	75.9	77.5	60.0	100.0	50.0	50.0	67.5	75.3	88.9	75.4

AN=Anantnag; BN=Bandipore; BA=Baramulla; BU=Budgam; DO=Doda; GA= Ganderbal; JM=Jammu; KA=Kathua; KI=Kishtwar; KL=Kulgam; KP=Kupwara; PN=Poonch; PU=Pulwama

RJ=Rajouri; RA=Ramban; RE=Reasi; SA=Samba; SH=Shopian; Sr=Srinagar; UD=Udhampur

Source Own calculations from GTD

Table 6.2 Success and failure of terrorist incidents by regions of Jammu & Kashmir

	Congress Government in New Delhi: 2004–2013		*Total*
	Jammu	*Kashmir*	
Total number of incidents	123	412	535
Total number of failed incidents	17	42	59
Total number of successful incidents	106	370	476
Success rate	86.2	89.8	89.0
	BJP Government in New Delhi: 2014–(June) 2021		
	Jammu	*Kashmir*	
Total number of incidents	163	1375	1538
Total number of failed incidents	49	330	379
Total number of successful incidents	114	1045	1159
Success rate (%)	69.9	76.0	75.4

The Jammu Region comprised the following districts: Doda; Jammu; Kathua; Kishtwar; Poonch; Rajouri; Ramban; Reasi; Samba; and Udhampur
The Kashmir Region comprised the following districts: Anantnag; Bandipore; Baramulla; Budgam; Ganderbal; Kulgam; Kupwara; Pulwama; Shopian; and Srinagar
Source Own calculations from GTD

buildings; police personnel and property; and military personnel and property. The first could, plausibly, be seen as a "soft" target and the last two as "hard" targets. It also distinguished between various modes of attack of which the most used were firearms and explosives: attacks using firearms and explosives accounted for, respectively, 32% and 45% of terrorist incidents in the three regions under study for the period 2004–(June) 2021.

Table 6.5 shows the success rate of terrorist attacks, in respect of their modes of attack and chosen targets, for J&K, the Red Corridor, and the Northeast with the success rate in each region subdivided according to whether it occurred during 2004–2013 or during 2014–(June) 2021. Three features of the data presented in the table stand out. First, the success rate when the attack used explosives (79.2% for all three regions combined) was generally lower than when it used firearms (93.5%). This is

Table 6.3 Success and failure of terrorist incidents by states of the Red Corridor

	Congress Government in New Delhi: 2004–2013							
	Andhra Pradesh	*Bihar*	*Chhattisgarh*	*Jharkhand*	*Orissa*	*Telangana*[a]	*West Bengal*	*Total*
Total number of incidents	75	329	356	445	366		314	1885
Total number of failed incidents	3	13	37	43	19		6	121
Total number of successful incidents	72	316	319	402	347		308	1764
Success rate (%)	96.0	96.0	89.6	90.3	94.8		98.1	93.6
	BJP Government in New Delhi: 2014–(June) 2021							
	Andhra Pradesh	*Bihar*	*Chhattisgarh*	*Jharkhand*	*Orissa*	*Telangana*	*West Bengal*	*Total*
Total number of incidents	78	205	896	506	261	55	13	2014
Total number of failed incidents	6	44	177	115	37	17	9	405
Total number of successful incidents	72	161	719	391	224	38	4	1609
Success rate (%)	92.3	78.5	80.2	77.3	85.8	69.1	30.8	79.9

Source Own calculations from GTD

[a]Telangana was formed on 2 June 2014

Table 6.4 Success and failure of terrorist incidents by states of the northeast

	Congress Government in New Delhi: 2004–2013							
	Arunachal Pradesh	*Assam*	*Manipur*	*Meghalaya*	*Mizoram*	*Nagaland*	*Tripura*	*Total*
Total number of incidents	3	586	556	120	5	50	33	1353
Total number of failed incidents	0	90	147	16	0	1	3	257
Total number of successful incidents	3	496	409	104	5	49	30	1096
Success rate (%)	100.0	84.6	73.6	86.7	100.0	98.0	90.9	81.0
	BJP Government in New Delhi: 2014–(June) 2021							
	Arunachal Pradesh	**Assam**	**Manipur**	**Meghalaya**	**Mizoram**	Nagaland	**Tripura**	**Total**
Total number of incidents	26	307	565	189	14	65	17	1183
Total number of failed incidents	3	83	147	31	4	18	3	289
Total number of successful incidents	23	224	418	158	10	47	14	894
Success rate (%)	88.5	73.0	74.0	83.6	71.4	72.3	82.4	75.6

Source Own calculations from GTD

not surprising—the expertise required to handle explosives is considerably greater than that required to load and fire a gun and is more likely to be in relatively short supply. Second, the success rate when the targets were private persons and their property (93.2% for all three regions combined) was higher than when the target was government (83.1%) or the military (86.6%).

6.3 Explaining the Likelihood of Terrorist Attacks Succeeding

This section analyses the probability of a terrorist attack "succeeding"—where the success of an attack was defined in the preceding section—taking into account both political and non-political factors.[6] The dependent variable Y, defined over the N incidents that occurred in the period 2004–(June) 2021, was assigned the value $Y_i = 1$ if, according to the GTD, incident i $(i = 1,...,N)$, was successful and $Y_i = 0$ if it was not. It was hypothesised that, in each terrorist region—J&K, the Red Corridor, the Northeast—Y was a function of *five* determining variables. These were: (i) the *party in government in New Delhi*; (ii) the *sub-regions* within the three conflict regions][7]; (iii) the main *terrorist groups* within the regions; (iv) the *targets*: private citizens and property, business, government, police, military; and (v) the main *weapon type* used: firearms or explosives.

The *party in government* variable reflects the commitment of the two parties to combatting terrorism. The *sub-regional* variable reflected the commitment of the local administration to fighting terrorism, the landscape in which the terrorists operated—both its physical features in terms of hills, forests, etc., and its psychological features in terms of support from the local population, all of which, collectively, aided or hindered an operation's success. *Terrorist groups* differed in the quality of their "equipment" where this might have been physical (quality of weapons and training, the size and quality of the support group) and psychological (ruthlessness, commitment, preparedness to die).[8] It is, therefore, possible that the fatalities resulting from a particular attack type (say, armed assault) might be different if it was carried out by an Islamic group

[6] The terms "probability" and "likelihood" are used interchangeably in this paper.

[7] For J&K these were the Jammu and Kashmir sub-regions; for the Red Corridor, it was the states within which the corridor lay, and for the Northeast it was the two main states which were affected by conflict, Assam and Manipur.

[8] They differ also in the quality of the opposition that they face: dealing with the might of the Indian army and Indian paramilitary forces in Kashmir would be a different proposition from dealing with the district police in Bihar and Andhra Pradesh.

Table 6.5 Success and failure of terrorist incidents by weapon and target of attack

	Congress: 2004–2013				*BJP: 2014–(June) 2021*			
	J&K	*Red Corridor*	*Northeast*	*Total*	*J&K*	*Red Corridor*	*Northeast*	*Total*
Weapon: Firearms								
Total number of incidents	235	696	391	1322	696	558	354	1608
Total number of successful incidents	214	664	359	1237	508	508	296	1312
Success rate (%)	91.1	95.4	91.8	93.5	73.0	91.0	83.6	81.5
Weapon: Explosives								
Total number of incidents	258	593	776	1627	626	853	631	2110
Total number of successful incidents	221	509	559	1289	473	511	418	1402
Success rate (%)	85.7	85.8	72.0	79.2	75.6	59.9	66.2	66.4
Target: Private Persons & Property & Business								
Total number of incidents	152	683	576	1411	298	816	510	1624
Total number of successful incidents	141	672	502	1315	259	801	451	1511
Success rate (%)	92.7	98.4	87.2	93.2	86.9	98.2	88.4	93.0
Target: Government								
Total number of incidents	86	316	227	629	133	163	149	445
Total number of successful incidents	69	296	158	523	105	137	102	344

(continued)

Table 6.5 (continued)

	Congress: 2004–2013				*BJP: 2014–(June) 2021*			
	J&K	*Red Corridor*	*Northeast*	*Total*	*J&K*	*Red Corridor*	*Northeast*	*Total*
Success rate (%)	80.2	93.7	69.6	83.1	78.9	84.0	68.4	77.3
Target: Police								
Total number of incidents	154	412	140	706	638	471	85	1194
Total number of successful incidents	145	363	121	629	520	367	62	949
Success rate (%)	94.2	88.1	86.4	89.1	81.5	77.9	72.9	79.5
Target: Military								
Total number of incidents	77	41	99	217	273	159	154	586
Total number of successful incidents	71	32	85	188	182	85	132	399
Success rate (%)	92.2	78.0	85.8	86.6	66.7	53.5	85.7	68.1

9*Source* Own calculations from GTD

in J&K compared to a "liberation" group in the Northeast. To account for this, the equation was estimated allowing the coefficients on the bombing and armed assault terms to vary by terrorist group.[9] The nature of the *target* reflects the ease with which assaults can be carried out—attacks on "soft" targets like private persons and businesses were more likely to be successful than attacks on "hard" targets like the government, police, and the military.

[9] For J&K, these were Hizbul Mujahideen, Jaish-e-Mohammad, and Lashkar-e-Taiba. For the Red Corridor, these were, Communist Party of India—Maoist (CPI (Maoist)) and the Maoists; for the Northeast, these were United Liberation Front of Assam (ULFA), the National Socialist Council of Nagaland (Khaplang and Isak Muivah factions), National Democratic Front of Bodoland (NDFB), and the United National Liberation Front (UNLF).

Given the binary nature of the dependent variable ("success" or "failure"), the estimated equation was formulated as a logit model. If $Pr[Y_i=1]$ and $Pr[Y_i=0]$ represent, respectively, the probabilities of a terrorist incident being successful or a failure, the logit formulation expresses the log of the odds ratio as a linear function of K variables (indexed $k = 1...K$) which take values, $X_{i1}, X_{i2}...X_{iK}$ with respect to incident i, $i = 1...N$:

$$\log\left(\frac{\Pr[Y_i = 1]}{1 - \Pr[Y_i = 1]}\right) = \sum_{k=1}^{K} \beta_k X_{ik} + u_i = Z_i \qquad (6.1)$$

where β_k is the coefficient associated with variable k, $k=1...K$.

From Eq. (6.1) it follows that:

$$\Pr[Y_i = 1] = \frac{e^{\sum X_{ik}\hat{\beta}_k}}{1 + e^{\sum X_{ik}\hat{\beta}_k}} \qquad (6.2)$$

where the term 'e' in the above equation represents the exponential term.

One of the K variables was a party variable, *BJP*, such that $BJP_i=1$ if the incident i occurred when the BJP was in government (that is, 2014–(June) 2021) and $BJP_i=0$ if the incident i occurred when the Congress was in government (that is, 2004–2013). The novelty about the econometric equation was that each of the non-party variables was made to interact with the variable *BJP* so that the estimated logit model was:

$$\log\left(\frac{\Pr[Y_i = 1]}{1 - \Pr[Y_i = 1]}\right) = \sum_{k=1}^{K} \beta_k X_{ik} + \sum_{k=1}^{K} \alpha_k \times BJP_i + u_i \qquad (6.3)$$

The coefficient associated with variable k in the context of a BJP government (that is, $BJP_i = 1$) was $(\beta_k + \alpha_k)$ while the coefficient associated with the *same* variable for a Congress government (that is, $BJP_i = 0$) was β_k: α_k, thus, represents the "party-in-government" effect associated with variable k. So, for example, if the terrorist sub-region was one of the variables—that is to say, the sub-region in which the incident occurred (for example, Jammu or Kashmir in J&K) influenced the incident's likelihood of being successful, the formulation in Eq. (6.3) suggests that the probability of an incident in Jammu or in Kashmir being successful would depend on whether the BJP or the Congress was the party of government in New Delhi. Testing the null hypothesis $\alpha_k = 0$, in Eq. (6.3), would be a test of whether inter-party differences in the average probability of terrorist success were significantly different with respect to the sub-region represented by the *k*th variable.

6.4 The Method of Recycled Proportions and Synthetic Probabilities

The results in this chapter are presented in terms of the probabilities computed from Eq. (6.3), which is the logit model interacts with the *BJP* variable, using the method of "recycled predictions". This underpins the results presented in this paper.[10] The variable Y_i in Eq. (6.3) is defined over incidents distinguished by different characteristics—by party in government, terrorist region, terrorist group, weapon used, and target. Suppose that one is interested in identifying the probabilities of terrorist incidents being successful which can be *entirely* ascribed to the party in government and, further, to test whether these differ significantly between the two parties—BJP and the Congress. The method of "recycled predictions" enables one to do this.

Using the logit estimates from Eq. (6.3) one can predict for each incident its probability of success. This probability is denoted $\hat{p}_i (i = 1...N)$ and is defined for each of the N incidents. Suppose that M and $N\text{-}M$ of these incidents occurred when, respectively, the BJP and the Congress were in government. The mean of the $\hat{p}_i$ defined over all the N incidents in the estimation sample will be the same as the (estimation) sample proportion of incidents that were successful. Similarly, the mean of the $\hat{p}_i$ defined over the M "under-BJP", and the $N\text{-}M$ "under-Congress", incidents will be the same as the (estimation) sample proportion of incidents that occurred under, respectively, BJP and Congress governments. In other words, the estimated logit equation passes through the sample means.[11]

However, the difference between the two sample means for the BJP ($\hat{p}^{BJP}$) and the Congress ($\hat{p}^{CNG}$) does not reflect the differences between the probabilities of successful incidents under-BJP and under-Congress

[10] As described in Long and Freese (2014) See also https://www.stata.com/manual s13/rmlogitpostestimation.pdf.

[11] It is important to draw a distinction between the *estimation* sample and the *total* sample; because the equation can only be estimated for non-missing values on *all* the variables, the estimation sample will, typically, be smaller than the total sample.

governments *which are due solely to party*. This is because the incidents differ not just in terms of the governments under which they occurred—BJP or Congress—but also with respect to the sub-region in which they occurred, the terrorist groups involved, the weapons used, and the nature of the targets. Comparing the mean probabilities of success under the BJP and Congress governments will reflect all these differences and, hence, differences between $\hat{p}^{BJP}$ and $\hat{p}^{CNG}$ cannot be attributed *solely*—though, of course, some part may be attributable—to differences in party.

The method of "recycled predictions" isolates the *party effect* on the average probability of terrorist incidents being successful. First, "pretend" that *all* N incidents in the estimation sample (2004–2018) occurred under a Congress government. Holding the values of the other variables constant (either to their observed sample values, as in this chapter, or to their mean values), compute the average probability of an incident being a success and denote it $\tilde{p}^{CNG}$. Next, "pretend" that *all* N incidents in the estimation sample happened under a BJP government and, again holding the values of the other variables constant, compute the average probability of an incident being a success and denote it $\tilde{p}^{BJP}$.

Since the values of the non-party variables are unchanged between these two hypothetical scenarios, the only difference between them is that, in the first scenario, the Congress coefficient is "switched on" (with the BJP coefficient "switched off"), while, in the other scenario, the BJP coefficient is "switched on" (with the Congress coefficient "switched off"), for *all* the N incidents in the estimation sample—that this, incidents which took place between 2004 and (June) 2021.[12] Consequently, the difference between $\tilde{p}^{CNG}$ and $\tilde{p}^{BJP}$, in the average probability of an incident being successful, is *entirely* due to differences between the parties when in government.

In essence, therefore, in evaluating the effect of two characteristics A and B on the likelihood of a particular outcome, the method of "recycled proportions" compares two probabilities: first, under an "all have the characteristic A" scenario and then, under an "all have the characteristic B" scenario with the values of the other variables remaining

[12] In operational terms, STATA's margin command will perform these calculations.

unchanged between the two scenarios. The difference in the two probabilities is then entirely due to the attribute represented by A and B (in this case, party-in-government differences).

These probabilities, respectively $\tilde{p}^A$ and $\tilde{p}^B$, are referred to in this paper as the *synthetic probabilities* (SP) of an event under A and B. So, for example, in the earlier exposition, $\tilde{p}^{CNG}$ and $\tilde{p}^{BJP}$ refer to the synthetic probabilities (SP) of incidents being successful under, respectively, Congress and BJP governments; these should be distinguished from $\hat{p}^{CNG}$ and $\hat{p}^{BJP}$ which are average predicted probabilities of incidents being successful under, respectively, Congress and BJP governments.

6.5 Estimation Results for the Synthetic Probabilities of Terrorist Success

Inter-party differences in the SP of terrorist incidents being successful are shown in Table 6.6 for J&K and in Tables 6.7 and 6.8 for, respectively, the Red Corridor, and the Northeast. The second and third columns of these tables show the synthetic probabilities) for, respectively, Congress and BJP governments. The SP against the 'Overall' row and the 'CNG' column in Tables 6.6, 6.7 and 6.8 were computed using the method of "recycled proportions", discussed above. So, for J&K, it was assumed all the 1688 incidents in its estimation sample occurred under a Congress government Table 6.6 shows that this calculation yielded a SP of 91.7% for "Congress-in-government".[13] A similar calculation, but now under the assumption that all 1688 incidents occurred under a BJP government yielded a SP of 79.8% for "BJP-in-government". The difference between the Congress and BJP probabilities for J&K was 11.9 points (Table 6.6: column 4).

Dividing this difference by its standard error (Table 6.6: column 5) yielded a z-value of 6.6: the observed difference of 11.9 points, in the probabilities of an attack being "successful" in J&K under, respectively, Congress and BJP governments, thus was significantly different from

[13] Or, in other words, by the applying the coefficients relevant to the Congress (that is, the β_k of Eq. (6.3)) to *all* the 1688 incidents and computing the average likelihood of incidents being successful.

Table 6.6 Synthetic probabilities of terrorist incidents being successful in J&K: Congress and BJP Governments compared

	Congress: 2004–2013	*BJP: 2014–(June) 2021*	*Difference*	*Standard error*	*z-value*
Overall	0.917	0.798	0.119**	0.018	6.6
J&K Region					
Jammu	0.869	0.851	0.019	0.049	0.4
Kashmir	0.924	0.790	0.133**	0.019	7.0
Target					
Private Persons & Property & Business	0.932	0.897	0.036	0.027	1.3
Government	0.803	0.821	−0.018	0.055	−0.3
Police	0.940	0.798	0.142**	0.026	5.5
Military	0.924	0.637	0.288**	0.042	6.8
Weapon Employed					
Firearms	0.931	0.717	0.213**	0.024	8.9
Explosives	0.905	0.888	0.017	0.024	0.7
Incendiary	0.894	0.749	0.145	0.116	1.2

** Significant at the 5% level; * Significant at the 10% level
The synthetic probabilities shown were computed from a logit model, incorporating interaction effects as set out in Eq. (6.3), estimated on data for 1688 incidents between 2004 and (June) 2021. During this period, the Congress was the party of government 2004–2013 and the BJP from 2014 onwards
Source Own calculations from GTD

zero (superscript ** in Table 6.6).[14] Since the only difference between the all-Congress and the all-BJP scenarios was the party under whose government, the 1688 incidents occurred, one can ascribe the (significant) difference of 11.9 points to inter-party differences in dealing with terrorists.

There were several important differences in the success rates between the two periods in their SP with respect to specific variables. First, although the SP of success in Jammu region was not significantly different between the Congress and BJP regimes, SP of success in the Kashmir region was significantly higher under the Congress (92.4%) compared to the 79% under the BJP. Secondly, the SP of success of attacks against the

[14] Meaning that the likelihood of observing this value, under the null hypothesis of no difference in between the SP of the Congress and the BJP, was less than 5%.

Table 6.7 Synthetic probabilities of terrorist incidents being successful in the Red Corridor: Congress and BJP governments compared

	Congress: 2004–2013	*BJP: 2014–(June) 2021*	*Difference*	*Standard error*	*z-value*
Overall	0.881	0.847	0.034	0.027	1.3
Red Corridor States					
Andhra Pradesh	0.942	0.848	0.094	0.091	1.0
Bihar	0.943	0.799	0.145**	0.049	3.0
Chhattisgarh	0.866	0.922	−0.057	0.026	−2.2
Jharkhand	0.824	0.782	0.041	0.038	1.1
Orissa	0.944	0.906	0.038	0.038	1.0
Telangana			Telangana was formed on 2 June 2014		
West Bengal	0.961	0.523	0.438**	0.197	2.2
Target					
Private Persons & Property & Business	0.957	0.968	−0.011	0.025	−0.4
Government	0.933	0.973	−0.040	0.041	−1.0
Police	0.841	0.789	0.051	0.054	0.9
Military	0.851	0.750	0.102**	0.042	2.4
Weapon Employed					
Firearms	0.912	0.861	0.051*	0.031	1.7
Explosives	0.855	0.834	0.021	0.033	0.7

** Significant at the 5% level; *Significant at the 10% level

The synthetic probabilities shown were computed from a logit mode, incorporating interaction effects as set out in Eq. (6.3), estimated on data for 1828 incidents between 2004 and (June) 2021. During this period, the Congress was the party of government 2004–2013 and the BJP from 2014 onwards

Source Own calculations from GTD

police and the military were both significantly higher under the Congress (94% and 92.4%, respectively) than under the BJP (79.8% and 63.7%, respectively). Thirdly, the SP of success in attacks involving firearms was significantly higher under the Congress (93.1%) compared to that under the BJP (71.7%).

Tables 6.7 and 6.8 perform identical calculations using, respectively, the 1828 incidents in the estimation sample for the Red Corridor and the 507 incidents in the estimation sample for the Northeast. For the Red Corridor, Table 6.7 shows that there was no significant different in the *overall* SP of successful attacks between the Congress (88.1%) and BJP (84.7%) periods. There were, however, significant differences with

Table 6.8 Synthetic probabilities of terrorist incidents being successful in the northeast: Congress and BJP governments compared

	Congress: 2004–2013	*BJP: 2014–(June) 2021*	*Difference*	*Standard error*	*z-value*
Overall	0.921	0.892	0.029	0.027	1.1
Northeast States					
Assam	0.935	0.854	0.082*	0.044	1.9
Manipur	0.907	0.932	−0.025	0.033	−0.8
Target					
Private Persons & Property & Business	0.923	0.932	−0.009	0.030	−0.3
Government	0.837	0.748	0.089	0.110	0.8
Police	0.953	0.811	0.142*	0.083	1.7
Military	0.971	0.941	0.030	0.051	0.6
Weapon Employed					
Firearms	0.961	0.906	0.056*	0.030	1.9
Explosives	0.874	0.875	−0.001	0.046	0.0

** Significant at the 5% level; *Significant at the 10% level
The synthetic probabilities shown were computed from a logit model, incorporating interaction effects as set out in (6.3), estimated on data for 577 incidents between 2004 and (June) 2021. During this period, the Congress was the party of government 2004–2013 and the BJP from 2014 onwards
Source Own calculations from GTD

respect to specific variables. First, the SP of success in Bihar was significantly higher under the Congress than under the BJP (94.3% versus 79.9%) but the SP of success in Chhattisgarh was significantly lower under the Congress than under the BJP (86.6% versus 92.2%). Second, the SP of success in attacks against the military were significantly higher under the Congress (85.1%) compared to that under the BJP (75%). Thirdly, the SP of success in attacks involving firearms was significantly higher, though only at the 10% level of significance, under the Congress (91.2%) compared to that under the BJP (86.1%).

The estimation sample for the Northeast was restricted to the states of Assam and Manipur because of insufficient observations for the other states. While there was no significant difference in the *overall* SP of successful attacks between the Congress (92.1%) and BJP (89.2%) periods, the SP of successful attacks in Assam was significantly higher, though only at the 10% level of significance, under the Congress (93.5%)

compared to that under the BJP (85.4%). On the other hand, the SP of successful attacks in Manipur was *numerically* lower under the Congress than under the BJP (90.7% versus 93.2%) but this difference was not statistically significant.

Echoing the experience of the Red Corridor, the SP of successful attacks against the military in the Northeast was significantly higher, though only at the 10% level of significance, under the Congress (95.3%) compared to that under the BJP (82.0%); the SP of successful attacks using firearms in Assam and Manipur was significantly higher, though only at the 10% level, under the Congress (96.1%) compared to that under the BJP (90.6%).

6.6 The Influence of Non-Party Variables on the Likelihood of Successful Attacks

Tables 6.6, 6.7 and 6.8 focused on differences *between* the Congress and the BJP with respect to each category of determining variable. This section turns to a different theme: differences between the various categories of the determining variables. For example, for each terrorist region, were incidents more likely to succeed in some sub-regions than in others? Against certain targets than others? Using certain weapons than others? Were incidents more likely to succeed when carried out by certain groups than by other groups? This section answers these questions using the methodology of synthetic probabilities (SP), based on the method of recycled proportions discussed earlier.

Between 2004 and (June) 2021, the primary mode of attack in 45% of all terrorist incidents in J&K was firearms and in 43% of all incidents it was explosives. Twenty-two percent of targets were private persons and property and businesses, 11% was government and 39% and 17% of attacks targeted, respectively, the police and the military. Eleven percent of all attacks were by Hizbul Mujahideen, 6% were by Jaish-e-Mohammad, 8% were by Lashkar-e-Taiba, and 75% were by "other groups".[15] Table 6.9 shows the SP of successful terrorist incidents in J&K associated with the non-party variables: the J&K regions (Jammu and Kashmir), the targets of attack, the modes of attack, and the terrorist groups responsible.

[15] For details of these groups, see Bose (2021), Tankel (2014), and Pandya (2024).

Table 6.9 Synthetic probabilities of terrorist incidents being successful in J&K by non-party variables

	Probability	*Marginal probability*	*Standard error*	*z-Value*
Region				
Jammu [R]	0.849			
Kashmir	0.819	−0.030	0.028	−1.1
Terrorist Group				
Hizbul Mujahideen [R]	0.923			
Jaish-e-Mohammed	0.897	−0.026	0.034	−0.8
Lashkar-e-Taiba	0.905	−0.018	0.028	−0.6
Other Groups	0.785	−0.138**	0.021	−6.6
Target				
Private Persons and Property & Business [R]	0.903			
Government	0.811	−0.092**	0.031	−3.0
Police	0.832	−0.071**	0.019	−3.7
Military	0.708	−0.195**	0.027	−7.1
Weapon Employed				
Firearms [R]	0.885			
Explosives	0.765	0.120**	0.019	6.5
Incendiary	0.777	0.108**	0.051	2.1

[R] denotes reference category

** Significant at the 5% level; *Significant at the10% level

The synthetic probabilities shown were computed from a logit mode, incorporating interaction effects, as set out in Eq. (6.3), estimated on data for 1688 incidents in J&K between 2004 and (June) 2021

Source Own calculations from GTD

The column headed "Probability" in Table 6.9 shows the synthetic probabilities (SP) associated with the various categories of variables. So, in terms of region, Table 6.9 shows that the SP of success was 84.9% in Jammu and 81.9% in Kashmir. The column in Table 6.9 headed "Marginal Probability" represents, for each category of variable, the ***difference*** in SP between its reference constituent, denoted by [R], and its other constituents. Dividing these marginal probabilities by their standard errors (shown in the next column) yielded the z-values. These showed whether the marginal probabilities were significantly different from zero at the 5% (superscript ** in Table 6.9) or the 10% (superscript *) level.

So, for example, in Table 6.9, the SP of a successful attack, when the targets were private persons and property, or business—the reference constituent of the category "Target"—was 90.3%. When the target was government, the SP fell to 81.1% or, in other words, the marginal probability was −9.2 points (81.1–90.3). Associated with this was a standard error of 3.1 yielding a z-value of −3.0 which implied that the fall in the SP (the marginal probability) was significantly different from zero.

The salient features of Table 6.9 are that, firstly, the SP of successful terrorist attacks by one of the main terrorist groups in J&K—Hizbul Mujahideen, Jaish-e-Mohammad, Lashkar-e-Taiba—was significantly higher than that for attacks by "other" groups. However, there was no significant difference between these three main groups in their SP of success.

Secondly, the SP of successful attacks against soft targets like private persons, their property, and businesses was significantly higher (90.3%) than that against hard targets like government (81.1%), the police (83.2%), and the military (70.8%). The SP of successful attacks against the military was significantly lower than for attacks against the government or the police but, between government and the police, there was no significant difference in the SP of successful attacks against them.

Thirdly, the SP of attacks using firearms (88.5%) was significantly higher than for attacks using explosives (76.5%) or incendiary devices (77.7%) but there was no significant difference in the SP of successful attacks using the latter two modes. Lastly, there was no significant difference between Jammu and Kashmir regions in the SP of a successful attack.

Table 6.10 reproduces the above analysis for the Red Corridor. Between 2004 and (June) 2021, the primary mode of attack in 32% of all terrorist incidents in the Red Corridor was firearms and in 37% of all incidents it was explosives. Thirty-nine percent of targets in the Red Corridor were private persons and property and businesses, 12% targeted government and 23% and 5% of attacks were on, respectively, the police and the military. Fifty-one percent of all attacks in the Red Corridor were by the Communist Party of India Maoist (CPI-Maoist-Maoist) and 44% were by Maoists.[16] Table 6.10 shows the SP of successful terrorist incidents in the Red Corridor associated with the non-party variables: the states which

[16] For details of these groups see Pandita (2011).

encompassed the Red Corridor, the targets of attack, the modes of attack, and the terrorist groups responsible.

The salient features of Table 6.10 are that, firstly, the SP of successful terrorist attacks by the identified terrorist groups in the Red Corridor—Communist Party of India Maoist and Maoists—was significantly higher than that for attacks by "other" groups. However, there was no significant difference between these the first two groups in their SP of success.

Table 6.10 Synthetic probabilities of terrorist incidents being successful in the Red Corridor by non-party variables

	Probability	*Marginal Probability*	*Standard Error*	*z-Value*
State				
Andhra Pradesh [R]	0.854			
Bihar	0.824	−0.030	0.058	−0.5
Chhattisgarh	0.883	0.029	0.054	0.5
Jharkhand	0.754	−0.100*	0.055	−1.8
Orissa	0.869	0.015	0.057	0.3
West Benga	0.684	−0.169*	0.103	−1.6
Terrorist Group				
Communist Party of India (CPI-Maoist)[R]	0.914			
Maoists	0.939	0.025	0.029	0.8
Other Groups	0.812	−0.102**	0.017	−6.1
Target				
Private Persons and Property & Business [R]	0.971			
Government	0.847	−0.124**	0.023	−5.5
Police	0.825	−0.146**	0.016	−9.2
Military	0.689	−0.282**	0.033	−8.5
Weapon Employed				
Firearms [R]	0.886			
Explosives	0.841	−0.045**	0.016	−2.9

[R] denotes reference category.

** Significant at the 5% level; *Significant at the10% level

Note that Telangana was only formed on 2 June 2014

The synthetic probabilities shown were computed from a logit model, incorporating interaction effects, as set out in Eq. (6.3), estimated on data for 2020 incidents in the states of the Red Corridor between 2004 and (June) 2021

Source Own Calculations from GTD

Secondly, the SP of successful attacks against soft targets like private persons, their property, and businesses was significantly higher (97.1%) than that against hard targets like government (84.7%), the police (82.5%), and the military (68.9%). The SP of successful attacks against the military was significantly lower than for attacks against the government or the police but, between government and the police, there was no significant difference in the SP of successful attacks against them.

Thirdly, the SP of successful attacks using firearms (88.6%) was significantly higher than for attacks using explosives (84.1%). Lastly, in Jharkhand and in West Bengal the SP of a successful attack was significantly lower, though only at a 10% level, than in the other states.

Table 6.11 reproduces the above analysis for the states of Assam and Manipur in the Northeast. Between 2004 and (June) 2021, the primary mode of attack in 27% of all terrorist incidents in Assam and Manipur was firearms and in 58% of all incidents it was explosives. Forty-three percent of targets in these two states were private persons and property and businesses, 15% targeted government and 8% and 11% of attacks were on, respectively, the police and the military. Twenty-eight percent of all attacks in Assam and Manipur were by the United Liberation Front of Assam (ULFA), 13% were by the National Socialist Council of Nagaland (Khaplang and Muivah factions), 12% were by the National Democratic Front of Bodoland, 4% were by the United National Liberation Front, and 43% were by other groups.[17]

Table 6.11 shows the SP of successful terrorist incidents in the Northeast associated with the non-party variables: the states of Assam and Manipur, the targets of attack, the modes of attack, and the terrorist groups responsible.

Firstly, the SP of successful terrorist attacks by the identified terrorist groups in Assam and Manipur—the United Liberation Front of Assam (ULFA), the National Socialist Council of Nagaland (Khaplang and Muivah factions), the National Democratic Front of Bodoland (NDFB), and the United National Liberation Front (UNLF) —was significantly higher than that for attacks by "other" groups. There was, however, no significant difference between the four identified groups in their SP of success.

[17] For details see Saikia (2021).

Table 6.11 Synthetic probabilities of terrorist incidents being successful in the northeast (Assam and Manipur) by non-party variables

	Probability	*Marginal probability*	*Standard error*	*z-Value*
State				
Assam [R]	0.9			
Manipur	0.915	0.016	0.034	0.5
Terrorist Group				
United Liberation Front of Assam)	0.964			
National Socialist Council of Nagaland (Khaplang and Muivah factions)	0.908	−0.056	0.047	−1.2
National Democratic Front of Bodoland (NDFB)	0.932	−0.032	0.033	−1.0
United National Liberation Front (UNLF)	0.922	−0.042	0.060	−0.7
Other Groups	0.859	−0.105	0.035	−3.0
Target				
Private Persons and Property & Business [R]	0.930			
Government	0.807	−0.123	0.051	−2.4
Police	0.898	−0.032	0.038	−0.8
Military	0.960	0.031	0.028	1.1
Weapon Employed				
Firearms [R]	0.943			
Explosives	0.883	−0.060	0.026	−2.3

[R] denotes reference category
** Significant at the 5% level; *Significant at the10% level
The synthetic probabilities shown were computed from a logit model, incorporating interaction effects, as set out in Eq. (6.3), estimated on data for 577 incidents in the states of Assam and Manipur between 2004 and (June) 2021
Source Own Calculations from GTD

Secondly, the SP of successful attacks against soft targets like private persons, their property, and businesses was significantly higher (93.0%) than against government (80.7%), but it was not significantly different from attacks against the police (89.8%), and the military (96%%). There was, however, no significant difference between the police and the military in the SP of successful attacks against them.

Thirdly, the SP of successful attacks using firearms (94.3%) was significantly higher than for attacks using explosives (88.3%). Lastly in terms of state, there was no significant difference between Assam and Manipur in their, respective, SP of successful attacks.

6.7 Conclusions

This chapter explored the likelihood of terrorist incidents being successful in India, focusing on three key regions in India in which terrorist incidents are rife: Jammu & Kashmir, the Red Corridor, and the Northeast. By analysing data from the Global Terrorism Database (GTD) and employing the method of recycled proportions and synthetic probabilities, the chapter provided several important insights.

First, the observed differences in the overall success rates rates of terrorist attacks between the Congress and BJP governments was examined. While in J&K, the SP of attacks being successful was significantly higher under the Congress, this was not the case for the Red Corridor and the Northeast. Underlying this overall conclusion, were several results relating to specific variables. For instance, the SP of success in attacks against the police and military in J&K, and against the military in the Red Corridor and Northeast, were significantly higher under the Congress. Similarly, the SP of success in attacks involving firearms was also often higher under the Congress.

Secondly, the analysis of non-party variables revealed consistent patterns across the three regions. Attacks targeting soft targets like private persons and businesses were significantly more likely to succeed than those targeting government, police, or military installations. Furthermore, attacks using firearms generally had a higher probability of success compared to those using explosives. The study also found that attacks by identified and known terrorist groups were more likely to succeed than those by other unidentified groups.

These findings highlighted the complex interplay of political and non-political factors affecting the success rate of terrorist activities. While government policies and counter-terrorism strategies undoubtedly played a crucial role in the context of terrorism in India, the likelihood of success was also significantly influenced by the choice of targets, the methods of attack, and the capabilities of terrorist groups. This research embodied in this chapter provides a framework for understanding these dynamics and can inform the development of more effective counter-terrorism measures in India.

References

Bose, S. (2021). *Kashmir at the Crossroads: Inside a 21st Century Conflict*. Yale University Press.

Global Terrorism Database. (2019). *Codebook: Inclusion Criteria and Variables*. University of Maryland.

Lafree, G., & Dugan, L. (2007). Introducing the Global Terrorism Database. *Terrorism and Political Violence, 19*, 181–204.

Lafree, G., Dugan, L., & Miller, E. (2015). *Putting Terrorism in Context: Lessons from the Global Terrorism Database*. Routledge.

Long, J. S., & Freese, J. (2014). *Regression Models for Categorical Dependent Variables using Stata*. Stata Press.

Pandita, R. (2011). *Hello Bastar, The Untold Story of India's Maoist Movement*. Penguin Random House.

Pandya, A. (2024). *Inside the Terrifying World of Jaish-e-Muhammad*, Harper Collins.

Saikia, J. (2021). *Insurgency in Northeast India: Strategic Encirclement & The New Concern*. Centre for Global Security Challenges, University of Leeds.

Tankel, S. (2014). *Storming the World Stage: The Story of Lashkar-e-Taiba*. Oxford University Press.

CHAPTER 7

Summary and Conclusions

This book addressed the issue of terrorism in India in its three main zones of conflict—the state of Jammu and Kashmir; the Red Corridor, which is a swathe of over 100 districts running through Eastern, Central and Southern India; and the Northeast comprising seven states. In addressing this topic, the book, in terms of presentation, comprised two parts.

Part 1, Chapters 2, 3, and 4 introduced the reader to the why of the conflicts: What were the grievances? What were the demands for redress? What was the means for getting redress? What was the official reaction to grievances/demands/methods? These chapters introduced many of the pertinent issues which underpinned unrest in these three regions.

Part 2 of the book (Chapters 5 and 6) was concerned with quantitative analysis in the context of political economy. As discussed in Chapter 1, circumstances in India provided a natural experiment for studying inter party-in-government differences in the effectiveness of dealing with terrorists and terrorism. Between the period 2004 and 2021 (which is the last year for which Global Terrorism Database data are available) India had two successive governments of different ideological make-ups. The United Progressive Alliance, headed by the Congress Party, and led by Prime Minister, Manmohan Singh of the Congress, governed India in the decade between 2004 and 2013. The subsequent general elections of 2014 and 2019 saw the Bhartiya Janata Party

V. K. Borooah, *The Political Economy of Terrorism*,
https://doi.org/10.1007/978-3-032-08553-5_7

(BJP) sweep into power and, since 2014, the BJP, led by Prime Minister Narendra Modi, has been India's party of government.

The two parties are very different in their beliefs and ambitions for India. The contrast was between a socialist-oriented and secular Congress which, at least in rhetoric, subscribed to the non-violent beliefs of its principal founder, Mahatma Gandhi, and the free-market oriented BJP, with substantial support from India's leading business houses. In contrast to the Congress' secularism, the BJP viewed India as a Hindu country, rooted in the Hindu religion. Therefore, the traditions, beliefs and practices of Hindus should take primacy over those of other religions and, particularly, over those of India's largest religious minority, Muslims.

These differences in attitudes were reflected in the way the two parties approached the protagonists in the three areas of terrorist activity. The mostly upper-caste, often foreign-educated, and generally left-wing members of the Congress party were sympathetic to Muslims, defending their laws, their customs, and their way of life. In the name of secularism, Indian history textbooks under Congress governments exalted the achievements of the 'great Moghuls' and *ipso facto* diminished those of the great Hindu rulers—*inter alia* the Maurya, the Gupta, and the Chola dynasties (Singh, 2025). The Congress Party's pro-Muslim slant carried over to its attitude towards Jammu and Kashmir.

As was pointed out in Chapter 2 of this book, the sentimentalist in Nehru saw Kashmir as his ancestral home—though the earliest recorded ancestor of the Nehru family moved from Kashmir to Delhi in 1716—and the idealist in Nehru saw also in Kashmir an opportunity to both burnish his secularist credentials, and to further his desire to be seen as an international statesman, by "peacefully" incorporating a Muslim majority state into a newly independent India. In this project, the secular and socialist Kashmiri leader assisted Nehru, Sheikh Abdullah, who, until he began harbouring dreams of Kashmiri independence, was Nehru's "friend". This led the Congress government in New Delhi to offer the most favourable terms to the state of Jammu and Kashmir—terms enjoyed by no other princely state which had acceded to India—as the price for it being part of India.

These privileges, which were offered under Article 370 of the Indian constitution, accorded special status to Jammu and Kashmir by allowing it to have its own constitution, with the Indian Parliament needing the state government's consent for all legislation pertaining to the state (except in defence, foreign affairs, finance, and communications). In addition, there was also Article 35A under which only permanent residents of Jammu and Kashmir could hold property and public jobs in the state.

By contrast, the BJP's attitude towards Jammu and Kashmir was business-like and devoid of the romanticism with which the Congress viewed the state. On 5 August 2019, the Government of India revoked Jammu and Kashmir's special status by abrogating Article 370 and Article 35A. This meant the region would follow the same laws as the rest of India and be subject to the Indian Constitution in its entirety, with Indians from other parts of the country free to own property, settle, and work in the state. Following this abrogation, the state was reorganised into two Union Territories: Jammu & Kashmir and Ladakh. This, by itself, was a demotion from the full statehood, with special status, that Jammu and Kashmir had previously enjoyed.

In terms of fighting terrorism, the most important change in Jammu and Kashmir brought about by the BJP was the willingness to fight terrorism by attacking terrorist bases in Pakistan. After the Pulwama attack of 14 February 2019, India responded with airstrikes against Jaish-e-Mohammad's bases in Balakot which is in Pakistan's north-western Khyber Pakhtunkhwa province. After the terrorist attack in Pahalgam on 26 April 2025, in which 26 Indian tourists were killed by The Resistance Front, an affiliate organisation of the Lashkar-e-Taiba, the Indian military launched Operation *Sindoor* which targeted nine different terrorist bases in Pakistan, including the Lashkar-e-Taiba's headquarters in Muridke and Jaish-e-Mohammad's headquarters in Balakot along with training camps in Muzaffarabad (the administrative capital of Pakistan Occupied Kashmir), the Neelum Valley, Kotli, and Rawalakot.

The BJP's muscular response to Pakistan's proxy war was in contrast to the Congress government's response to the Pakistan-trained Islamic militants' attack on Mumbai on 26 November 2008. Then, with Manmohan Singh as the Prime Minister, India never retaliated militarily against Pakistan or against the Lashkar-e-Taiba camps in Pakistan. Instead, it came up with several reasons, detailed in S.S. Menon's, who was India's Foreign Secretary at that time, book , Menon (2016)—to explain away its pacific stance: any military response would have quickly obscured just how outrageous and terrible was the raid on Indian civilians and tourists; an Indian attack on Pakistan would have united Pakistan behind the Pakistan Army; it would have weakened the civilian government in Pakistan, which had just been elected to power; a military response would have imposed costs and set back the progress of the Indian economy.

But a more realistic appraisal of Pakistan, and of Pakistan's army which controls the country, shows just how futile is this policy of "turning the other cheek".[1] Fair (2014), after exhaustively examining Pakistan's archives of its defence literatures, concluded that the Pakistan army's war with India was more ideological than territorial, with Islamist Pakistan's aim being to undermine Hindu India's position in the world. In pursuit of this, it was willing to undergo any number of military defeats. As Zulfikar Ali Bhutto famously declared in 1974, "We will eat grass, even go hungry, but we will have our own [nuclear bomb]". More recently, Pakistan's leading general (now Field Marshal), Asim Munir, speaking in Muzaffarabad on 5 February 2025, vowed that: "Pakistan has already fought three wars for Kashmir, and if ten more wars are required, Pakistan will fight them"; on 17 April 2025, he declared that "we [Pakistanis] are different from the Hindus in every way".[2]

Against this backdrop, those in India and in the international community who feel that the root of hostilities between Pakistan and India is the issue of Kashmir, and that the two nations could live amicably side-by-side if that was resolved, are doomed to disappointment.[3] The Pakistan Army—which, in effect means Pakistan—guards not just Pakistan's external borders but also patrols its ideological territory (Fair, 2014). This ideology is Islam and the war against "Hindu" India is akin to *jihad*. It goes beyond Kashmir. It pursues the broader revisionist aim of, at the minimum, restoring Muslim-Hindu parity on the sub-continent. From Pakistan's perspective, its relationship with India is a zero-sum game: every Indian gain, is Pakistan's loss and vice-versa.

Congress and BJP attitudes towards insurgency in the Red Corridor and in the Northeast were also quite different. In 2005, in response to left-wing terrorism in the district of Bastar in Chhattisgarh, the Congress government established the para-military organisation *Salwa Judum* whose purpose was to conscript villagers by moving entire villages to what were essentially detention camps, and to engage in warfare with left-wing extremists (Ramasubbu, 2008). After the catalogue of human rights abuses engendered by the *Salwa Judum* became too grave to be

[1] A joke which bears repeating is that most countries have an army, but it is only in Pakistan where the army has a country.

[2] Farhat Javed, "Pakistan army chief's Kashmir remarks cause anger in India. " *BBC*, 30 April 2025. https://www.bbc.co.uk/news/articles/c39j3p14mg4o.

[3] For example, Rubin and Ahmed (2008).

ignored, the Indian Supreme Court declared the organisation to be illegal and ordered its immediate disarming.

By contrast, the BJP's attitude towards left-wing terrorism was effective but shorn of the human-rights abuses of the Congress. The BJP administration markedly increased the deployment of security forces in Maoist-affected regions, particularly in Chhattisgarh, Jharkhand, and Orissa and created specialised task forces within the paramilitary and state police—detailed in Chapter 3—to specifically address left-wing terrorism. This was allied to investments in modern equipment and technology, including drones and surveillance systems, for combat and intelligence-gathering. All these measures led to a number of successes so that India's Home Ministry was sufficiently confident to proclaim, on 17 May 2025, that the government of India is committed to "completely eliminating Naxalism [left-wing extremism] by 31st March 2026, since Naxalism is seen as the biggest obstacle in the development of remote areas and tribal villages, as it prevents education, healthcare, connectivity, banking, and postal services from reaching these villages" (Government of India, 2025).[4]

In terms of the Northeast, the Congress Party's attitude in the 1950s and 60s towards the Mizos and Nagas was one of neglect laced with cruelty. The Mizos were not taken seriously by the Indian and the Assam governments when they predicted a famine based on the flowering of the bamboo tree (see Chapter 4). Sure enough, when the famine occurred, help was scanty and five percent of the entire Mizo population died of starvation (Dalrymple, 2025).

When, in response to this neglect, the Mizos began an armed insurrection, the egregious village resettlement program, initiated in Nagaland in the 1950s, was extended by the government to the Mizos in the 1960s. This program assumed that all people in an insurgency area were potentially hostile and, for the larger public good, they had to be quarantined in camps with their original villages burnt down (Sundar, 2011). This happened in Nagaland in the 1950s, in Mizoram in the 1960s and was reprised in Chhattisgarh in 2005 showing that, in the intervening half-century, the Congress governments had not learned anything about the inhumanity of this practice. and of the human rights abuses it embodied.

[4] For a list of these successes see Pradeep Bhandari, "Modi-Shah's Unwavering Resolve Against Naxalism is bearing Results," Indian Express 31 May 2025. https://indianexpress.com/article/opinion/columns/modi-shah-naxalism-maoists-10040206/

Since 2004, however, the Congress did not have a significant political presence in the Northeastern states, except in Assam and, to an extent, in Meghalaya. Its political influence in the Northeast was blunted by the rise of identity politics, engendered by concerns about the alleged presence of "outsiders" in territories "belonging" to various ethnic groups. Ethnic and cultural identity became central to the politics of the region. This, in turn, led to the emergence of local political parties—such as, the Asom Gana Parishad (AGP) in Assam and the Nationalist Congress Party (NCP) in Manipur– pandering to the notion of autochthony, that is to the belief that a group of persons "belonged" to an area by virtue of being 'rooted in its soil'.

The conflation of ethnicity with territory, particularly when in large parts of the Northeast it was predicated on resentment about the presence of Muslim "outsiders", was meat and drink to the BJP. It set about extending its reach in the states of the Northeast by making strategic alliances with regional parties and focusing on issues of development, ethnicity, and territorial security. At the BJP's initiative, the Northeast Democratic Alliance (NEDA) was formed in May 2016 as a coalition of non-Congress parties in Northeast India. The result of this alliance was that the BJP was able to enter government as a coalition partner in Arunachal Pradesh, Assam, Manipur, and Nagaland.

The BJP's strategy in the India's Northeast is a lesson in fighting terrorism through astute and agile political and economic policies. In terms of economics, the BJP's "Act East policy " sees the Northeast of India as the gateway to increased trade and contact with South-East Asian countries with a view to counteracting growing Chinese ambitions in this region. The key to this is connectivity and the BJP government has been energetic in pushing for agreements with other countries—Japan, Singapore, Bangladesh—to establish road and air links with the Northeast of India (Yhome, 2015).

The Act East policy introduced infrastructure projects, such as the Agartala-Akhaura Rail Project (the first railroad connecting Northeastern India and Bangladesh) and the Asian Trilateral Highway (a new highway connecting Moreh, India to Thailand via Myanmar). The soon-to-be-launched Bairabi-Sairang railway line links Bairabi on Mizoram's northern border to Sairang near Aizawl, bringing the Indian Railways to the state capital for the first time. Work on the 51.38-km line was completed in June 2025. With that, Aizawl will become the fourth northeastern capital—after Guwahati, Agartala, and Itanagar—to be linked to the

Indian Railways' grid.[5] A consequence of all these infrastructural investments is that terrorists in the Northeast of India are in the process of being defanged.

So, what is the likely course of terrorism in India over the next few years. This author's prognosis, based on the assumption that the BJP continues in government for the next decade, is that both left-wing extremism in the Red Corridor and militant activity in the Northeast will fade away leaving Jammu and Kashmir as the only theatre of serious militancy. (If the Congress and its allies come to power then all predictions are off the table because it is impossible to say what the Nehru-Gandhi dynasts will do).

Jammu and Kashmir poses three problems. The first is the tension that exists between "Hindu" Jammu and "Muslim" Kashmir which could be exacerbated with the BJP in government at the Centre and, possibly, as a coalition partner, in the state. The second problem is the dependence of the residents in the Kashmir valley on tourism—about 7% of the state's GDP emanates from tourism compared to 4.6% for India as a whole and it provides employment (directly or indirectly) to approximately 70,000 people.[6]

This, however, is the sector that is most vulnerable to terrorist activity, a fact known to terrorists aiming to cripple the state's prosperity. After the Pahalgam attack on 26 April 2025, new bookings fell and existing bookings were cancelled resulting in empty rooms in several guest houses and hotels.[7] The third problem is that Pakistan's army regards its proxy war in Jammu and Kashmir, prosecuted through its agents Jaish-e-Mohammad and Lashkar-e-Taiba, as a "holy war", a *jihad* against "Hindu" India. This has led the Indian government to cross international borders and attack terrorist bases in Pakistan. But, therein, lies a further problem.

The *Economist* newspaper reported that five Indian Airforce planes were shot down by the Pakistan Air Force during the post-Pahalgam hostilities because of tactical errors made on the first night of fighting:

[5] https://indianexpress.com/article/long-reads/when-train-comes-aizawl-new-railway-line-hope-hesitation-in-mizoram-10135902/

[6] https://risingkashmir.com/tourism-in-kashmir-A-catalyst-for-economic-growth-and-development/

[7] https://www.reuters.com/world/india/kashmir-prepares-tourism-long-lull-war-cries-ring-loud-2025-05-06/#:~:text=All%20the%20nearly%20370%20hotels,to%20take%20on%20more%20work.%22

India lost some aircraft because its political leadership had ordered its air force not to hit Pakistan's air defences but to only target militant bases.[8] After the loss of aircraft, India changed tactics and attacked Pakistani military bases with missiles that overcame Pakistan's air defences. So, by way of corollary, future hostilities should involve attacks on terrorist *and* on military bases in Pakistan. It will need to be a determined Indian government that would be prepared to do so.

Such future attacks on Pakistani military bases come, however, with a warning. This is that the nature of warfare has changed radically, and, through a use of drones, small countries can hold off much larger and more powerful countries. Ukraine's ability to hold off Russia depends on its ability to produce millions of small, accurate, and cheap drones which are capable of inflicting heavy casualties on Russian forces (Filkins, 2025). In this paradigm, boots on the ground, allied to tanks and heavy artillery are less important than agility in the air which has made the Ukraine-Russia equation less unbalanced than it might have been in the absence of drones. There is no reason Pakistan cannot do the same—either by itself or with the assistance of China—vis-a-vis India. And that is why India must reconfigure its defence systems to consider this possibility so that, when engaging militarily with Pakistan, it treads firmly, decisively, and purposefully. The second change in the nature of warfare is the transformation of open battlefield conflict into "hybrid" warfare. It is the unpredictable and varied nature of assaults embodied in hybrid warfare that makes the West fearful of Russia—not so much because of Russian tanks or Russian infantry but because of the conventional and non-conventional, and ultimately unpredictable, forms of attack (cyber-attacks, kidnappings, naval blockades, strategic alliances) chosen to exploit specific vulnerabilities. Masala (2025) constructs a compelling a scenario for this in his eponymously titled book, *If Russia Wins*. It is not implausible that even now some officers in the Pakistan Army's ISI are dreaming of such a scenario for their own country.

[8] *The Economist*, "How Did Pakistan Shoot Down India's Fighter Jets"? 16 July 2025. https://www.economist.com/asia/2025/07/16/how-did-pakistan-shoot-down-indias-fighter-jets.

References

Dalrymple, S. (2025). *Shattered Lands: Five Partitions and the Making of Modern Asia*. Harper Collins.

Fair, C. C. (2014). *Fighting to the End: The Pakistan Army's Way of War*. Oxford University Press.

Filkins, D. (2025, July 14). The Next War: Is the U.S. Ready for the Future of Combat? *The New Yorker*.

Government of India. (2025). *Breaking the Red Grip: India's Triumph Over Left-Wing Extremism*. Government of India, Press Information Bureau.

Masala, C. (2025). *If Russia Wins: A Scenario*, Atlantic Books: London.

Menon, S. S. (2016). *Choices: Inside the Making of India's Foreign Policy*. Allan Lane.

Ramasubbu, K. (2008). How the Salwa Judum Experiment Went Wrong. Retrieved April 28, 2020, from https://www.livemint.com/Politics/aegTjKka79aqBcS2ZbFrQJ/How-the-Salwa-Judum-experiment-went-wrong.html

Rubin, B. R., & Rashid, A. (2008). From Great Game to Grand Bargain. *Foreign Affairs* (Nov.–Dec.), *87*: 30–44.

Singh, T. (2025, July 20). Time to Get Beyond History Books and Address Problems of Today. *The Indian Express*.

Sundar, N. (2011). Interning Insurgent Populations: The Buried Histories of Indian Democracy. *Economic and Political Weekly, 46*, 47–57.

Yhome, K. (2015). From "Look East" to "Act East": What it Means for India's Northeast. *Eastern Quarterly, 2*, 18–29.

INDEX

V. K. Borooah, *The Political Economy of Terrorism*,
https://doi.org/10.1007/978-3-032-08553-5

N

GPSR Compliance

The European Union's (EU) General Product Safety Regulation (GPSR) is a set of rules that requires consumer products to be safe and our obligations to ensure this.

If you have any concerns about our products, you can contact us on ProductSafety@springernature.com

In case Publisher is established outside the EU, the EU authorized representative is:

Springer Nature Customer Service Center GmbH
Europaplatz 3
69115 Heidelberg, Germany

Batch number: 09655825

Printed by Printforce, the Netherlands